MARVEL
SPIDER-MAN

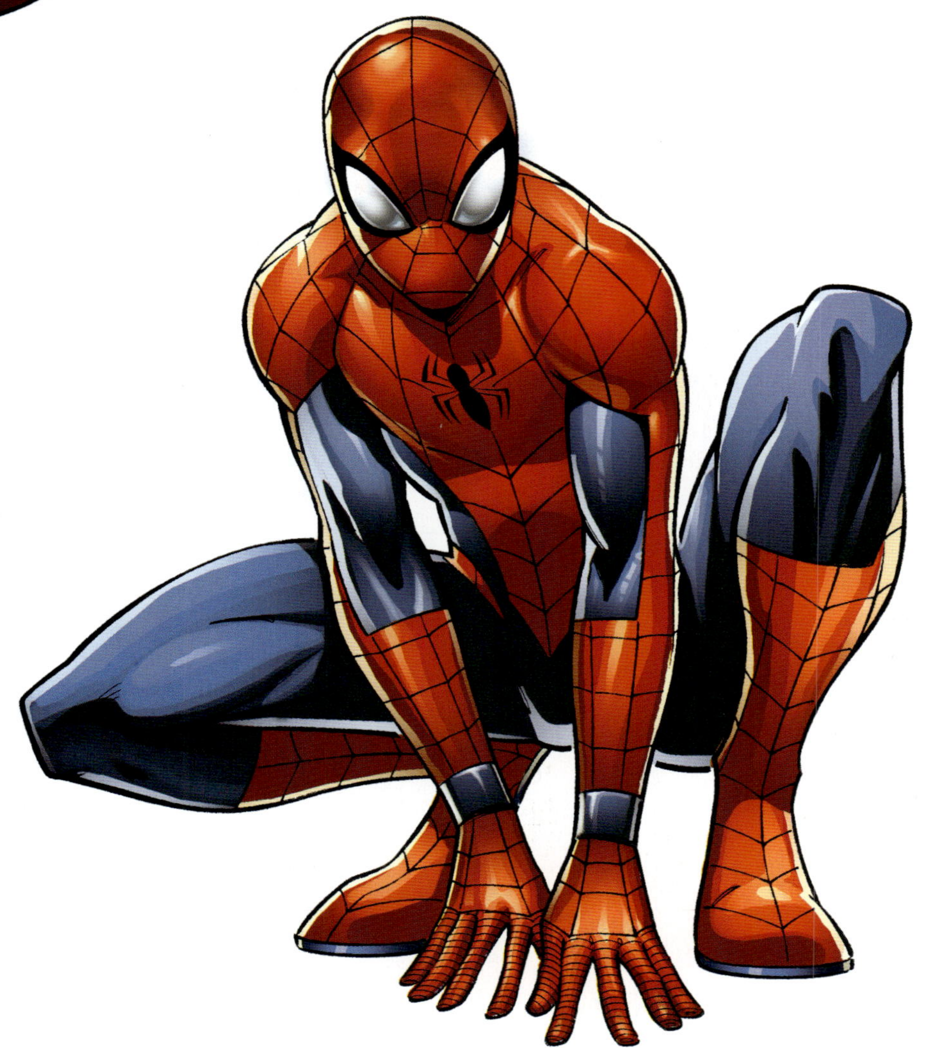

First Published in 2017 by Walter Foster Publishing, an imprint of The Quarto Group.
6 Orchard Road, Suite 100, Lake Forest, CA 92630, USA.

ISBN: 978-1-63322-261-8

Printed in China
10 9 8 7 6 5 4 3 2

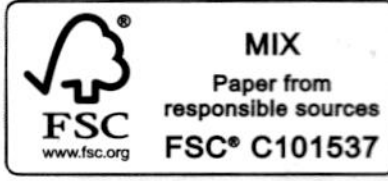

TABLE OF CONTENTS

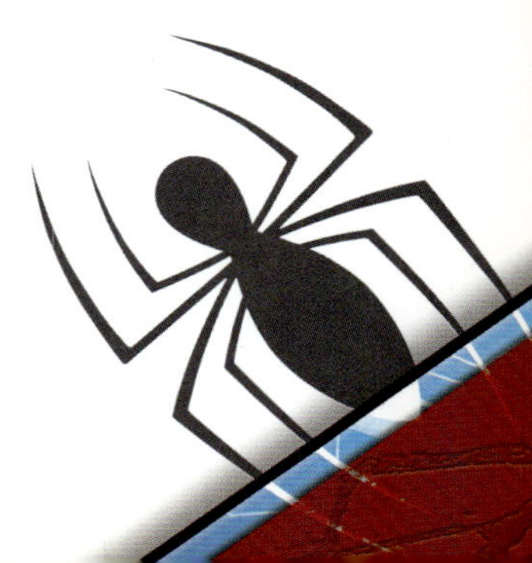

THE STORY OF SPIDER-MAN

Orphaned as a baby when his parents were killed overseas in a plane crash as U.S. government spies, only child Peter Parker was raised by his Uncle Ben and Aunt May. Academically gifted, Peter displayed an affinity for science that was nothing short of genius. Socially, however, he was shy and the target of much cruelty by his peers at Midtown High School.

Attending a public science exhibit when Peter was 15 years old, he was bitten on the hand by a radioactive spider irradiated by a particle beam, empowering Peter with the arachnid's proportional strength and agility, and the ability to cling to almost any surface. Most incredibly, he had gained a sixth sense that provided him with early warning of impending danger. Using his scientific prowess, he constructed a pair of artificial web-shooters that attached to his wrists.

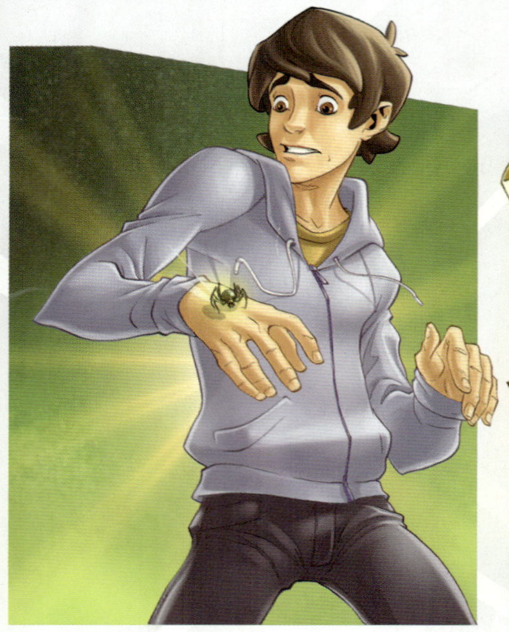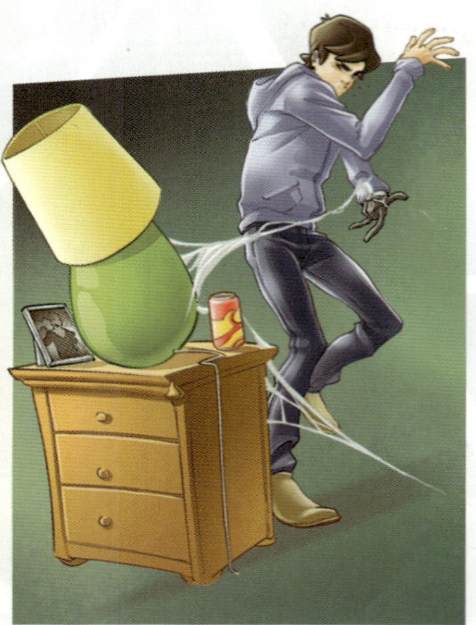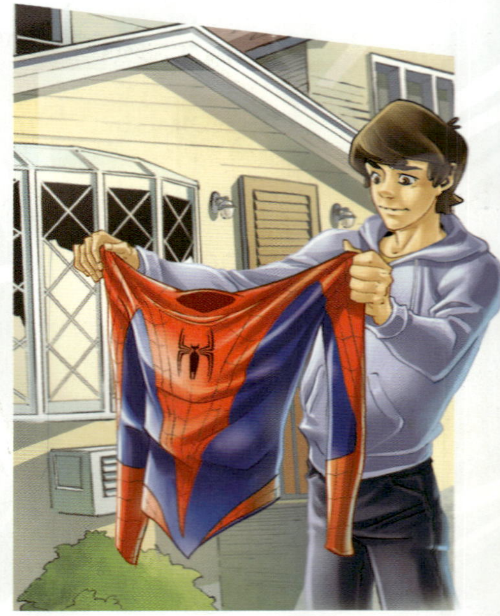

Wearing a disguise, Peter tested his new abilities and defeated professional wrestler Crusher Hogan in the ring, and earned some cash. Unconcerned with the rest of the world, he allowed a burglar that he could have easily restrained to run past him and escape. A few days later, Peter's Uncle Ben was shot and killed by this same burglar. Consumed with guilt, Peter became aware at last that with great power comes great responsibility, just as his uncle had once said.

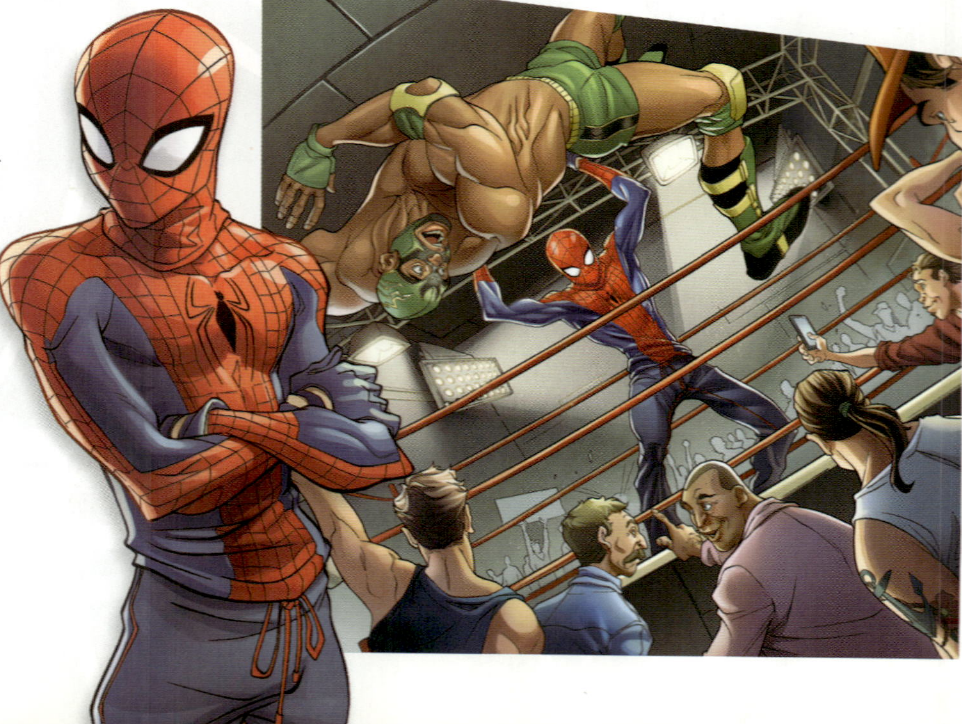

To help his Aunt May with finances, Peter took a freelance job at the *Daily Bugle* selling pictures of himself as Spider-Man to publisher J. Jonah Jameson. Jameson used his newspaper to publicly condemn Spider-Man as a menace. Spider-Man was mistrusted and feared by the public. At school, Peter's popularity was no greater, as "Puny Parker" frequently clashed with bully Flash Thompson and his followers.

In addition to his personal problems, Spider-Man soon found himself facing a rogue's gallery of powerful thieves, gangsters, and megalomaniacs, including the Chameleon, the Tinkerer, the Vulture, Doctor Octopus, Lizard, the Sandman, the Green Goblin, and more.

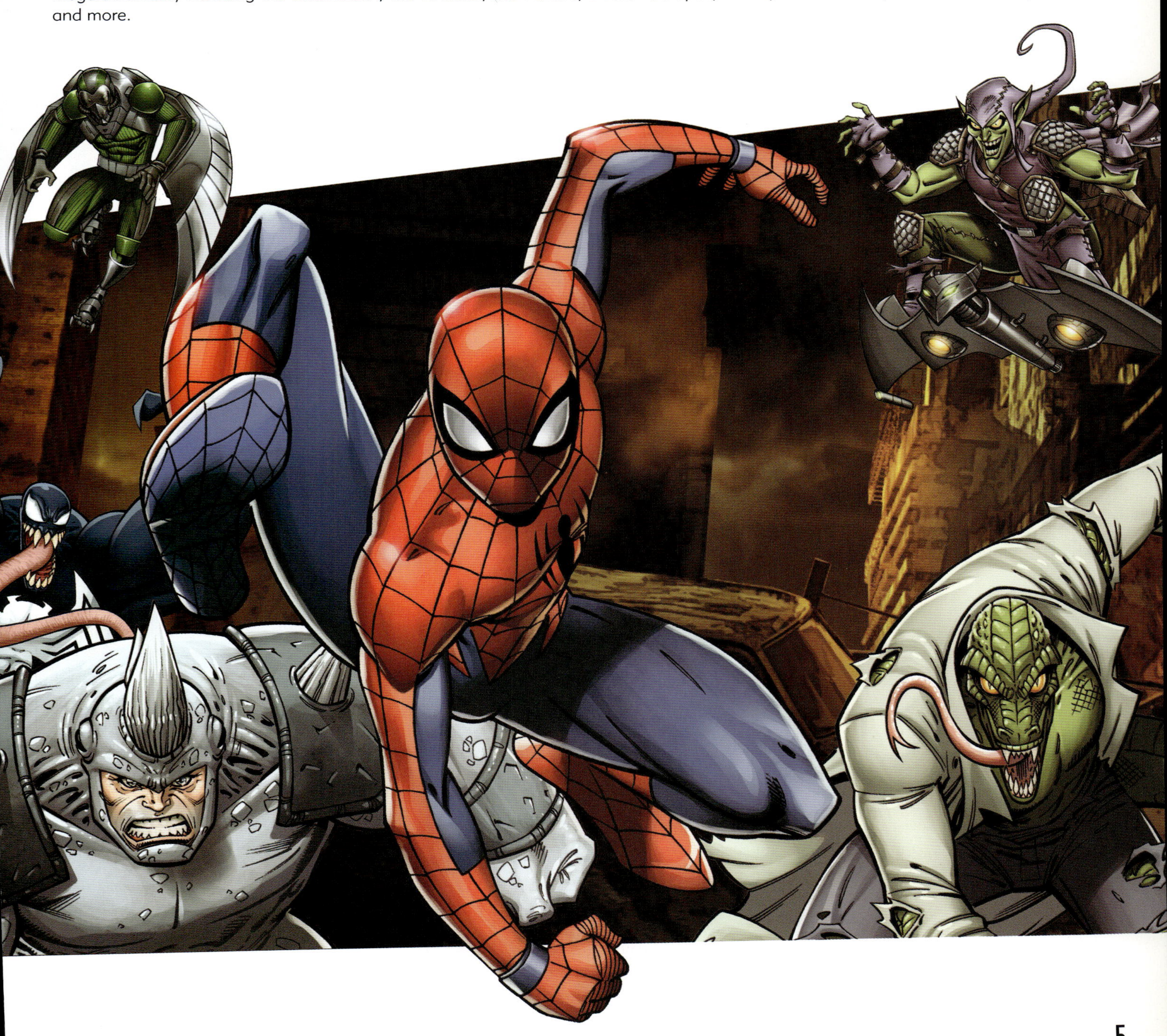

TOOLS & MATERIALS

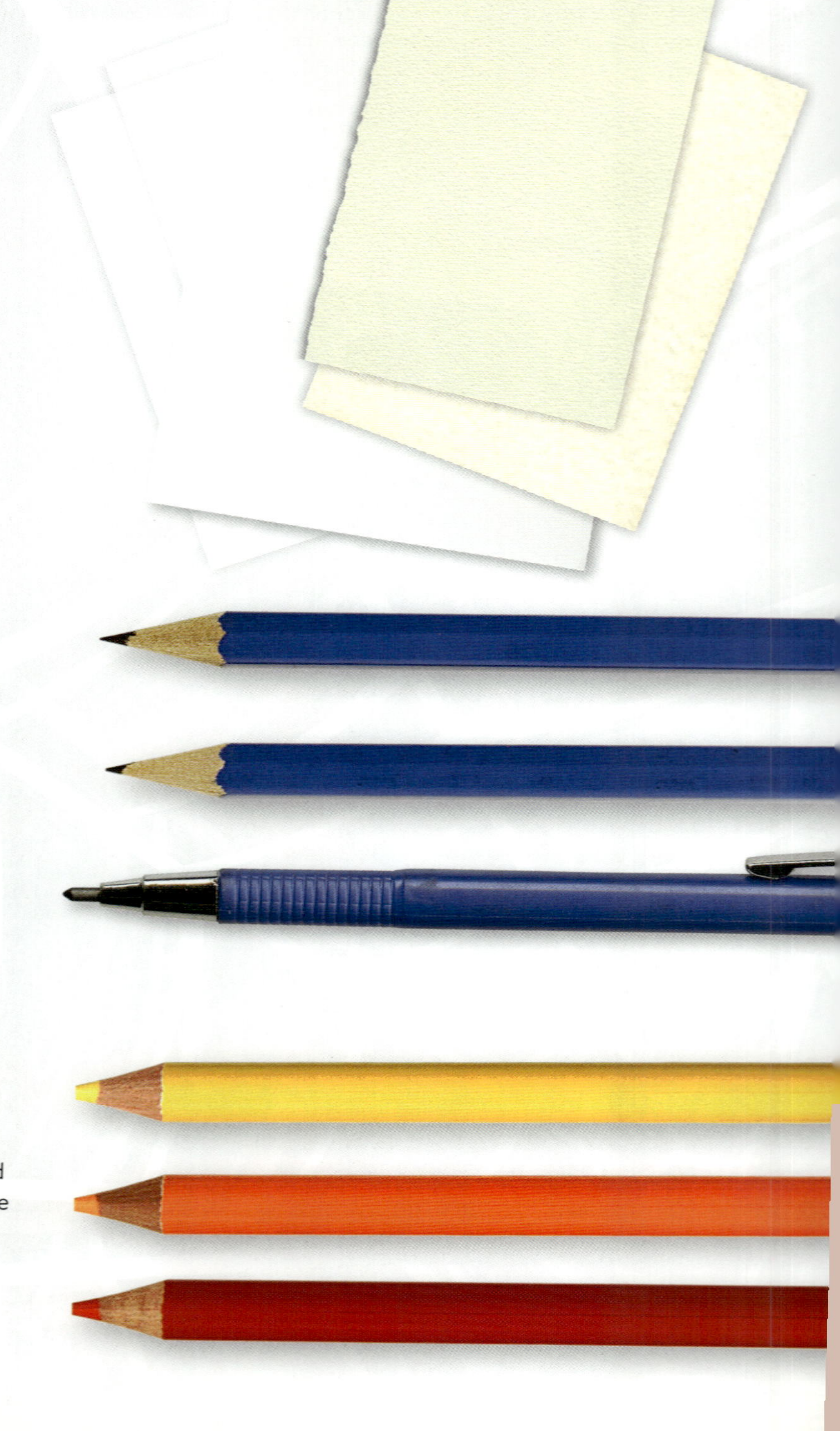

PAPER

Sketch pads and inexpensive printer paper are great for sketching and working out your ideas. Tracing paper can be useful for creating a clean version of a sketch using a light box. Just be sure to use quality tracing paper that is sturdy enough to handle erasing and coloring. Cardstock is sturdier than thinner printer paper, which makes it ideal for drawing repeatedly or for heavy-duty artwork. You may also want to have illustration board on hand.

PENCILS

Pencil lead, or graphite, varies in darkness and hardness. H pencils have harder graphite, which marks paper more lightly, while B pencils have softer graphite, which makes darker marks. A good pencil for sketching is an H or HB, but you can also use a regular #2 pencil.

COLORED PENCILS

Colored pencils layer over each other easily. They come in wax-based, oil-based, and water-soluble versions. Oil-based pencils complement wax-based pencils nicely. Water-soluble pencils react to water in a manner similar to watercolor. In addition to creating finished art, colored pencils are useful for enhancing small details.

ART MARKERS

Alcohol-based art markers are perfect for adding bold, vibrant color to your artwork. They are great for shading and laying down large areas of color. Markers and colored pencils can be used in combination with paint to enhance and accent your drawings.

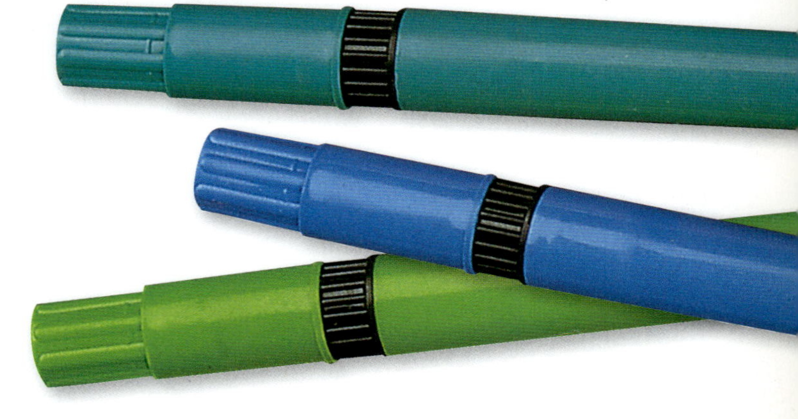

ERASERS

Vinyl and kneaded erasers are both good to have on hand. A vinyl eraser is white and rubbery and gentler on paper than a pink eraser. A kneaded eraser is like putty. It can be molded into shapes to erase small areas. You can also use it to lift graphite off paper to lighten artwork.

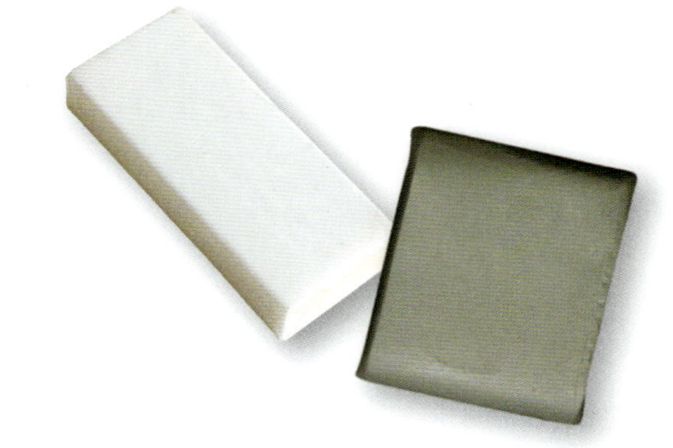

PAINT

Have fun exploring acrylic and watercolor paint. Watercolor paints are available in cakes, pans, and tubes. Tube paints are fresher and the colors are brighter. Acrylic paint dries quickly, so keep a spray bottle of water close to help keep the paint on your palette fresh. It's a good idea to have two jars of water when you paint: one for diluting your paints and one for rinsing your brushes.

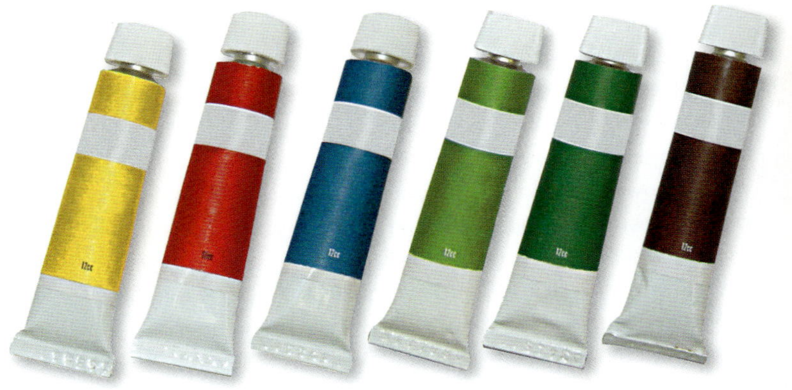

DRAWING BASICS

Drawing consists of three elements: line, shape, and form. The shape of the object can be described with simple one-dimensional lines. The three-dimensional version of the shape is known as the object's "form." In pencil drawing, variations in *value* the (relative lightness or darkness of black or a color) describe form, giving an object the illusion of depth.

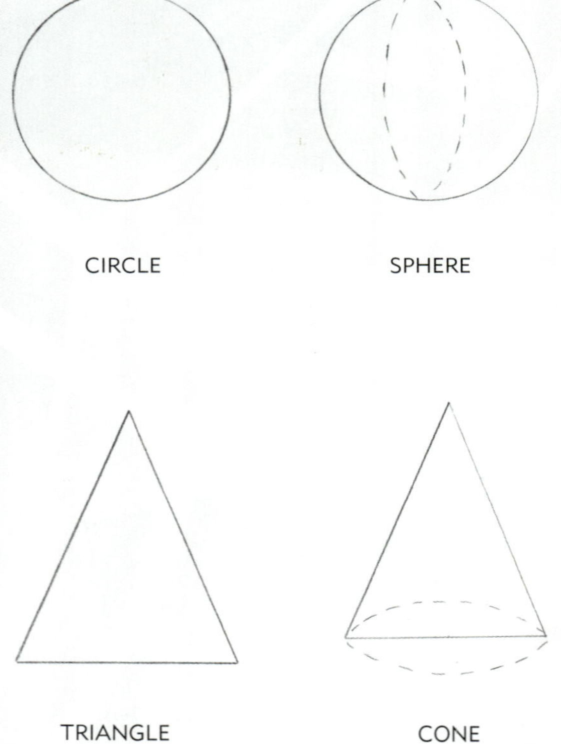

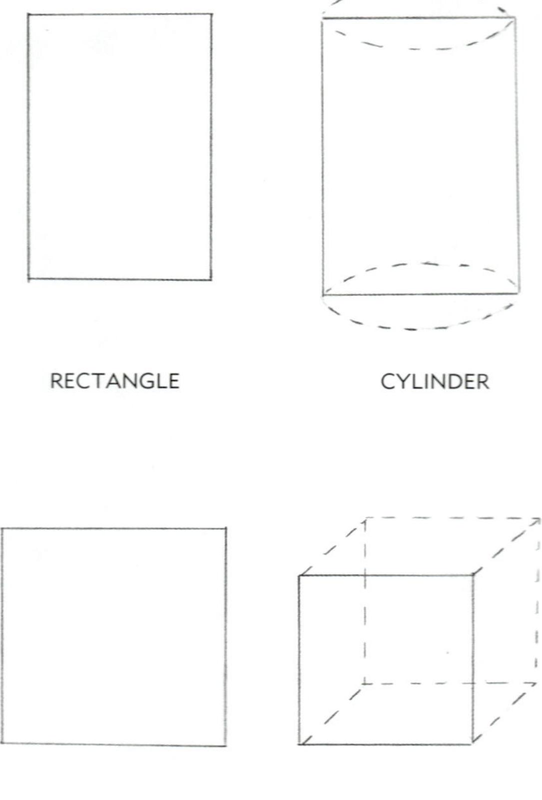

ADDING VALUE TO CREATE FORM

A shape can be further defined by showing how light hits the object to create highlights and shadows. First note from which direction the source of light is coming. In this example, the light source is shining from the upper right. Then add the shadows accordingly. The *core shadow* is the darkest area on the object and is opposite the light source. The *cast shadow* is what is thrown onto a nearby surface by the object. The *highlight* is the lightest area on the object, where the reflection of light is strongest. *Reflected light*, often overlooked by beginners, is surrounding light that is reflected into the shadowed area of an object.

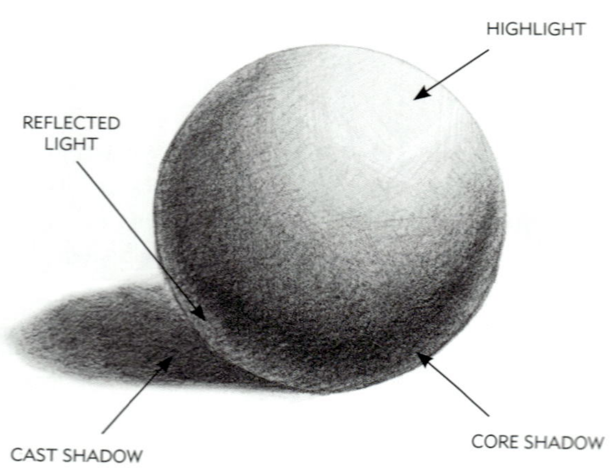

STEP-BY-STEP DRAWING METHOD

This book teaches the step-by-step drawing method and shows you how to draw a character using basic shapes. You will always begin by drawing very basic shapes, like lines and circles.

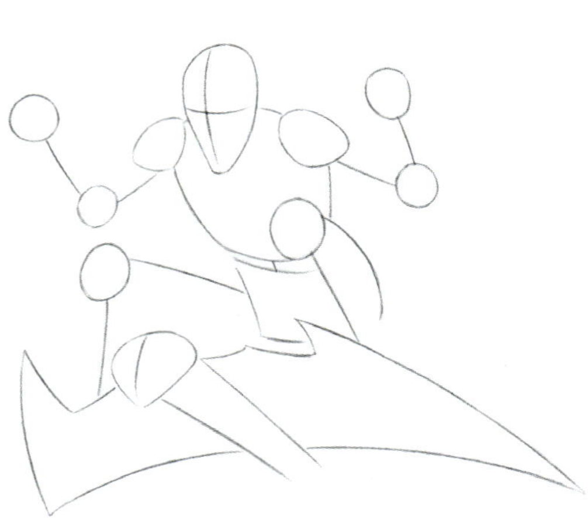

STEP 1

First draw the basic shapes, using light lines that will be easy to erase.

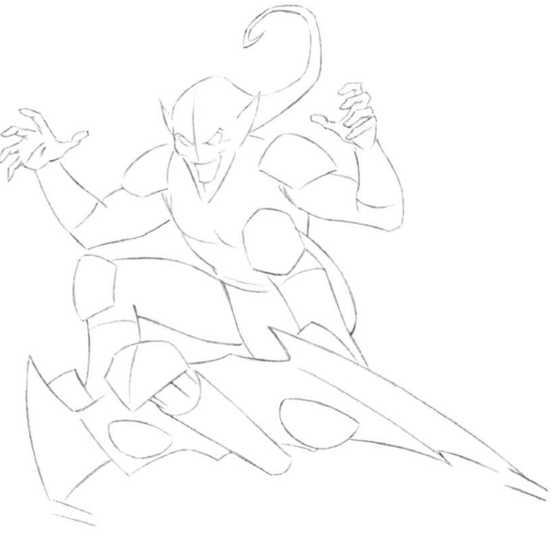

STEP 2

Erase guidelines and add more detail. Pay attention to the new lines added in each new step.

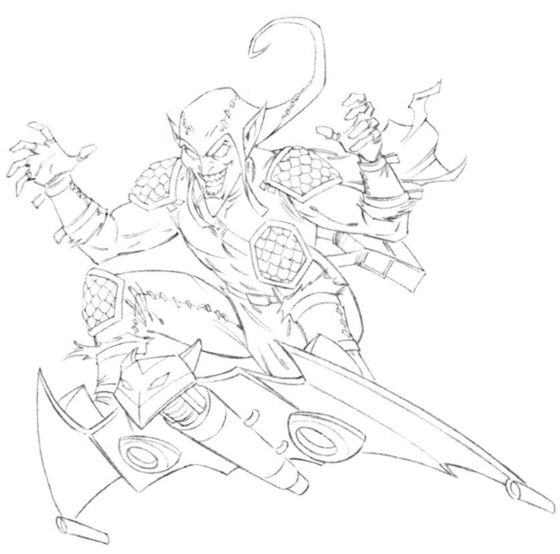

STEP 3

In each new step, add more defining lines. Take your time adding detail and copying what you see.

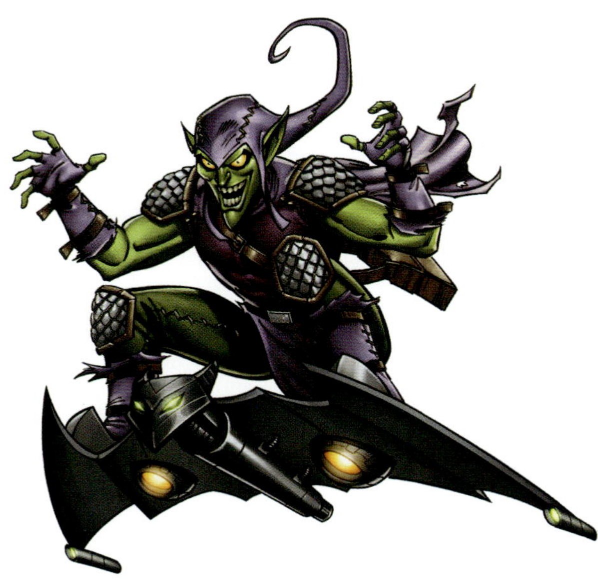

STEP 4

Add final details and shading. Then ink and color your drawing using whichever method you choose!

BASIC ANATOMY

The musculature of different individuals varies, but we all have the same muscles underneath. Become familiar with basic anatomy so you can better envision the way the skin lays over the muscles to create the human form.

Front

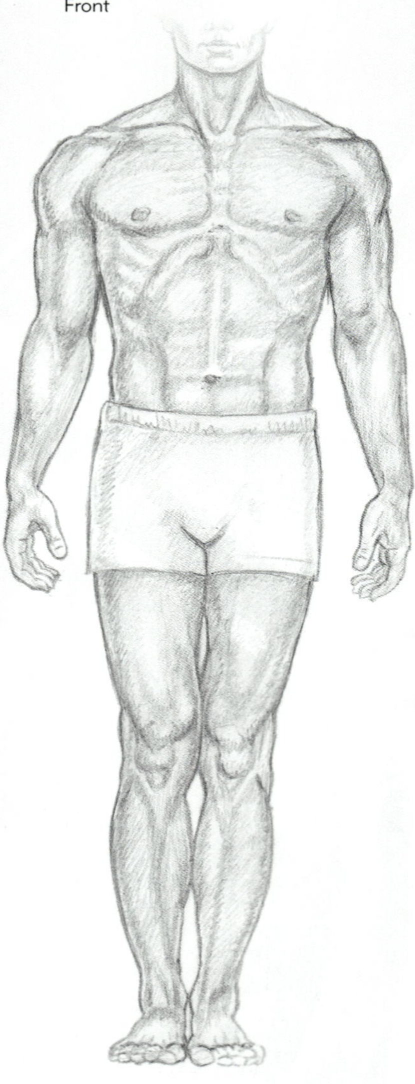

Back

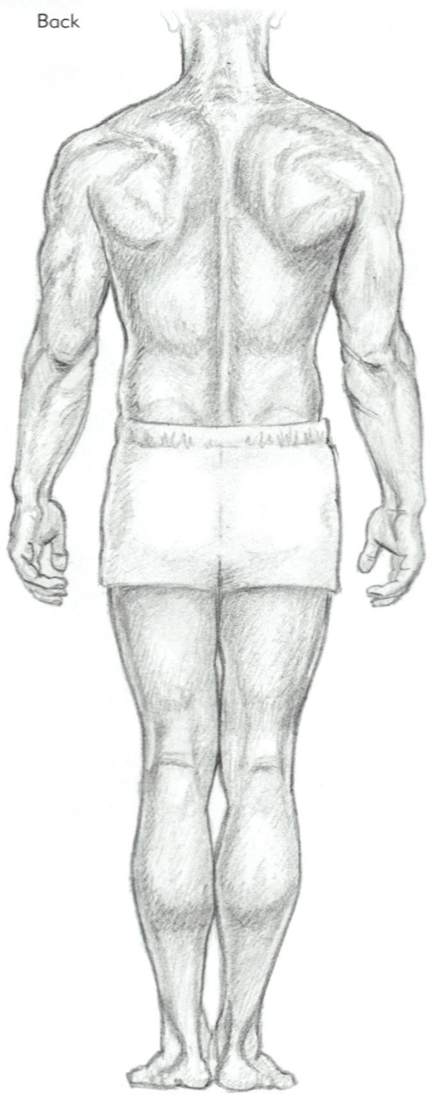

TORSO MUSCULATURE
(Front) The torso muscles—from the neck to the shoulders, across the chest, down and around the rib cage, and then from the hips to the legs—control the movement of the body and give form to the skeleton.

TORSO MUSCULATURE
(Back) The muscles in the back of the torso generally extend across the body, rather than up and down as in the front. They hold the body erect, stretching tightly across the back when the limbs move forward.

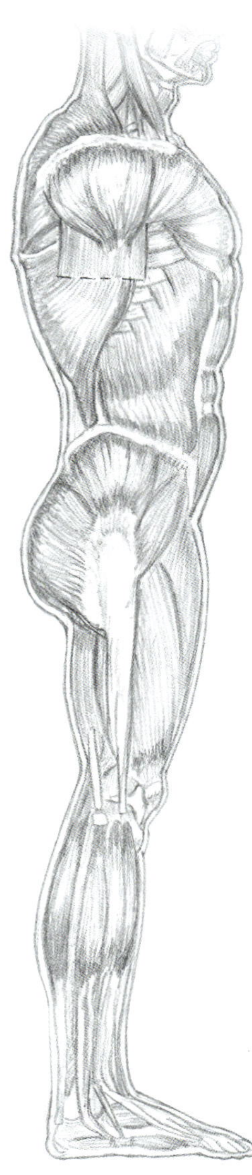

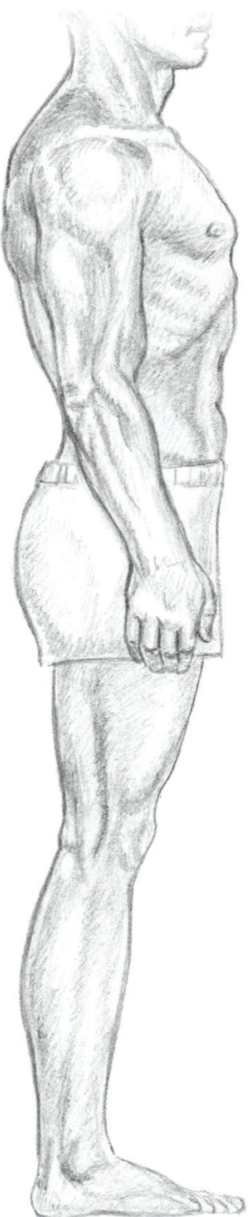

BODY MUSCULATURE

Proportion doesn't apply to length alone—the thickness of the body also must be proportionate. This aspect of proportion varies depending on the fitness of the individual, but the drawing above will help you assess these proportions based on an ideal human musculature.

MALE PROPORTIONS

The average male is approximately 7½ heads high; of course, these proportions vary with different body types. Often artists use an 8-head-high figure of the male as an ideal proportion.

BASIC ANATOMY

Using what you know about human anatomy—its muscles and proportions—apply this to a thin and lean Spider-Man. Spider-Man is not overly muscular, like a lot of Super Heroes. His strength comes from his super spider powers, not bulky muscles.

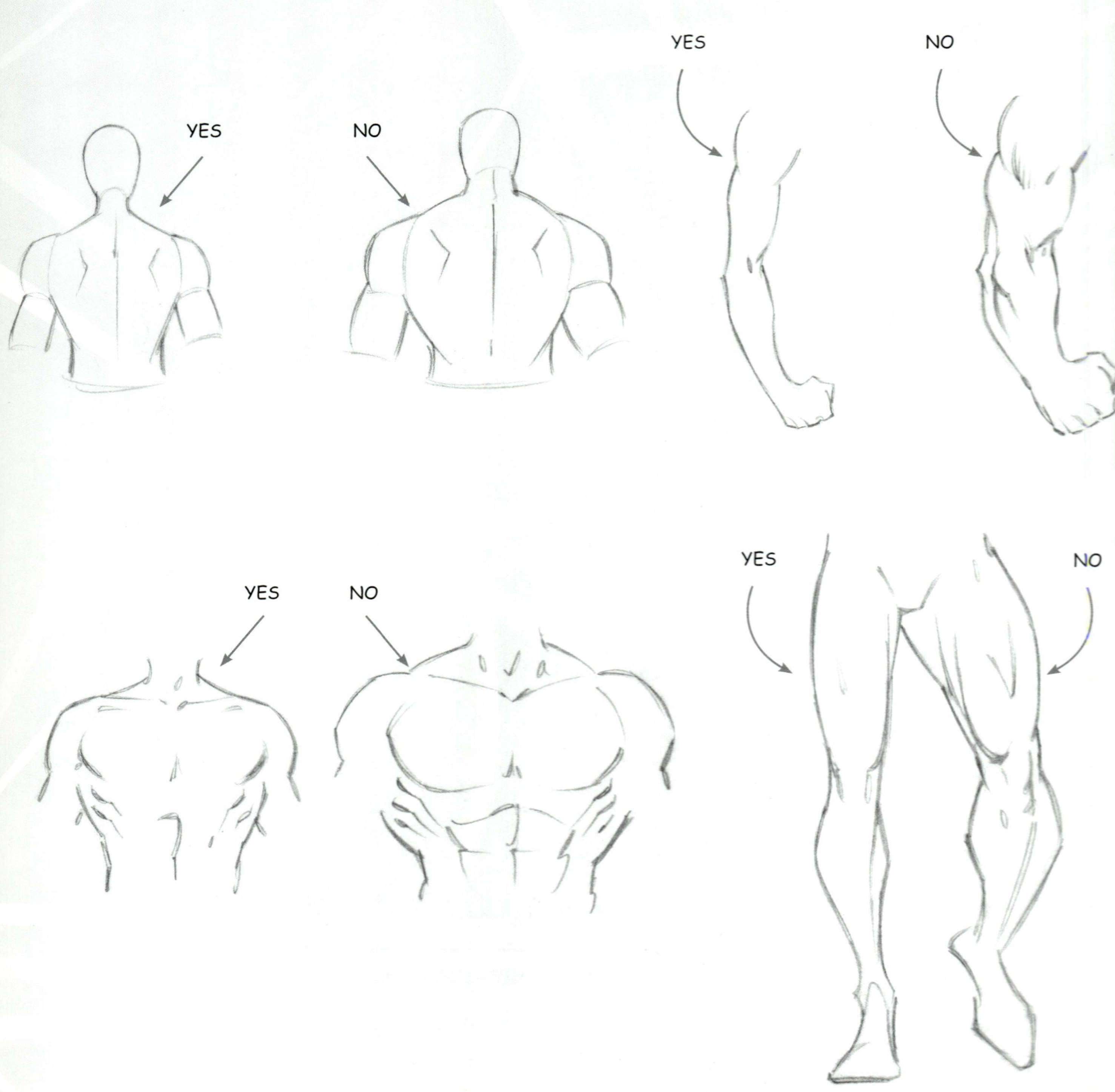

When drawing Spider-Man, use the eyes to show emotion. You don't have a mouth or facial muscles to draw, so the only way to convey what he's thinking is through subtle changes in the mask's eye shapes. Note that in profile, Spider-Man's nose is visible. In a three-quarter view, the bulge of his ears is visible.

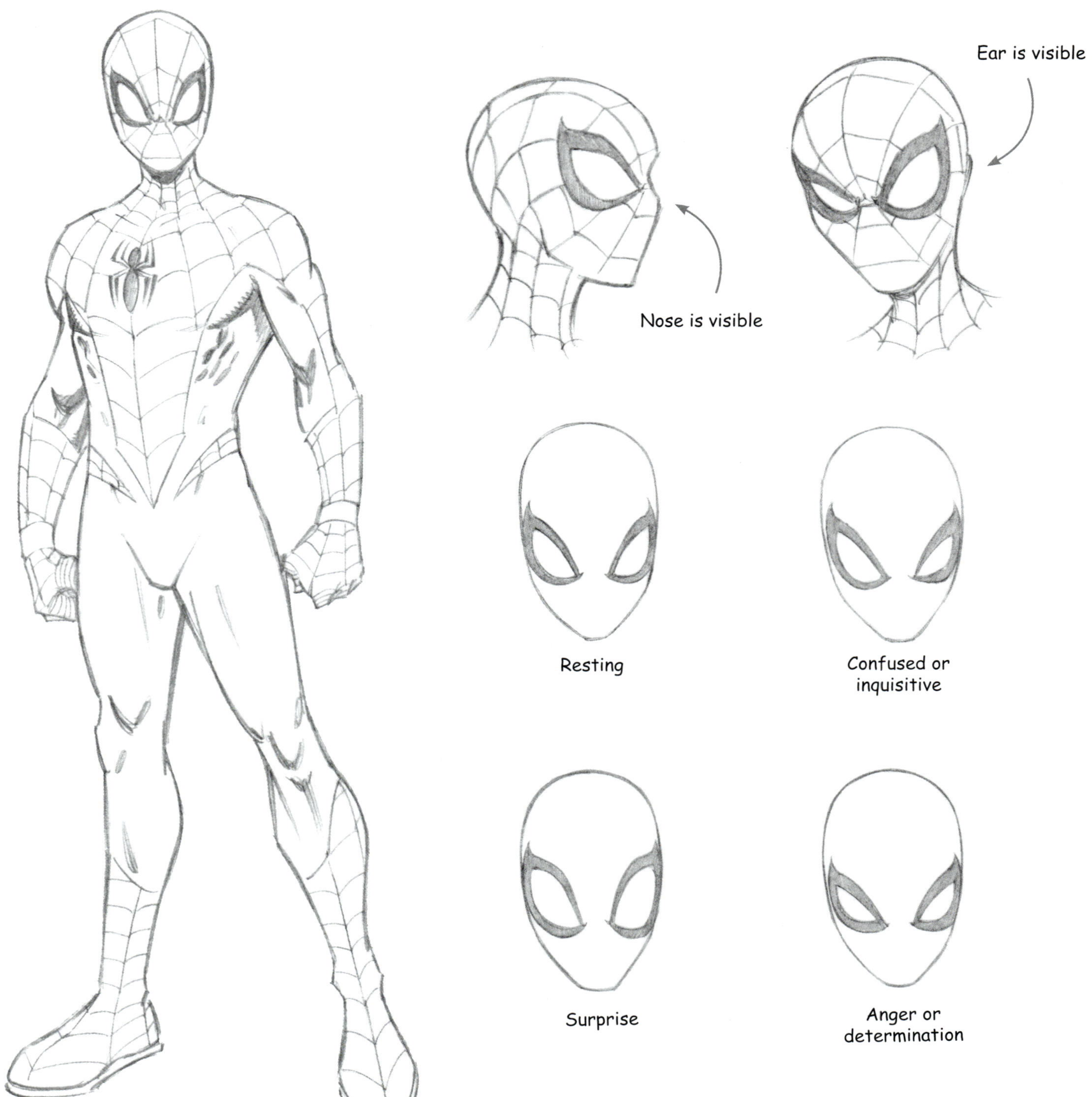

INKING TECHNIQUES

In the early days of comic books, images were reproduced inexpensively using a very simple black-and-white photographic process. Most inking was done with India ink—preferred for its extremely dense black value. To create subtle tonal changes from solid black shadows to lighter areas, artists used hatching, cross-hatching, or "feathered" brushstrokes or pen strokes.

Today, improved reproduction techniques allow artists to explore various inking styles—but the iconic look of comic-style art owes much to those early inking techniques.

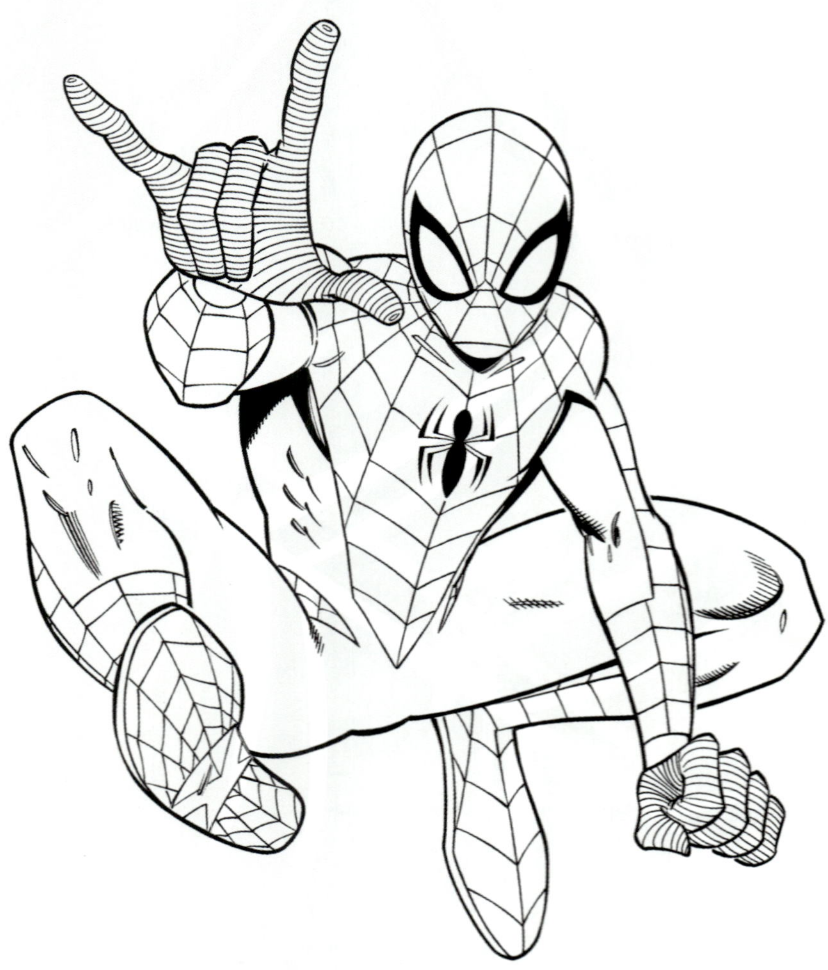

When inking, use various line weights and textures
to define the shapes and the image as a whole.

COLORING TECHNIQUES

You can color your drawings any way you'd like, using colored pencils, markers, paints, or digitally. Here, a professional comic book colorist describes the process for coloring Spider-Man digitally using Adobe Photoshop®.

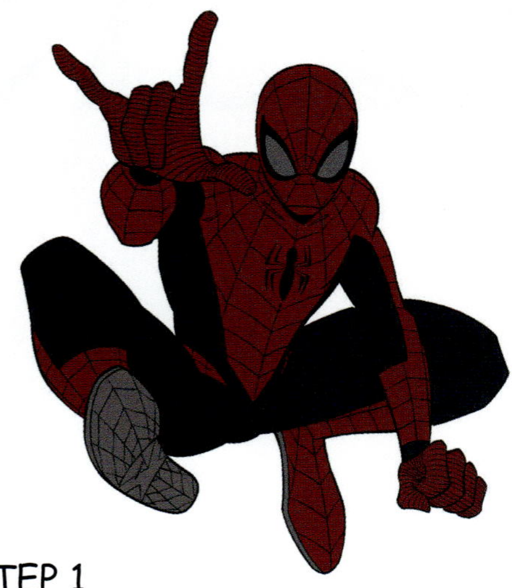

STEP 1

Start by blocking out the entire form, and then block out your different colors.

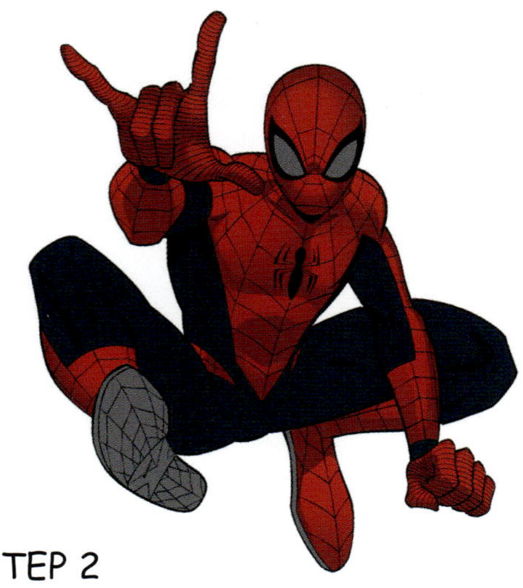

STEP 2

Look at the linework for signs of light placement and begin to work in your colors to create highlights and shadow. The colorist chose a bluish red for the base and a more pure red for the shapes that are in more direct light.

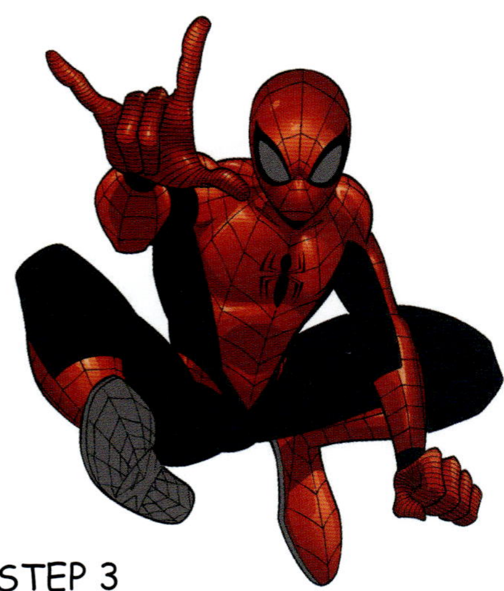

STEP 3

To bring out the reds, the colorist used brighter shades of orange. Remember not to use black or white, as it will bleach out or muddy your work.

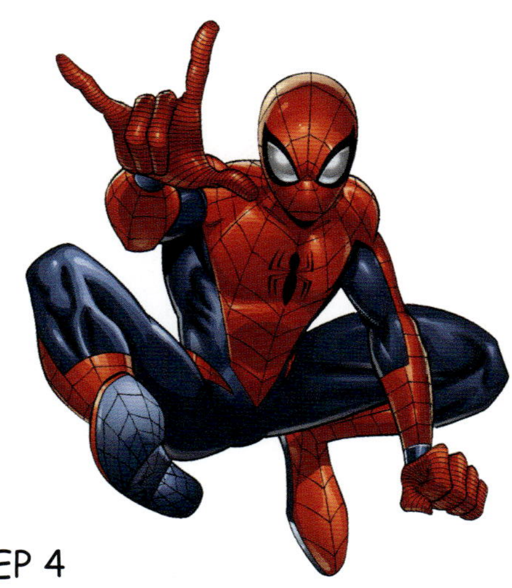

STEP 4

Now focus on the places that reflect light strongest. Using a mild yellow or near-white, highlight these areas. Work the contours to round out the highlights not leave things looking flat. Repeat through each color group until finished.

SPIDER-MAN

Bitten by a radioactive spider, high school student Peter Parker gains the speed, strength, and powers of a spider. Adopting the name Spider-Man, Peter hopes to start a wrestling career using his new abilities. But taught that with great power comes great responsibility, Spidey instead vows to use his powers to help people.

STEP 1

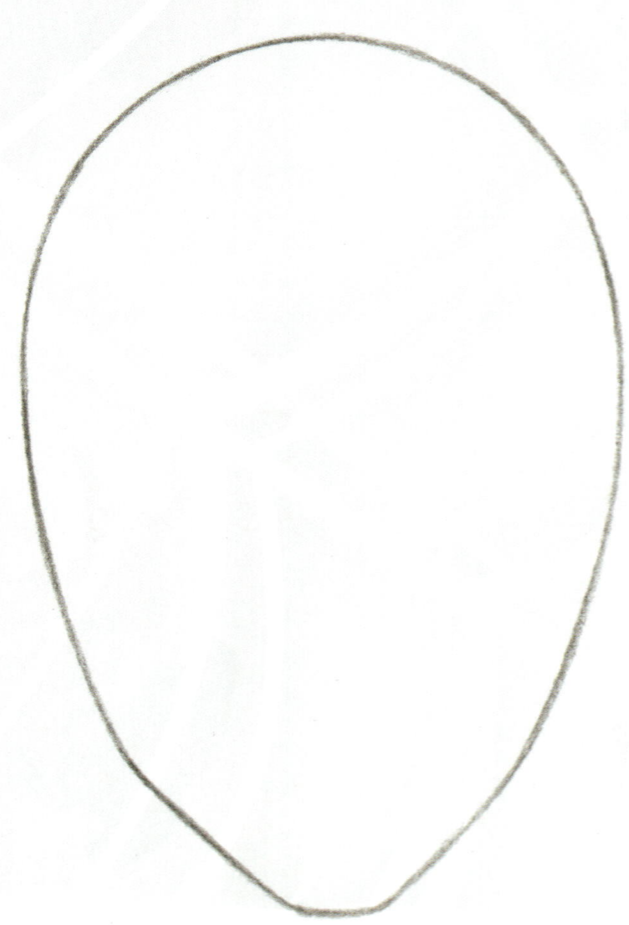

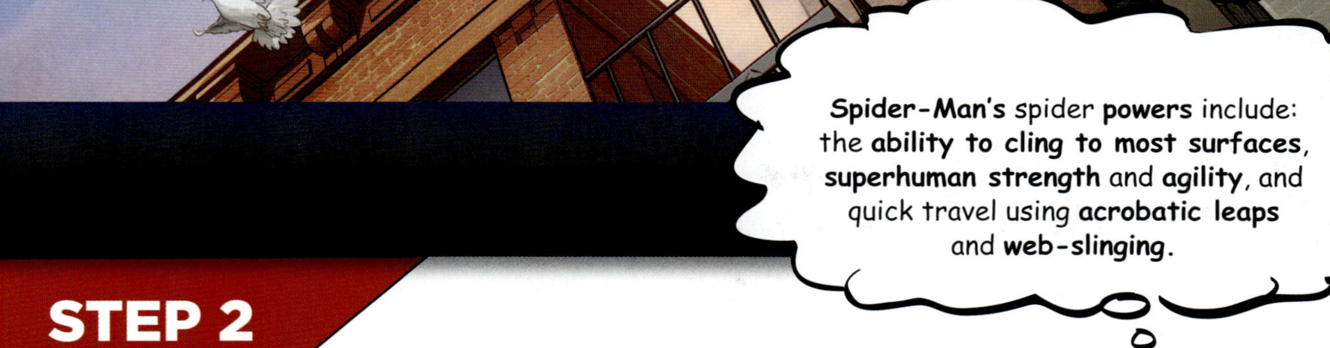

Spider-Man's spider powers include:
the ability to cling to most surfaces,
superhuman strength and agility, and
quick travel using acrobatic leaps
and web-slinging.

STEP 2

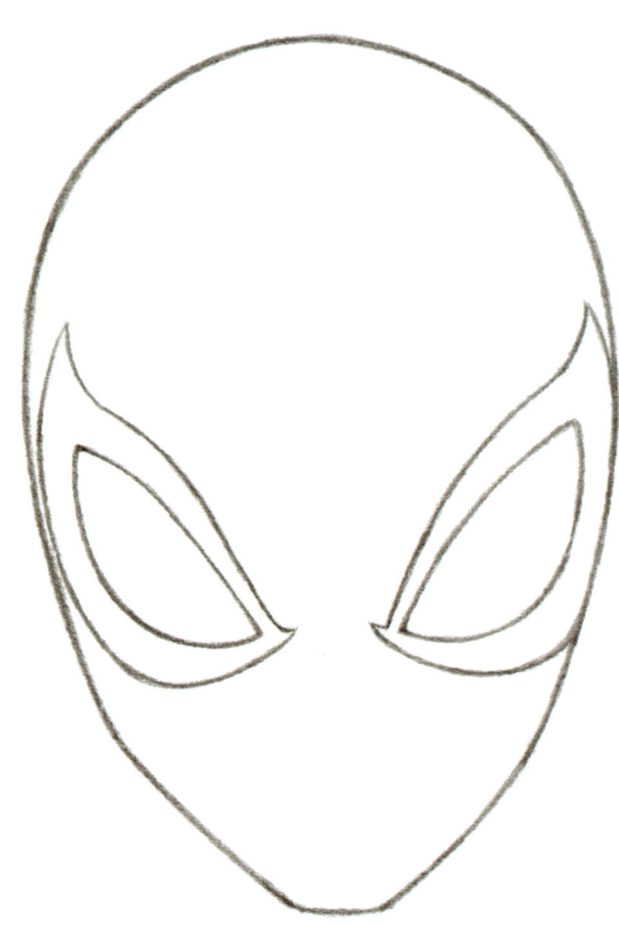

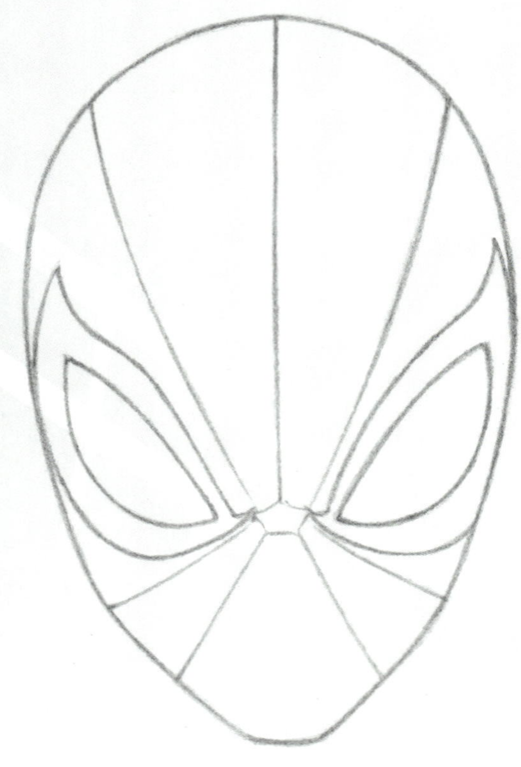

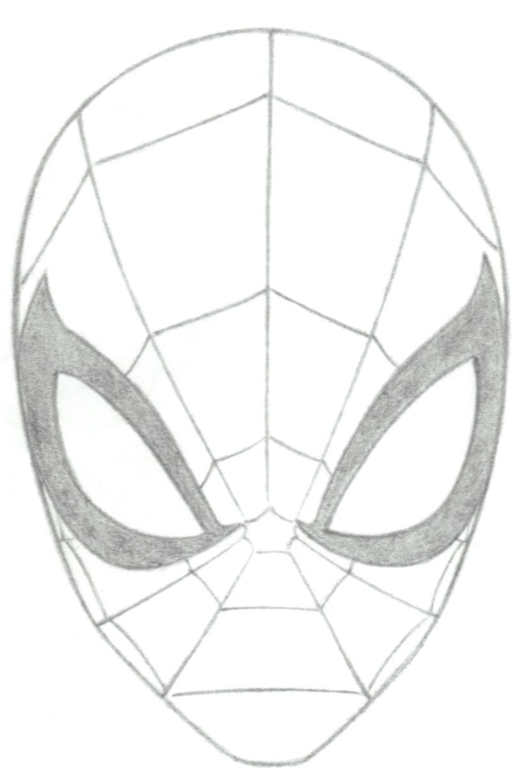

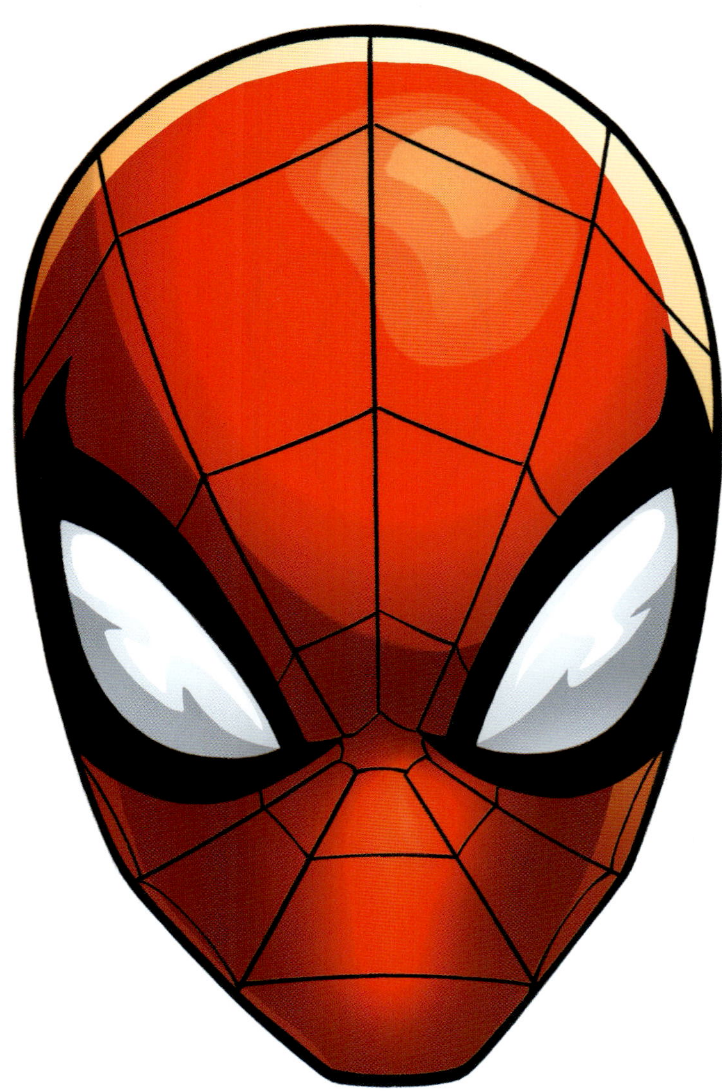

SPIDER-MAN

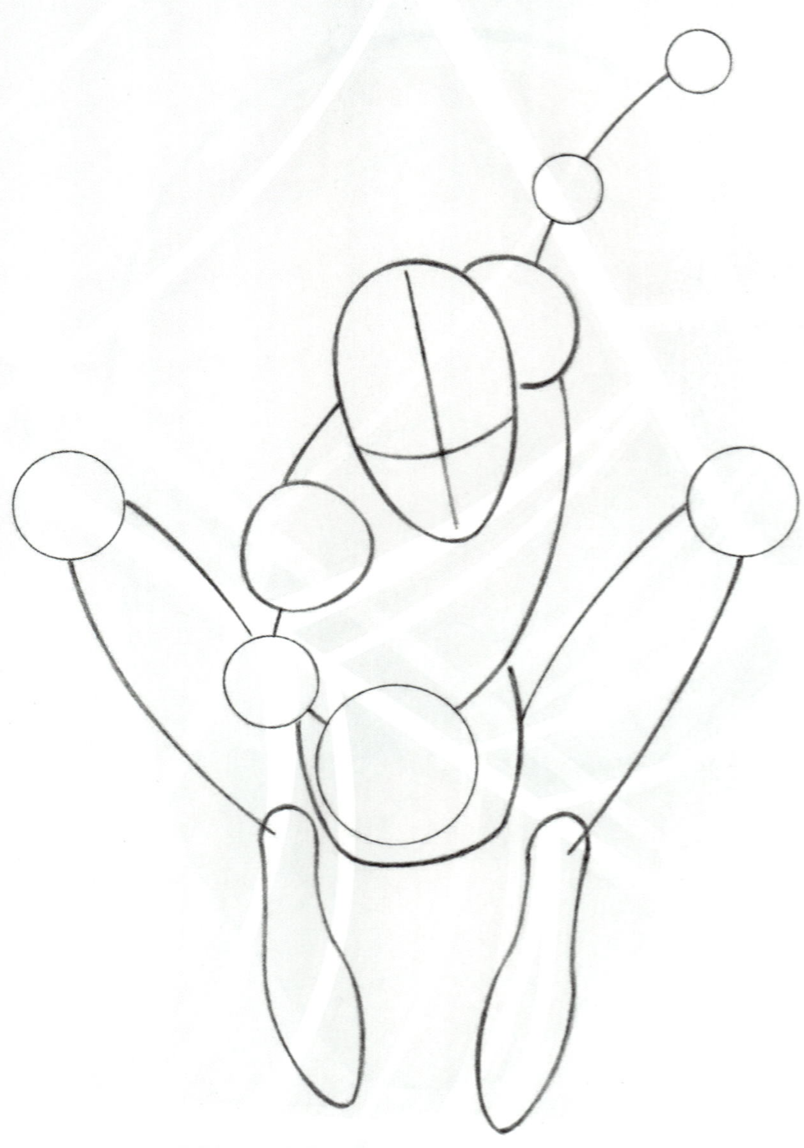

Spider-Man's first appearance is in *Amazing Fantasy #15*,
the **last** issue of *Amazing Fantasy*, published in **1962**.

STEP 2

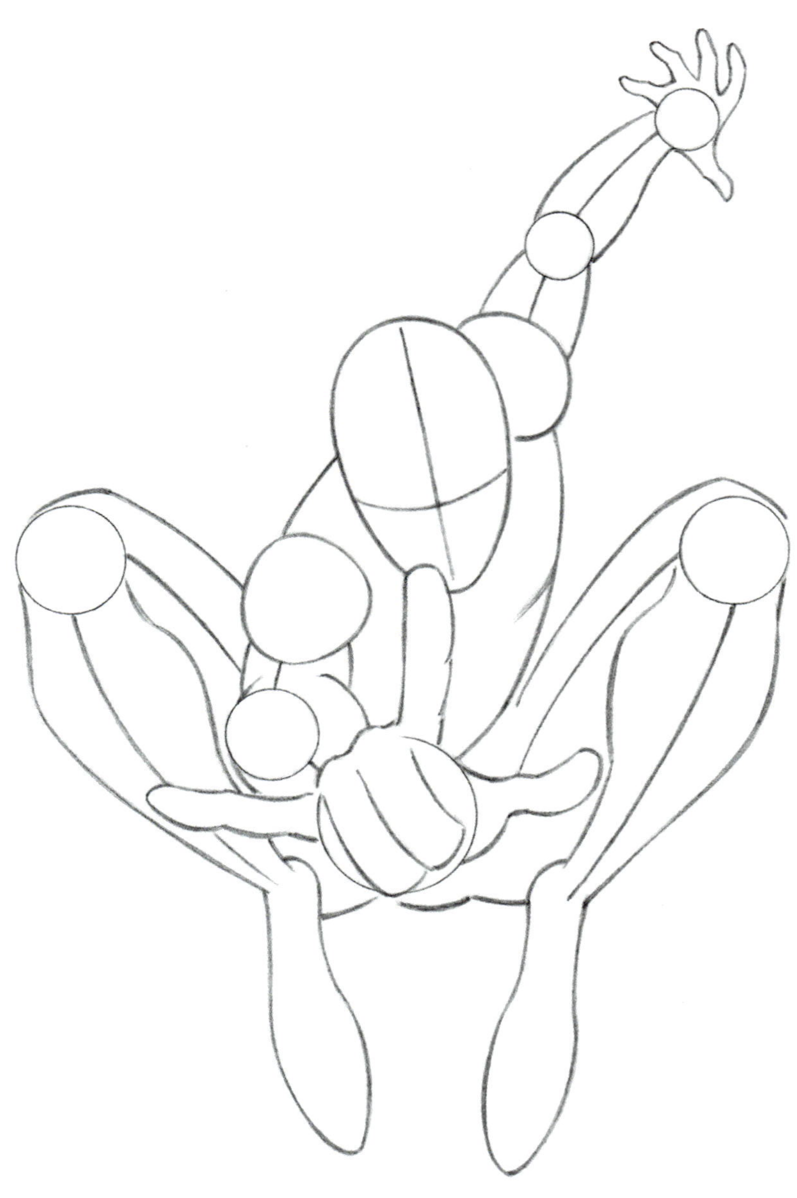

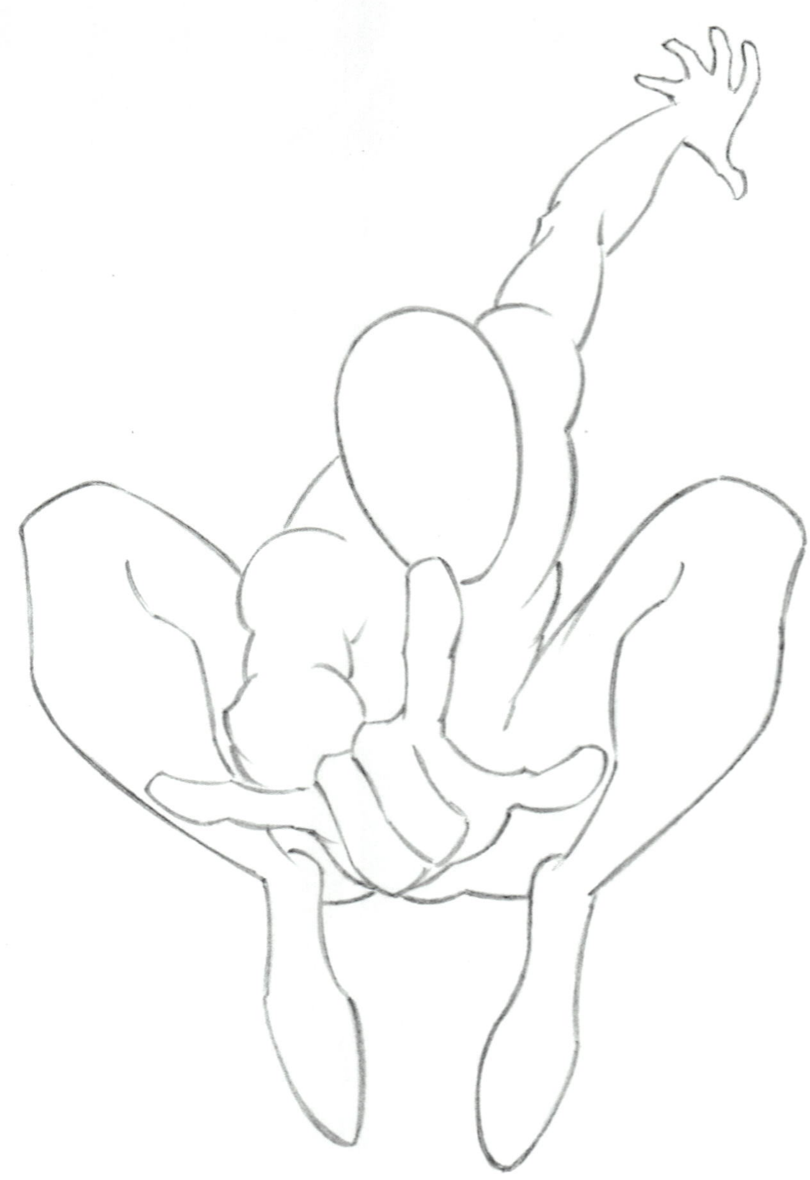

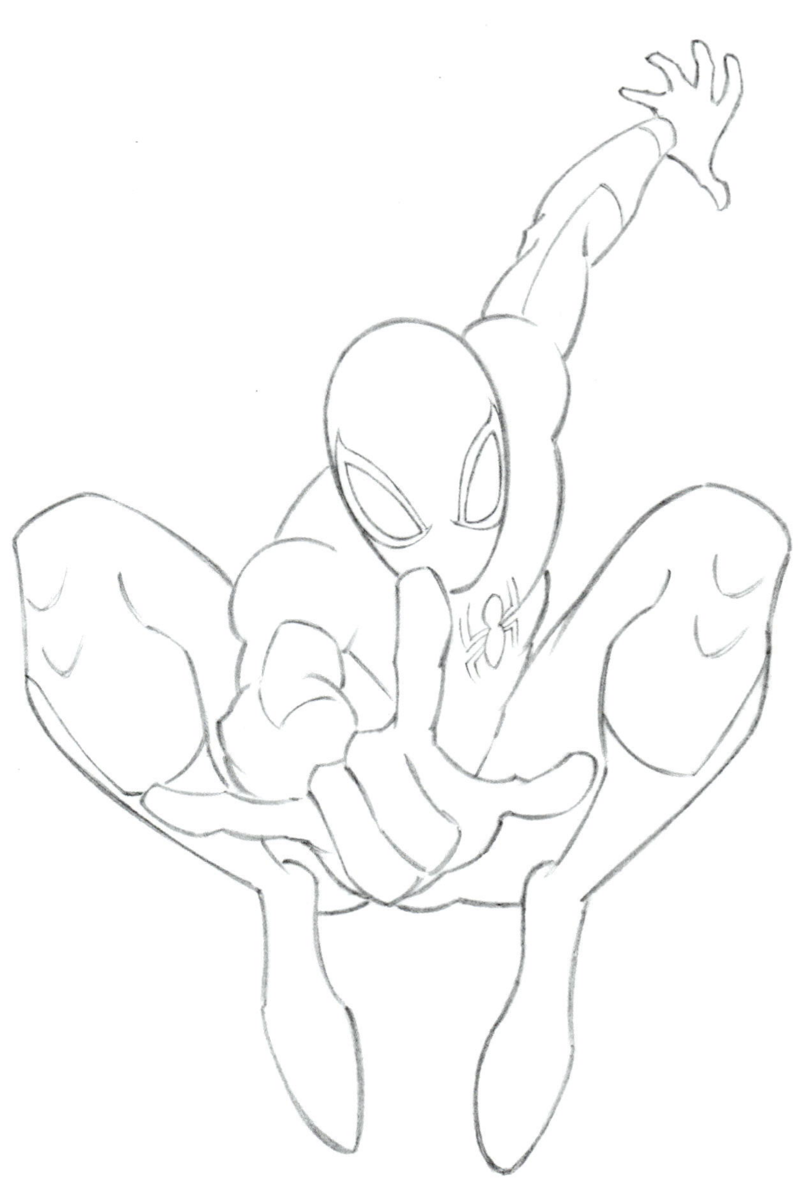

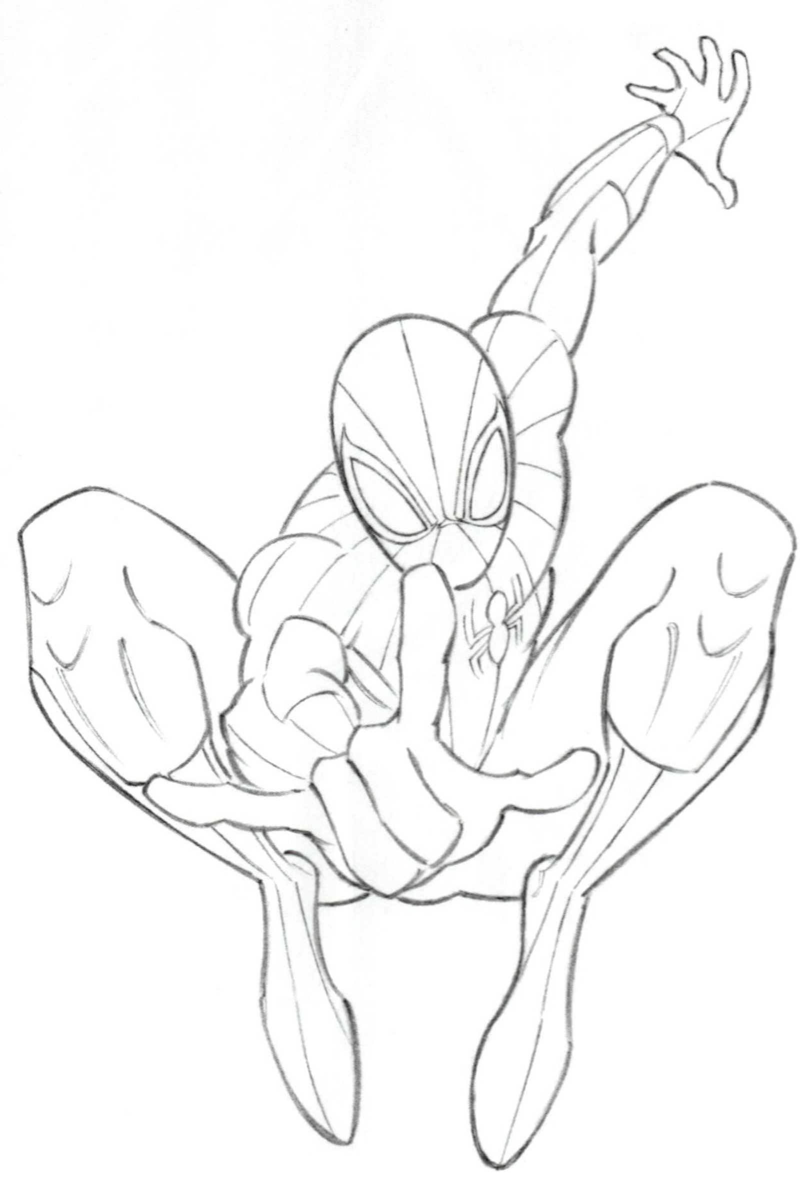

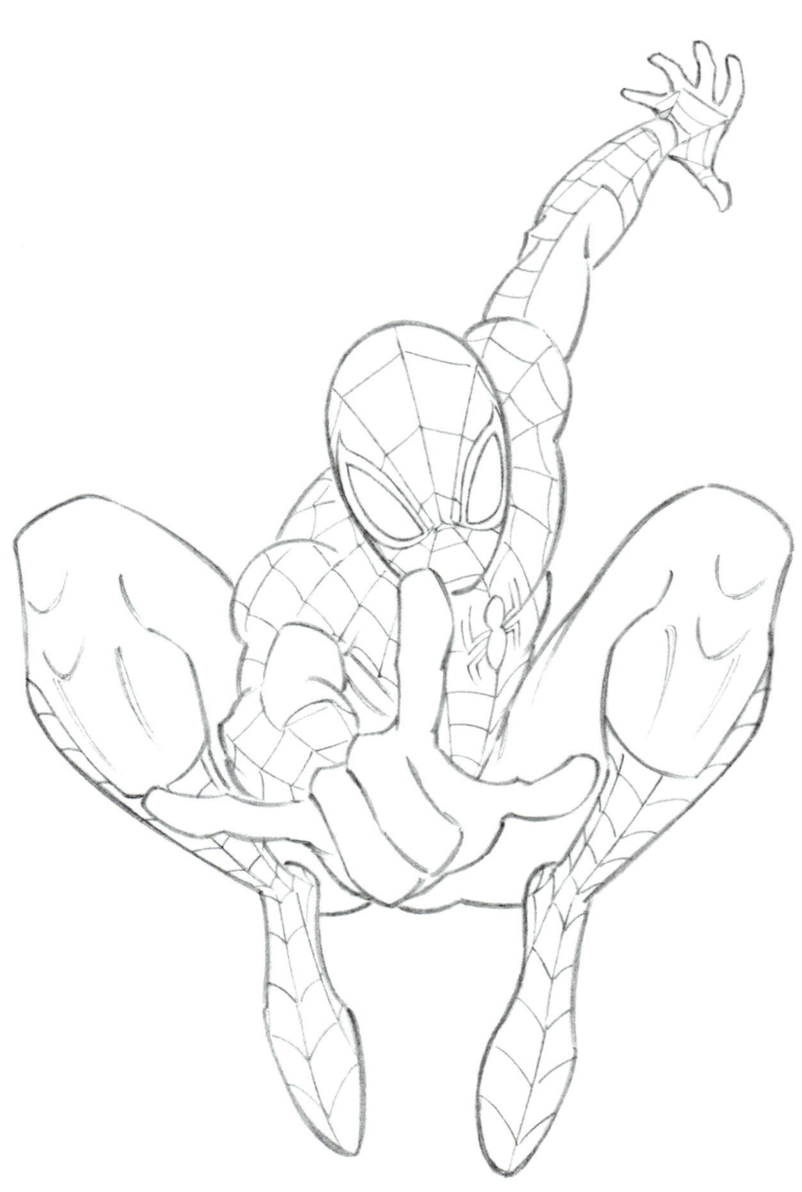

Note that the costume's web pattern
continues onto the hands.

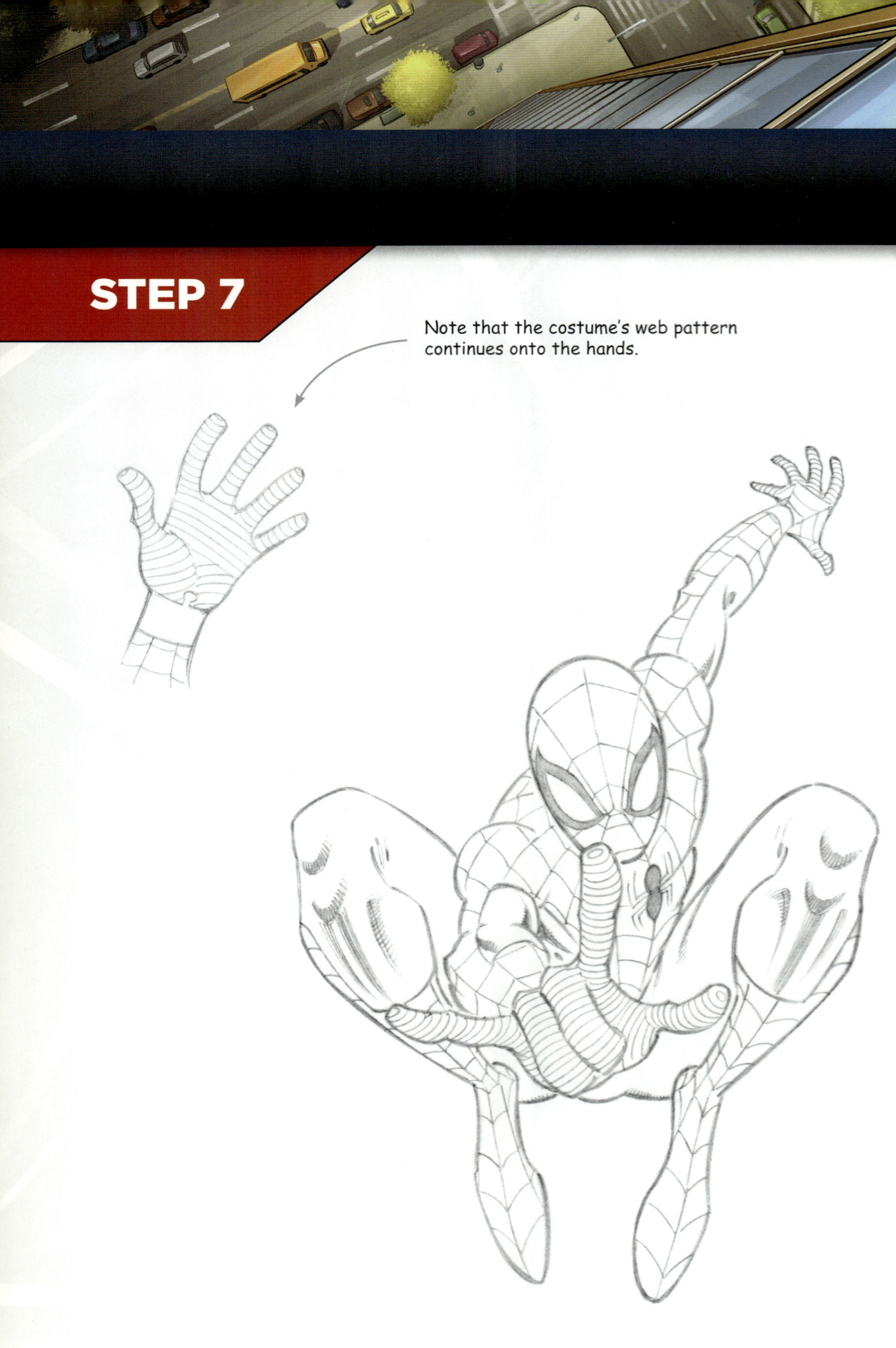

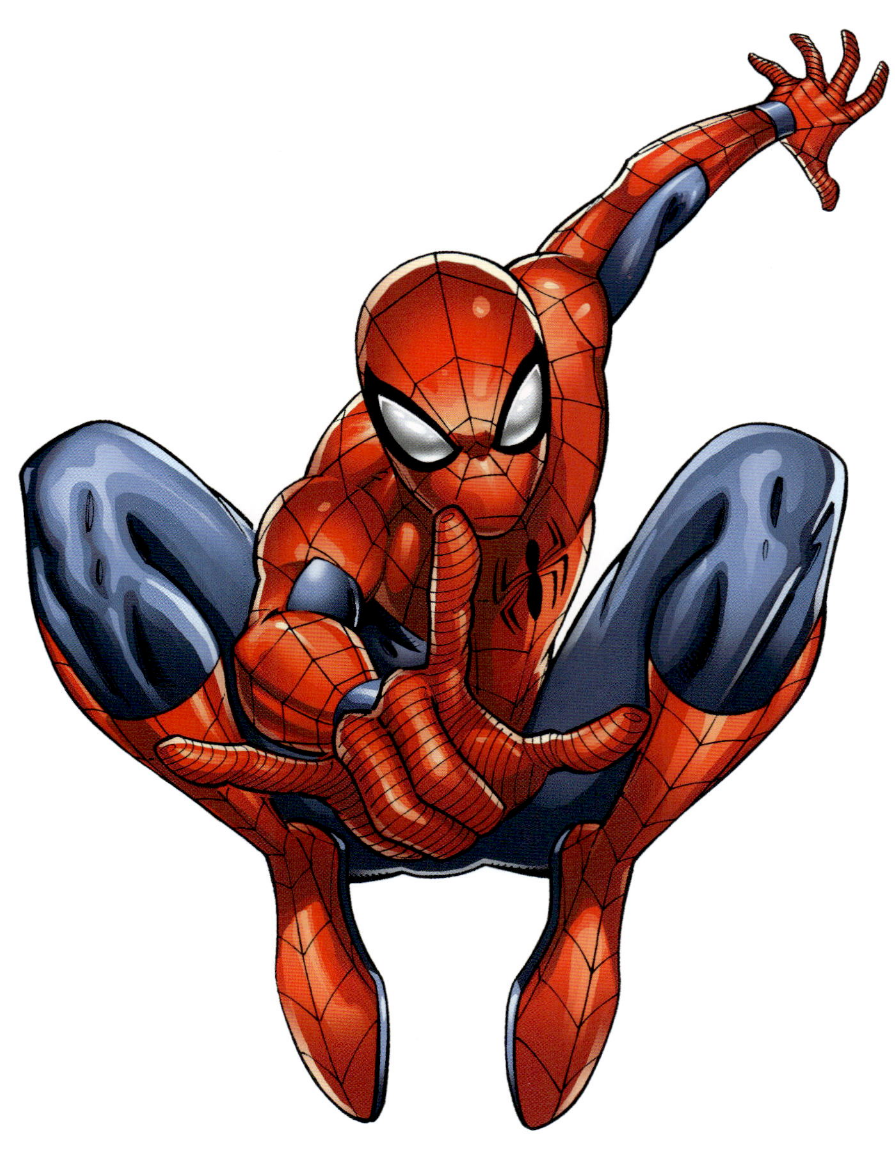

SPIDER-MAN

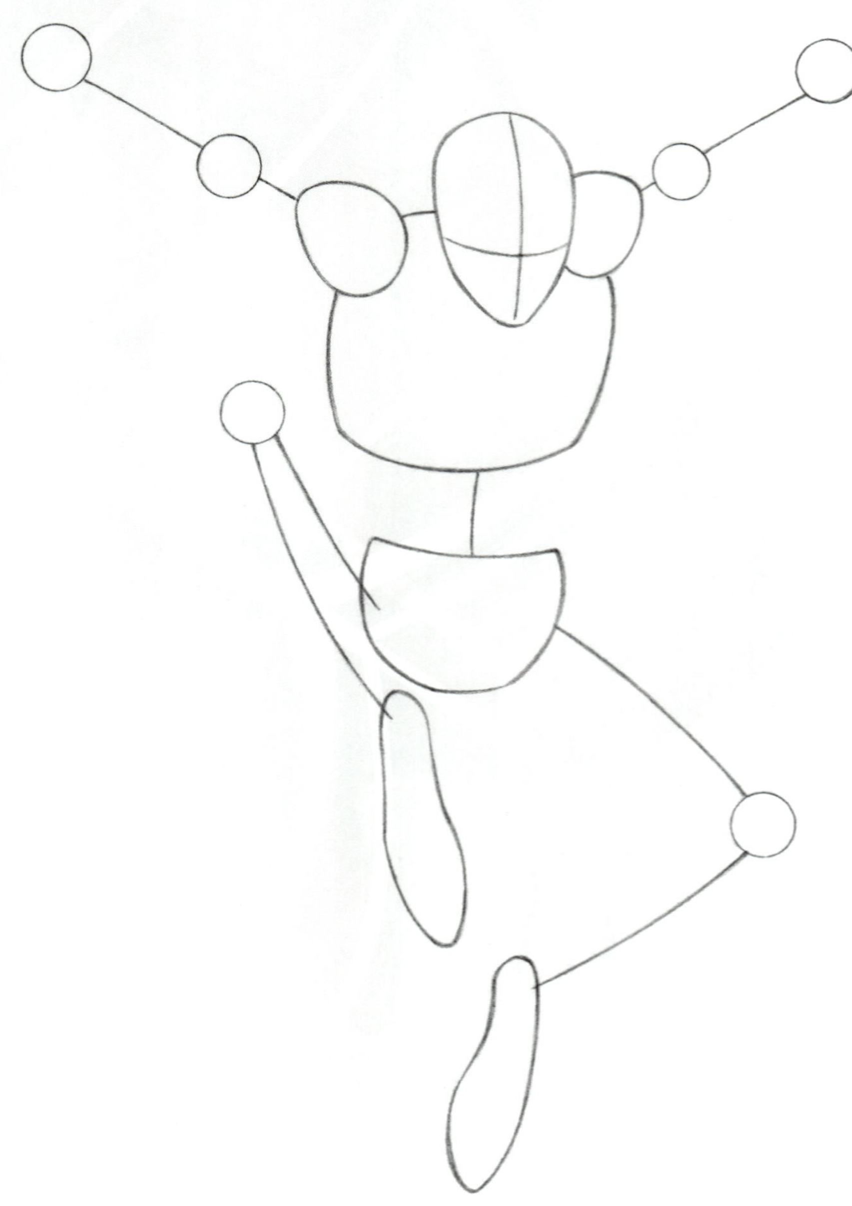

Originally priced at **13 cents**, a near-mint copy (*9.6 CGC*) of *Amazing Fantasy* sold in **2011** for **$1.1 million**.

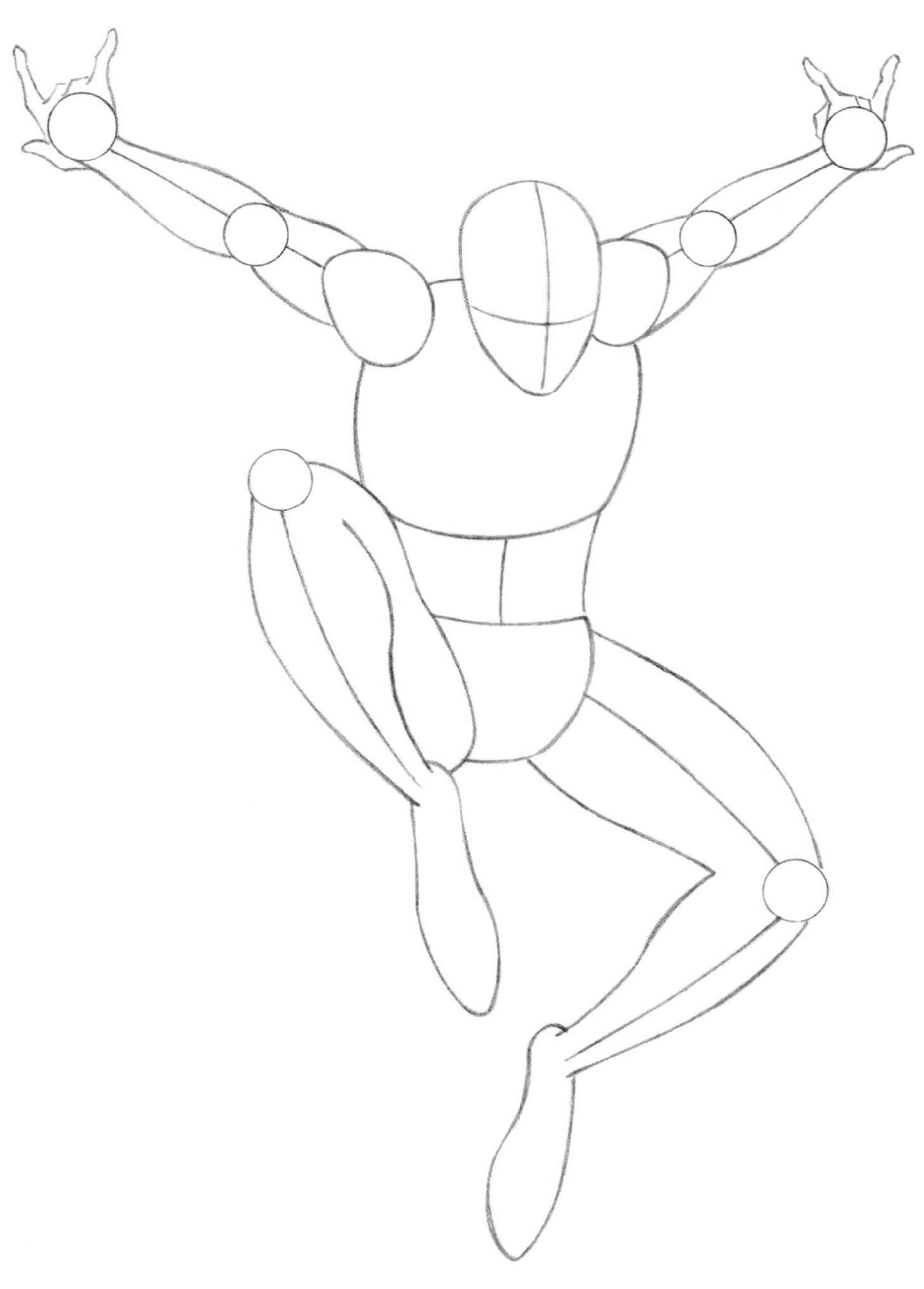

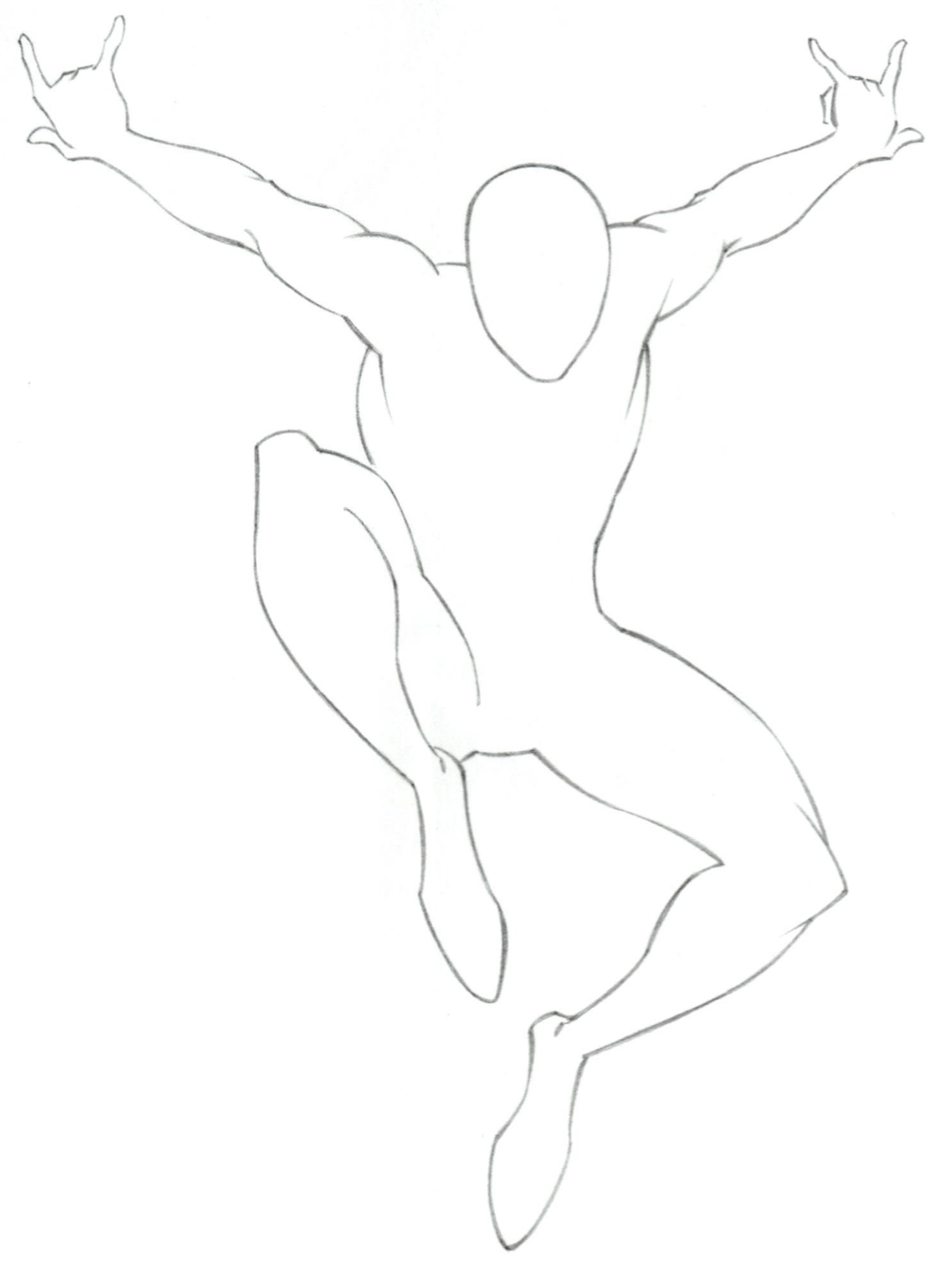

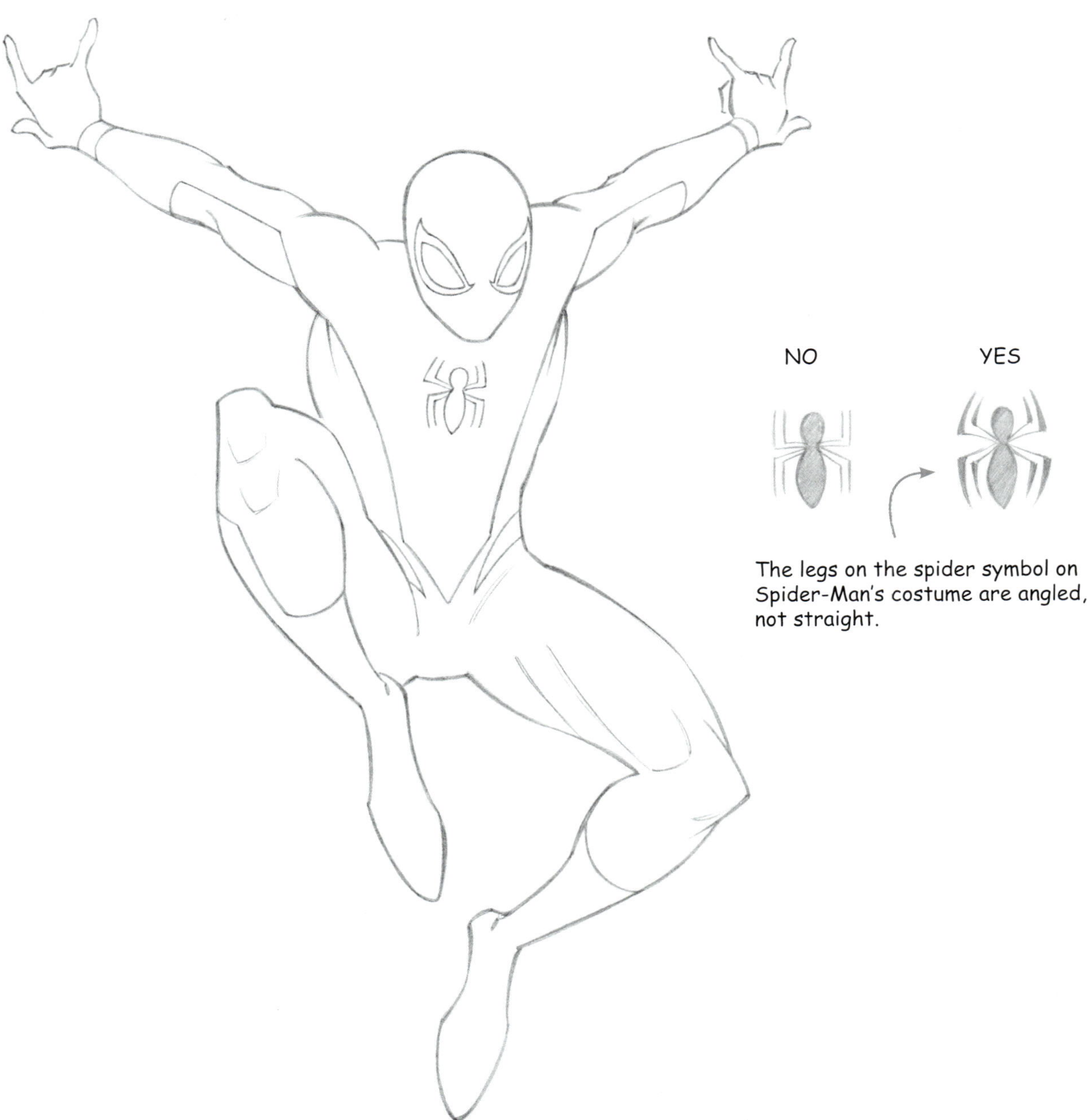

NO   YES

The legs on the spider symbol on Spider-Man's costume are angled, not straight.

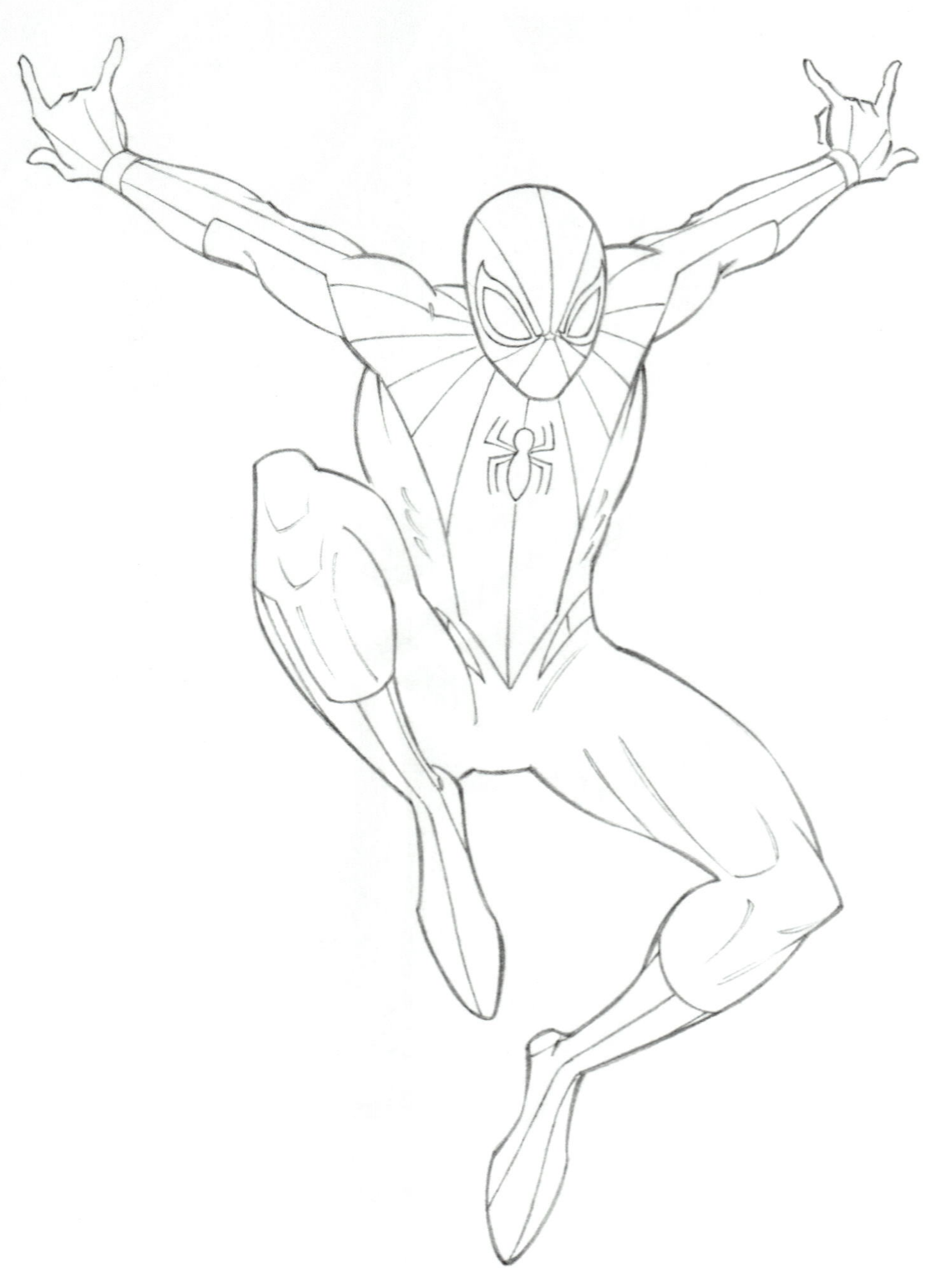

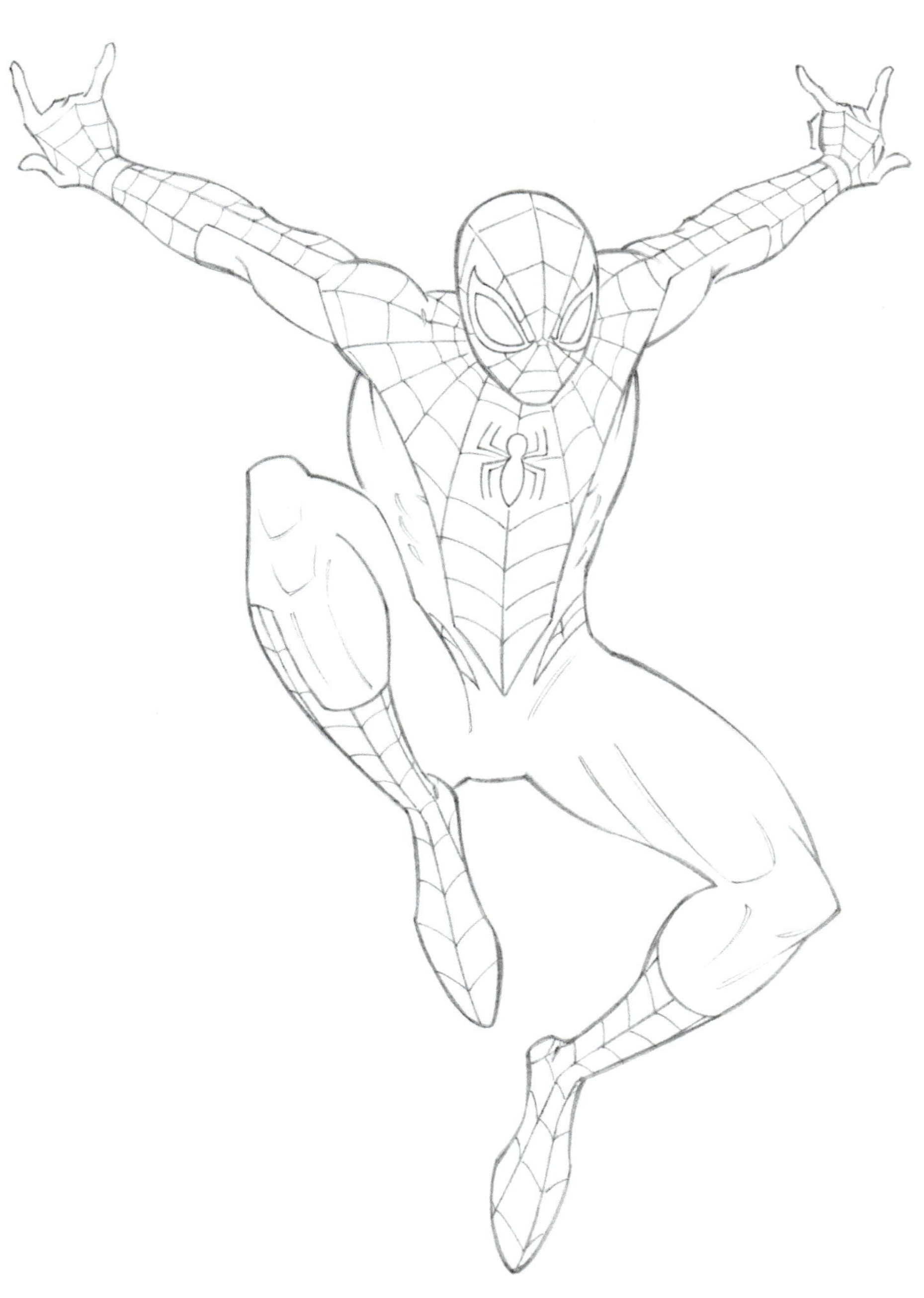

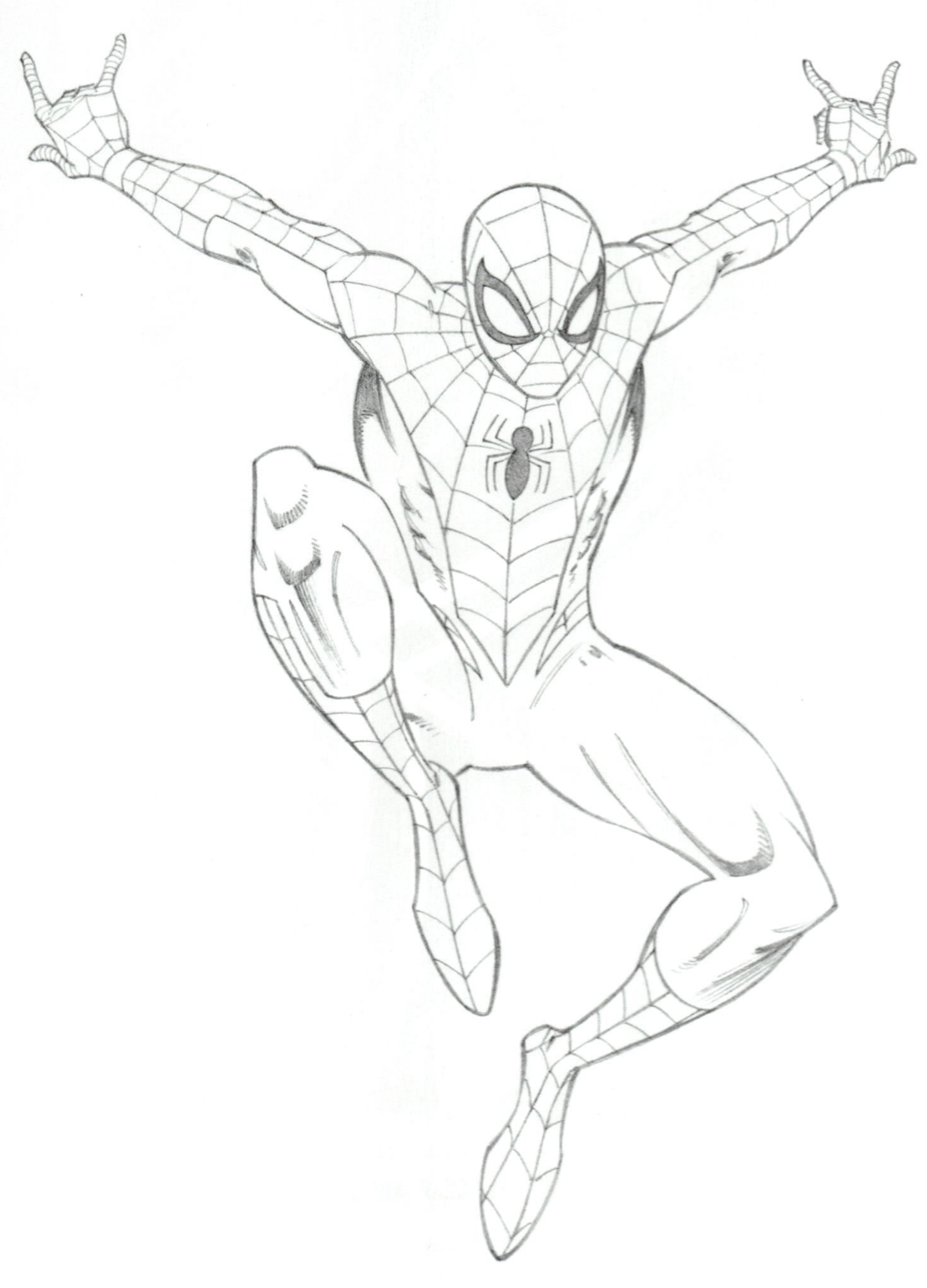

STEP 8

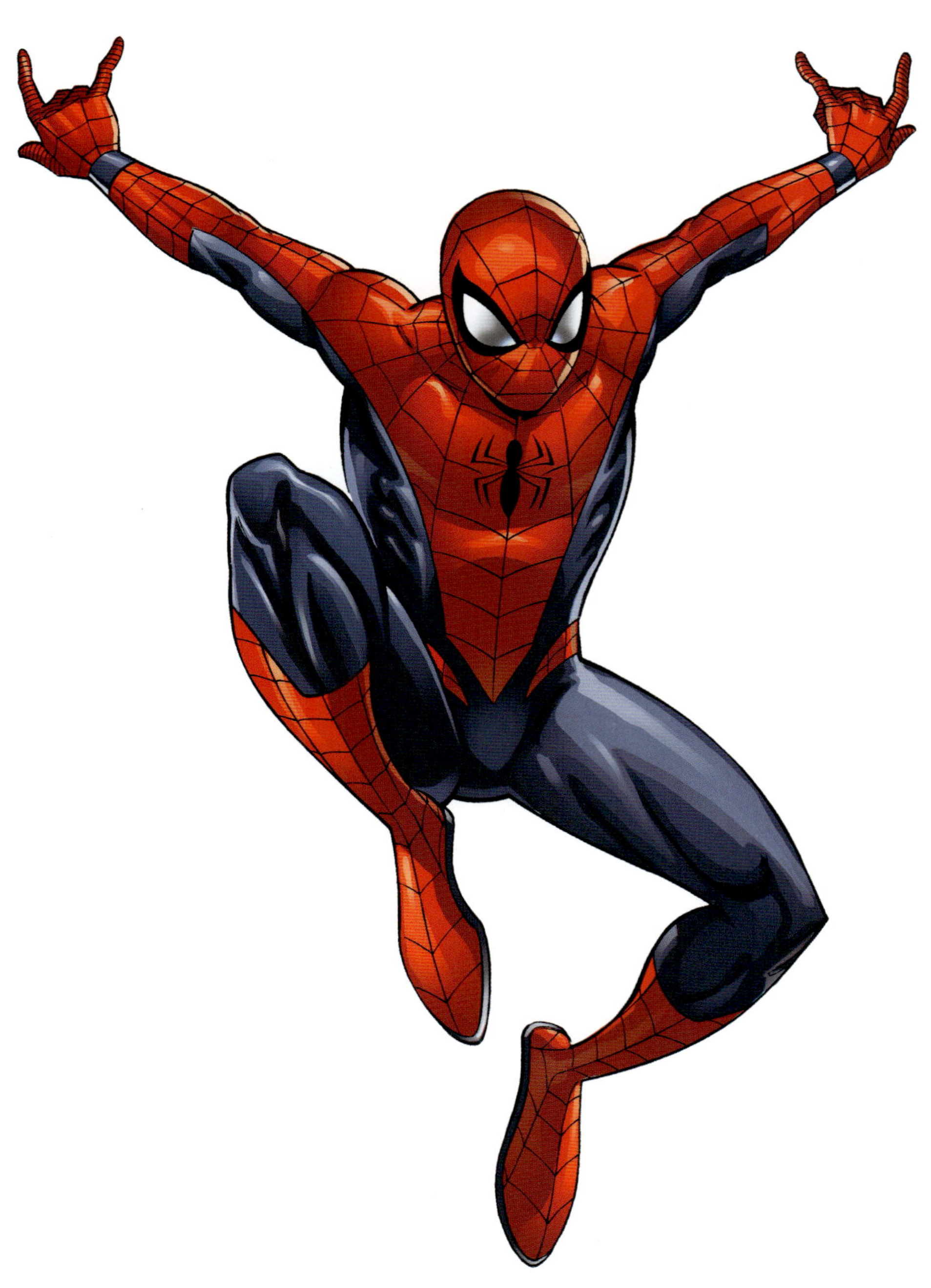

SPIDER-MAN

STEP 1

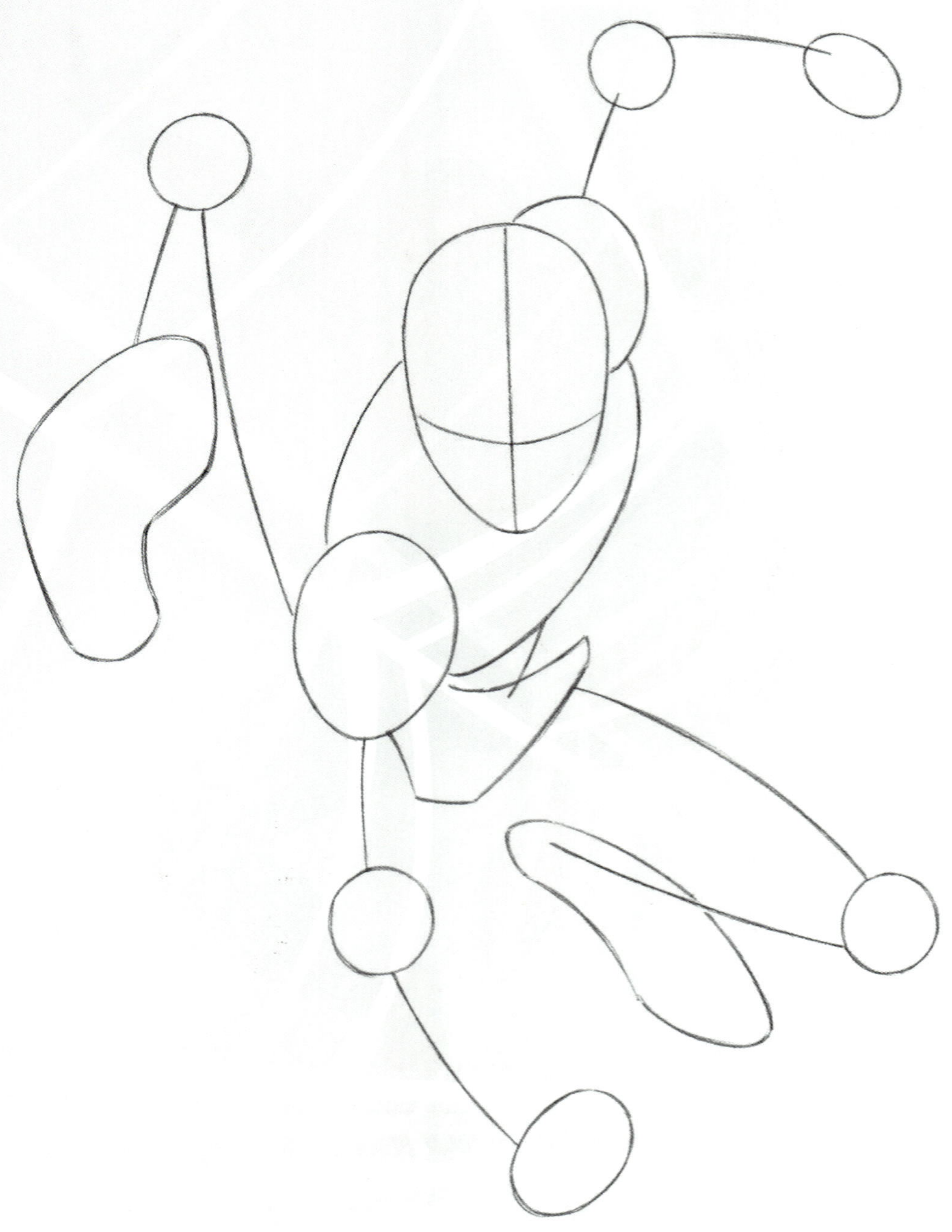

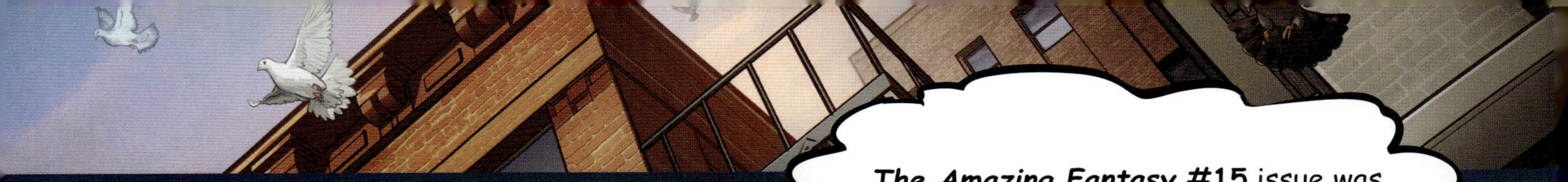

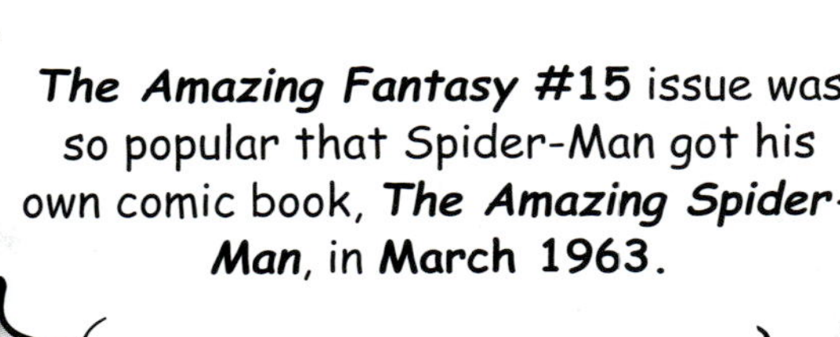

The Amazing Fantasy #15 issue was so popular that Spider-Man got his own comic book, *The Amazing Spider-Man*, in March 1963.

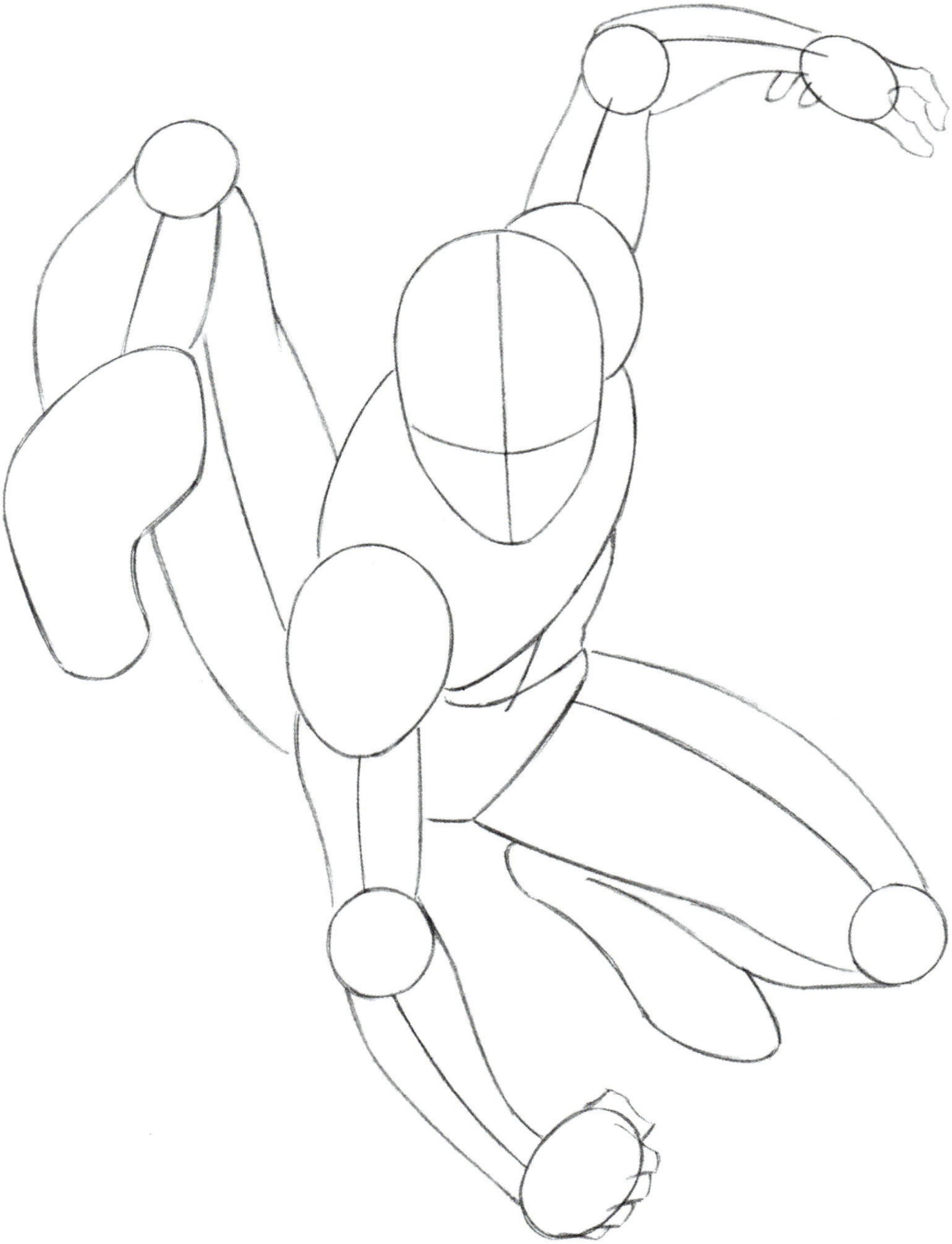

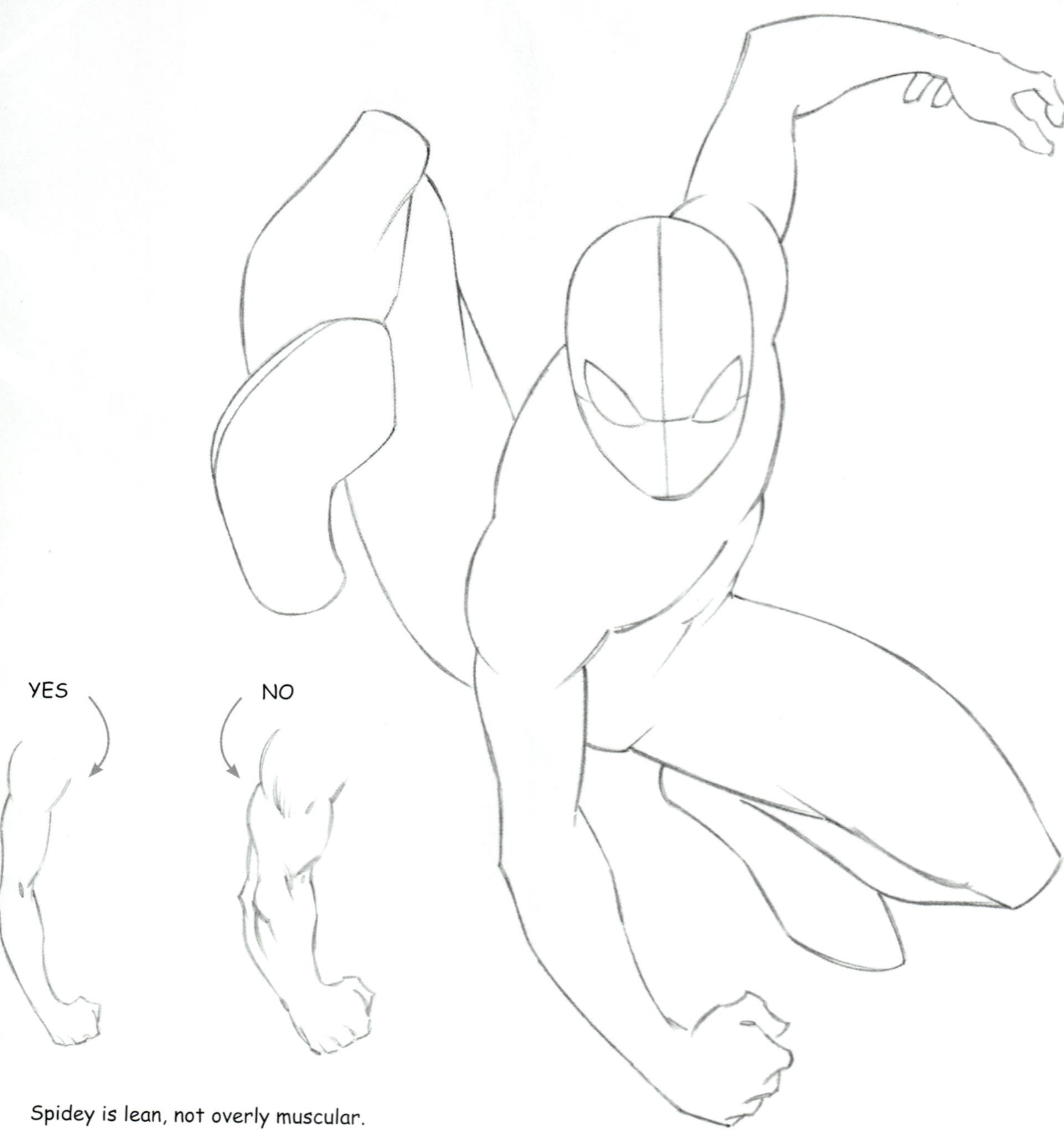

Spidey is lean, not overly muscular.

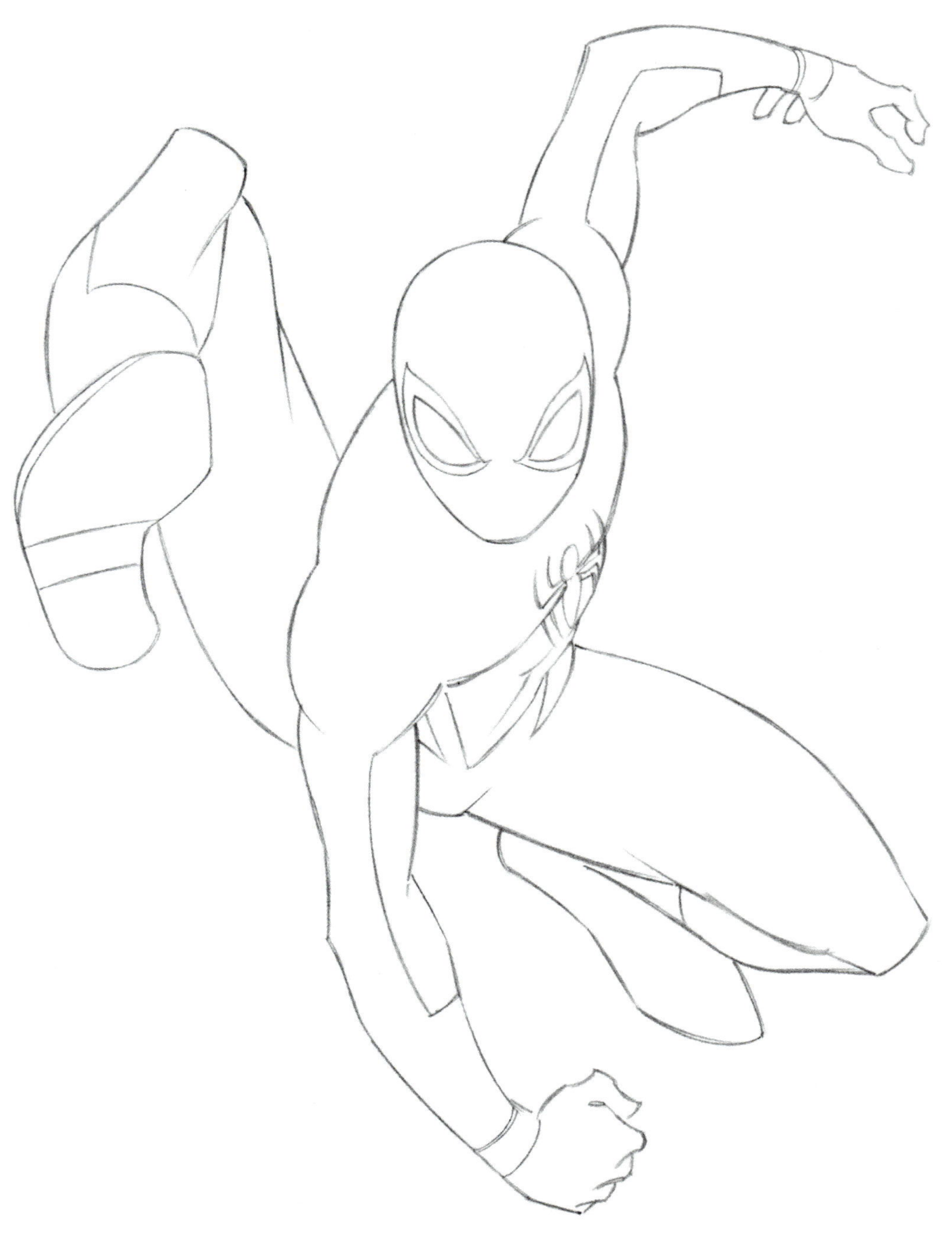

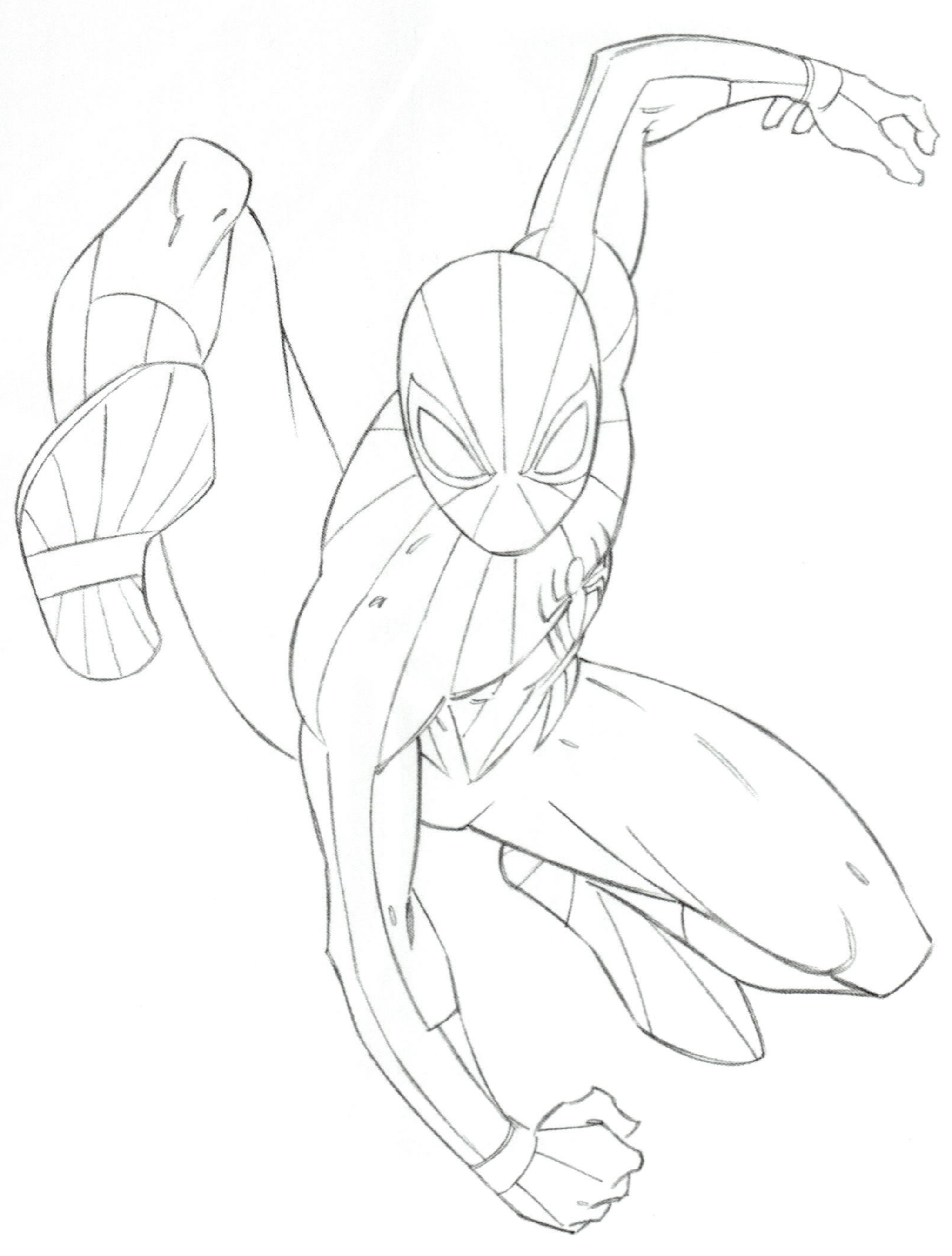

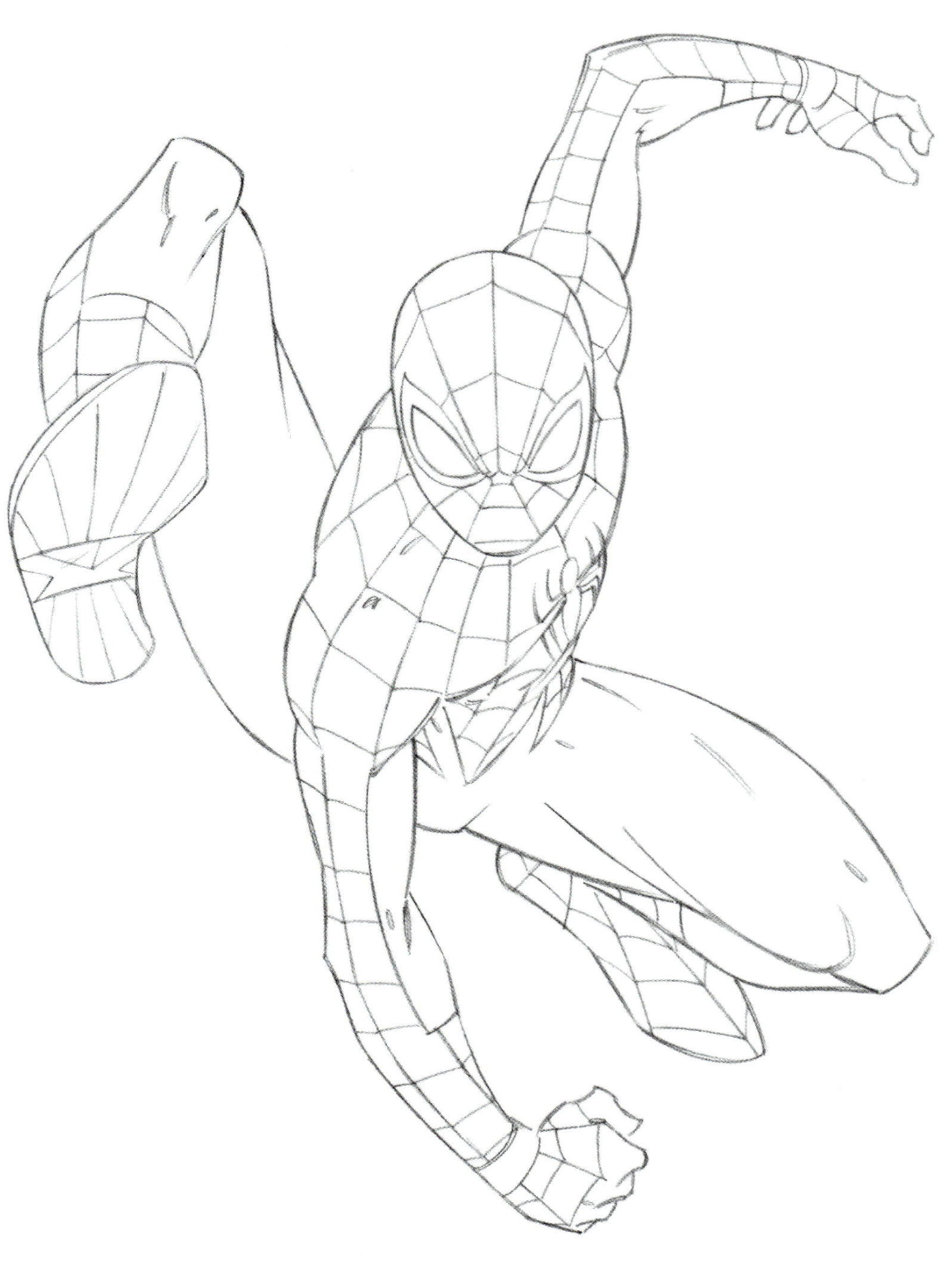

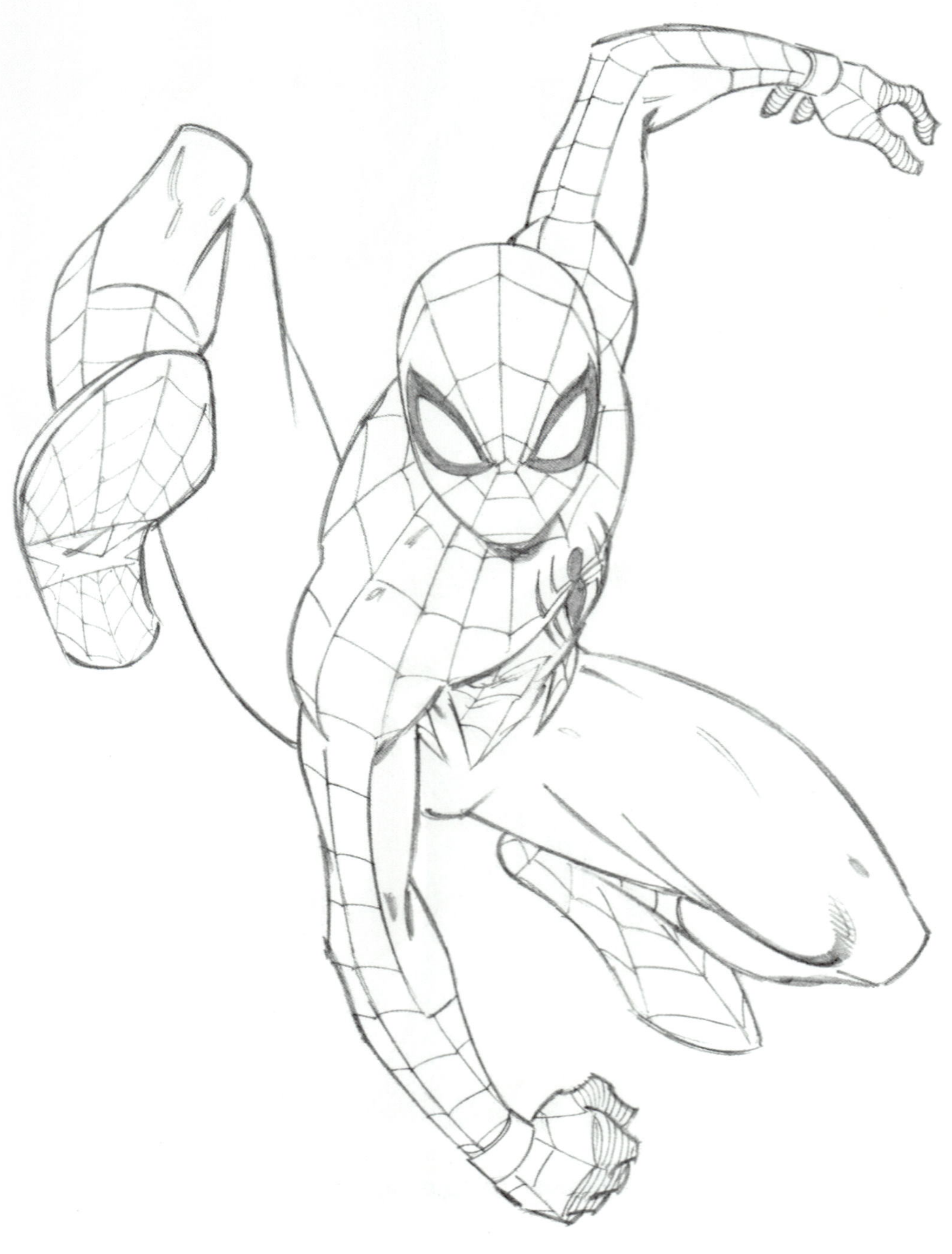

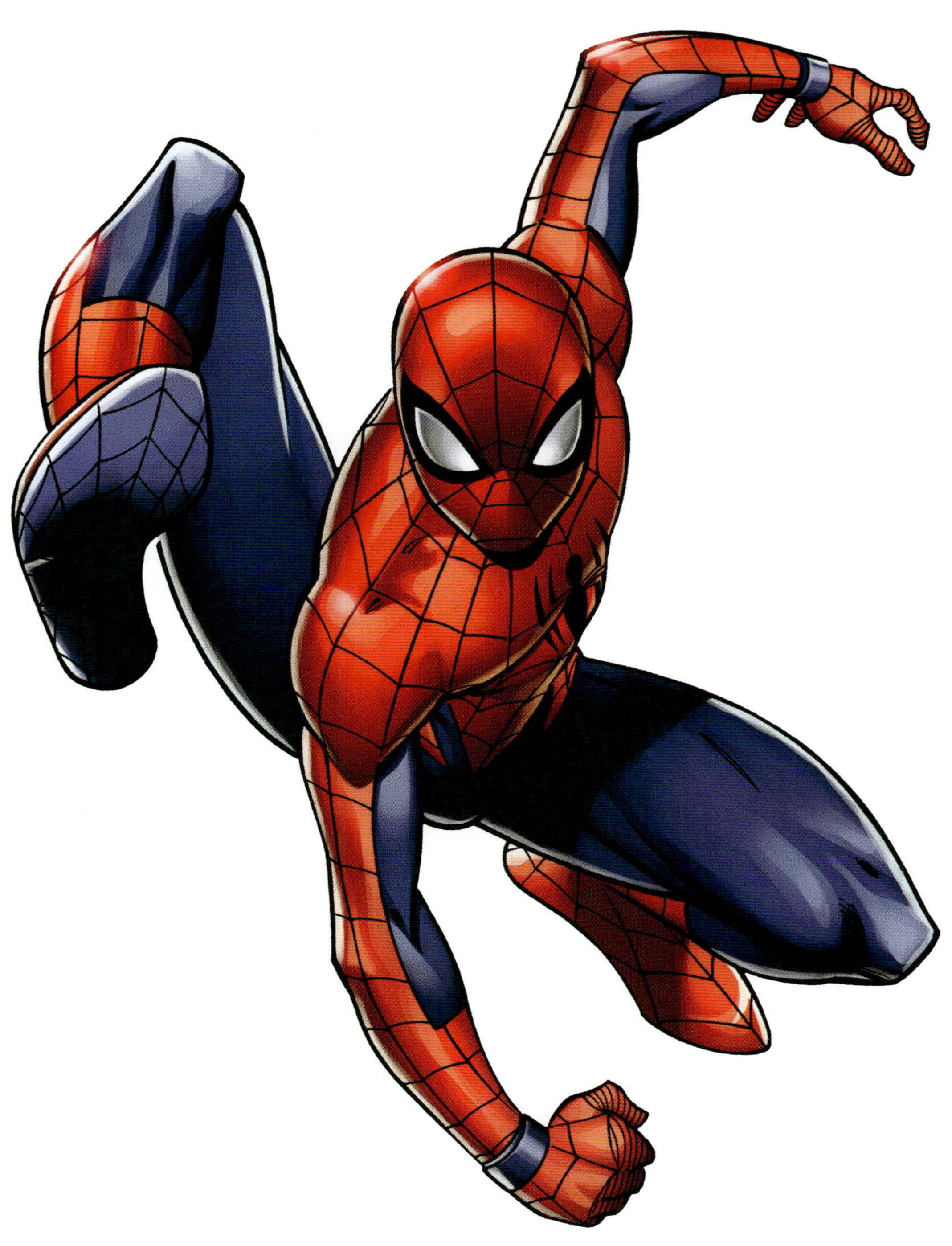

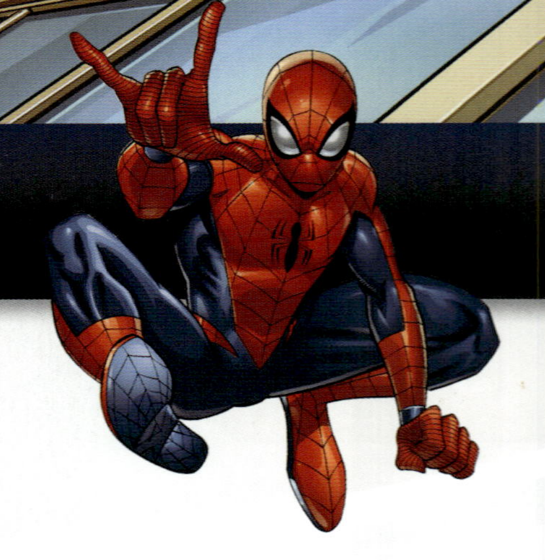

STEP 1

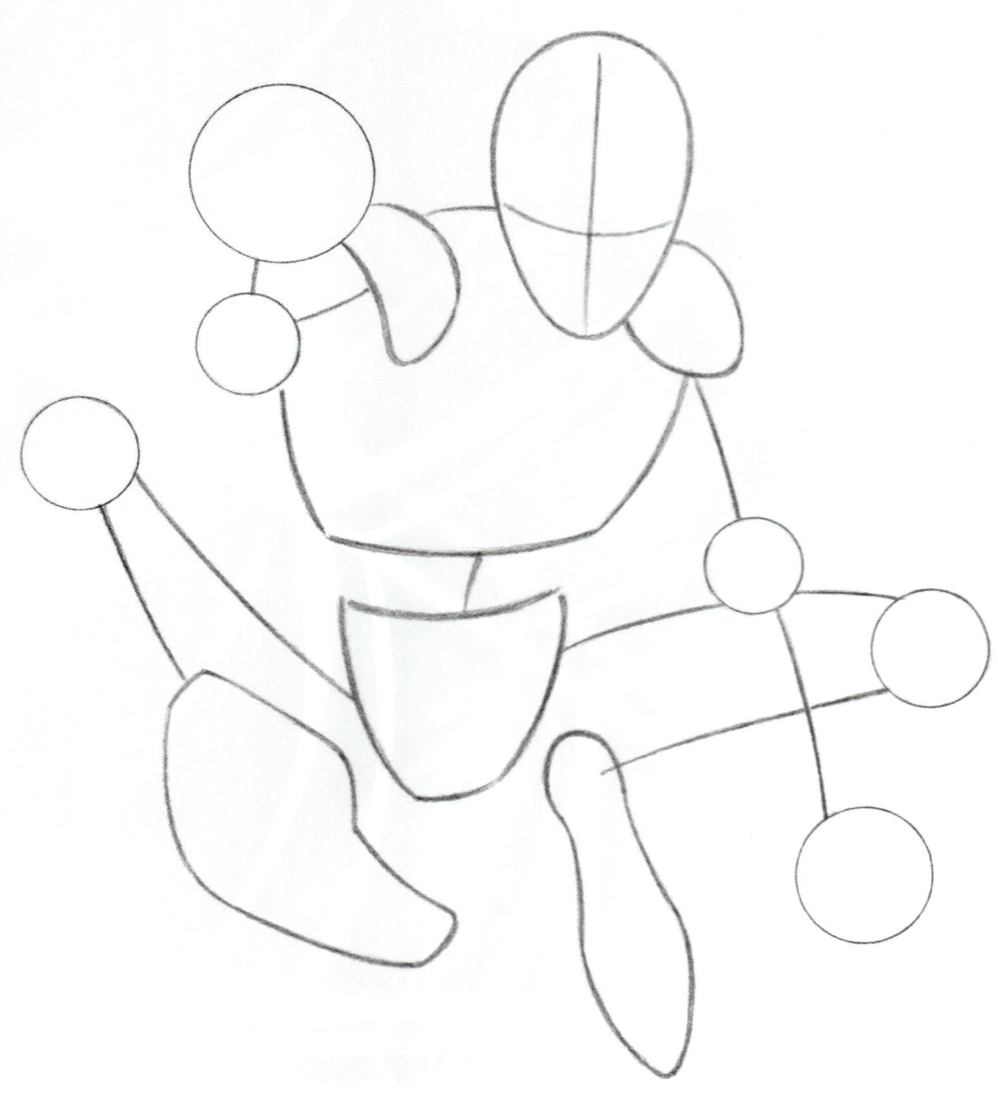

STEP 2

Spider-Man is Marvel's most popular **Super Hero**, very likely due to his relatability with Marvel's core audience of young males.

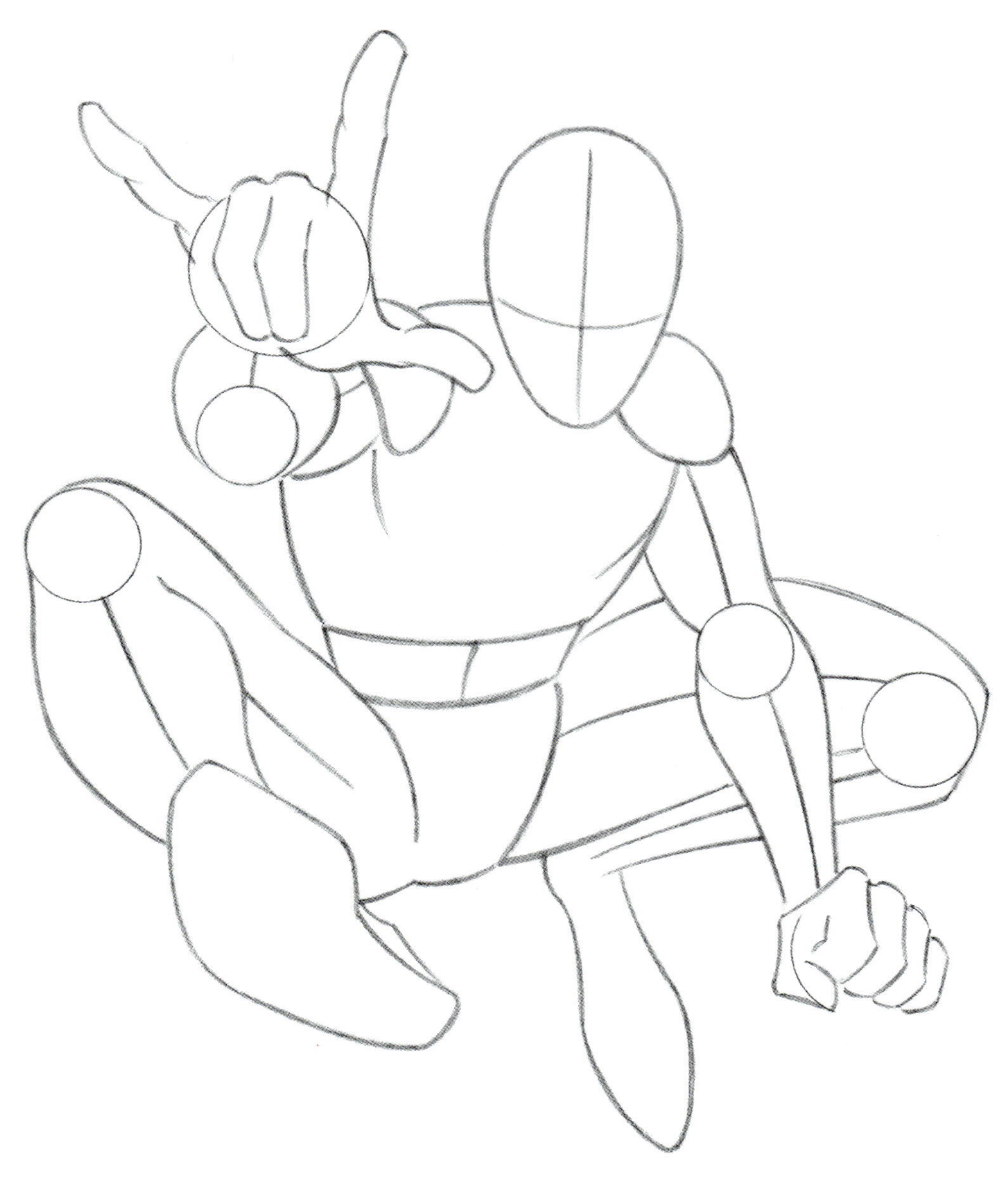

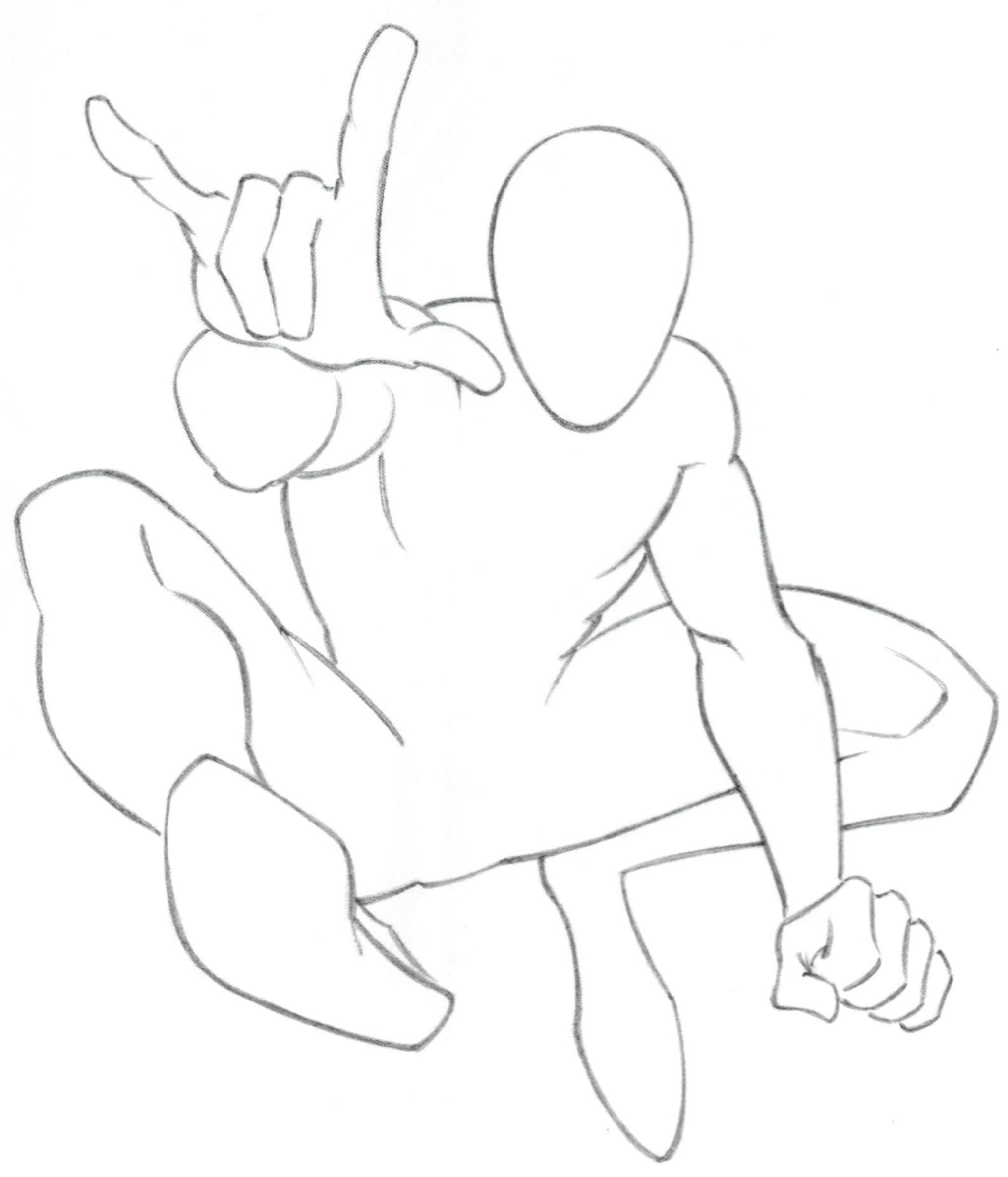

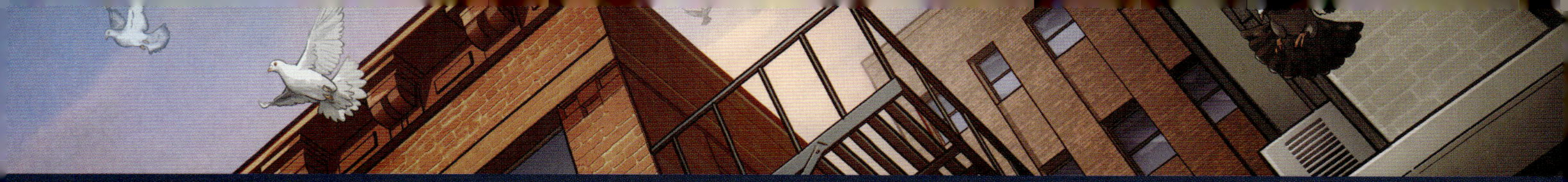

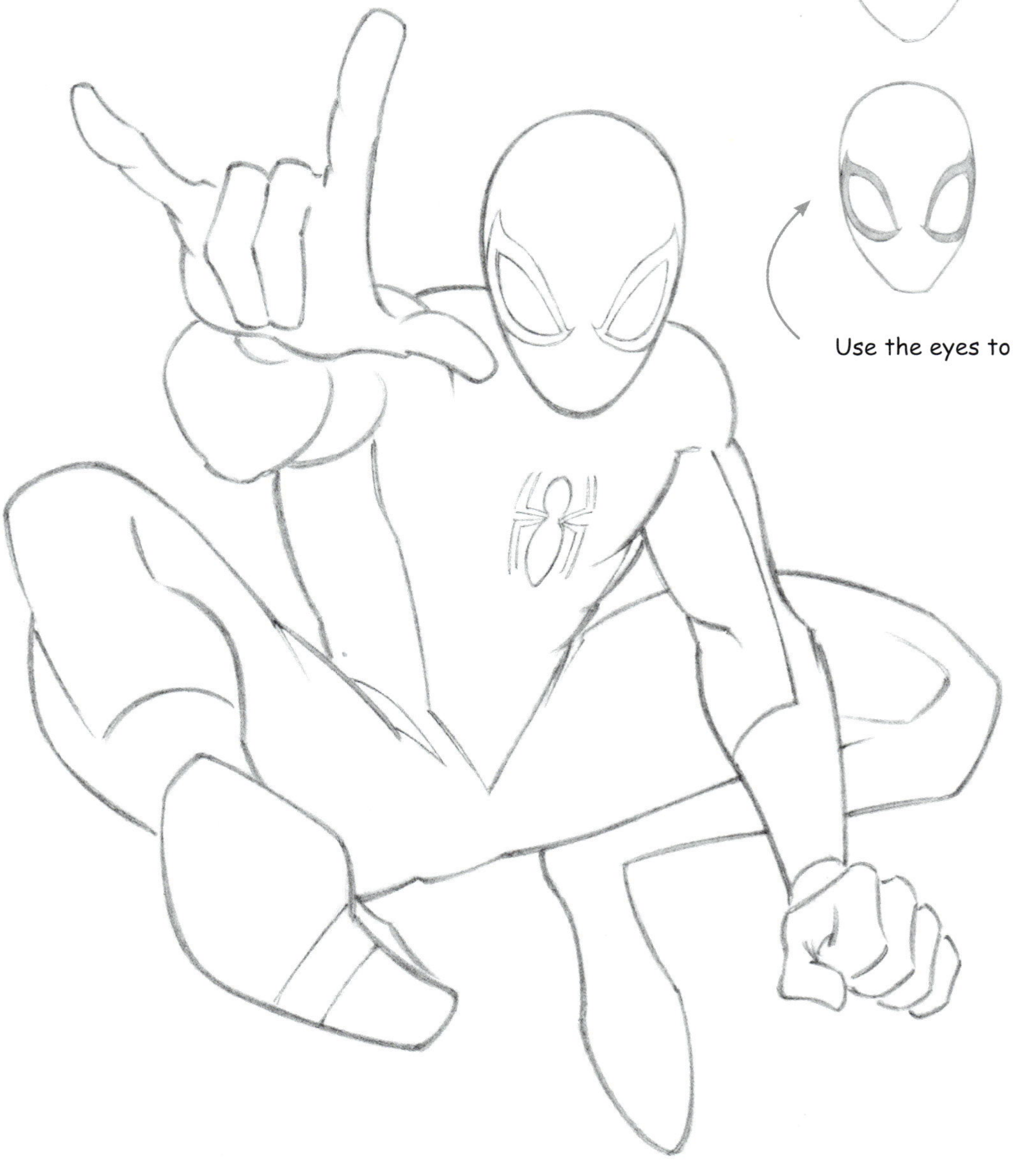

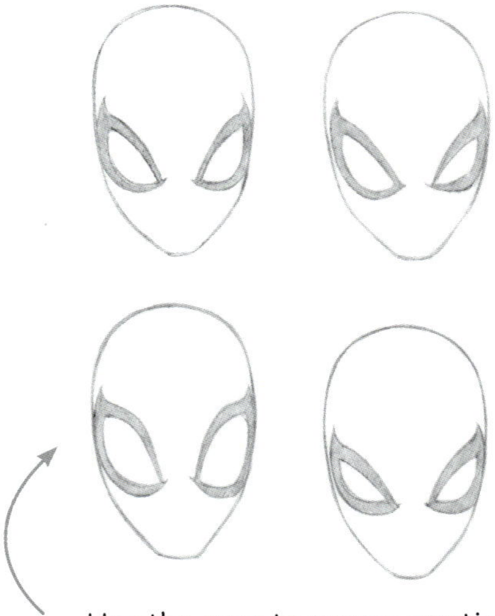

Use the eyes to convey emotion.

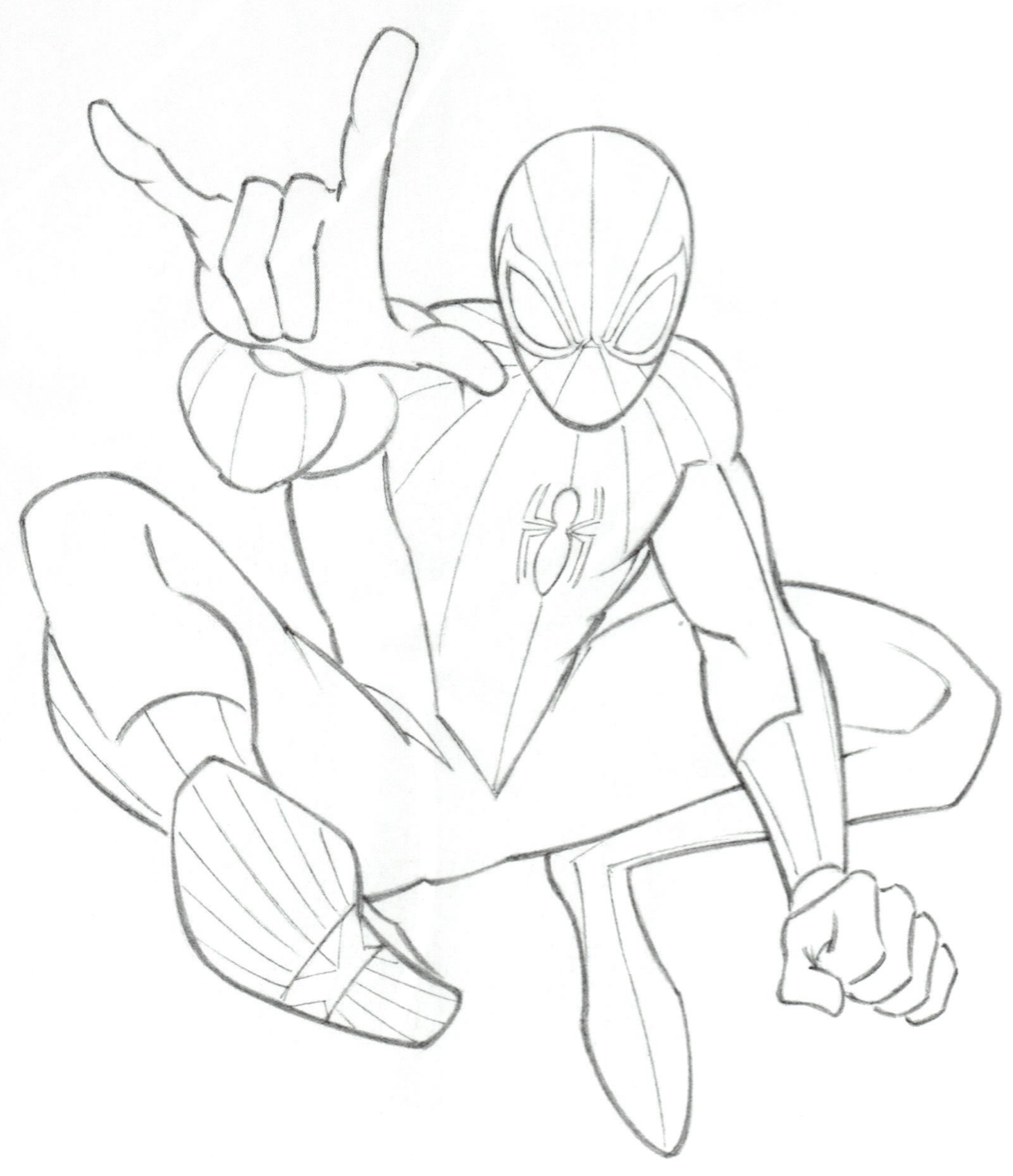

STEP 6

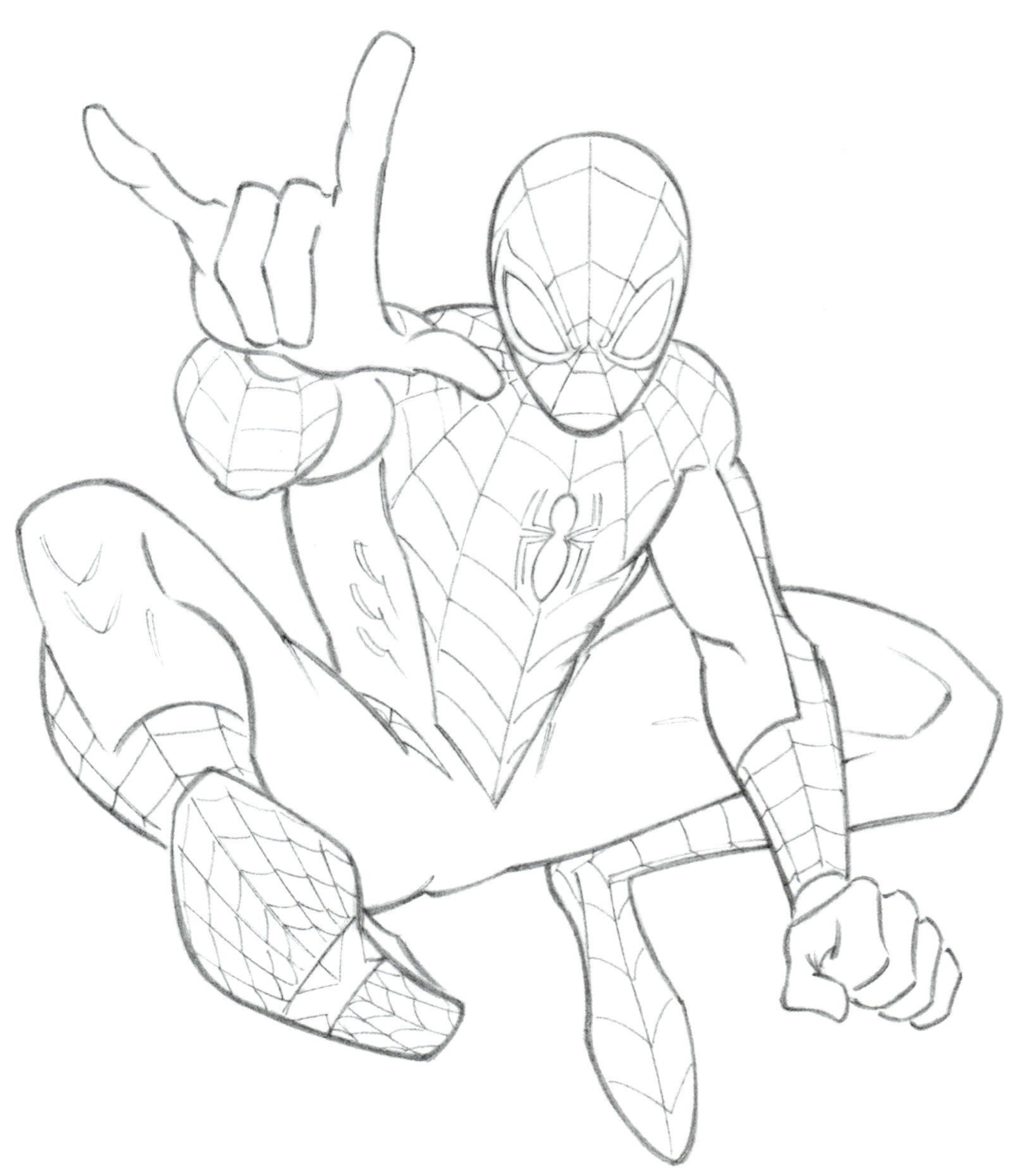

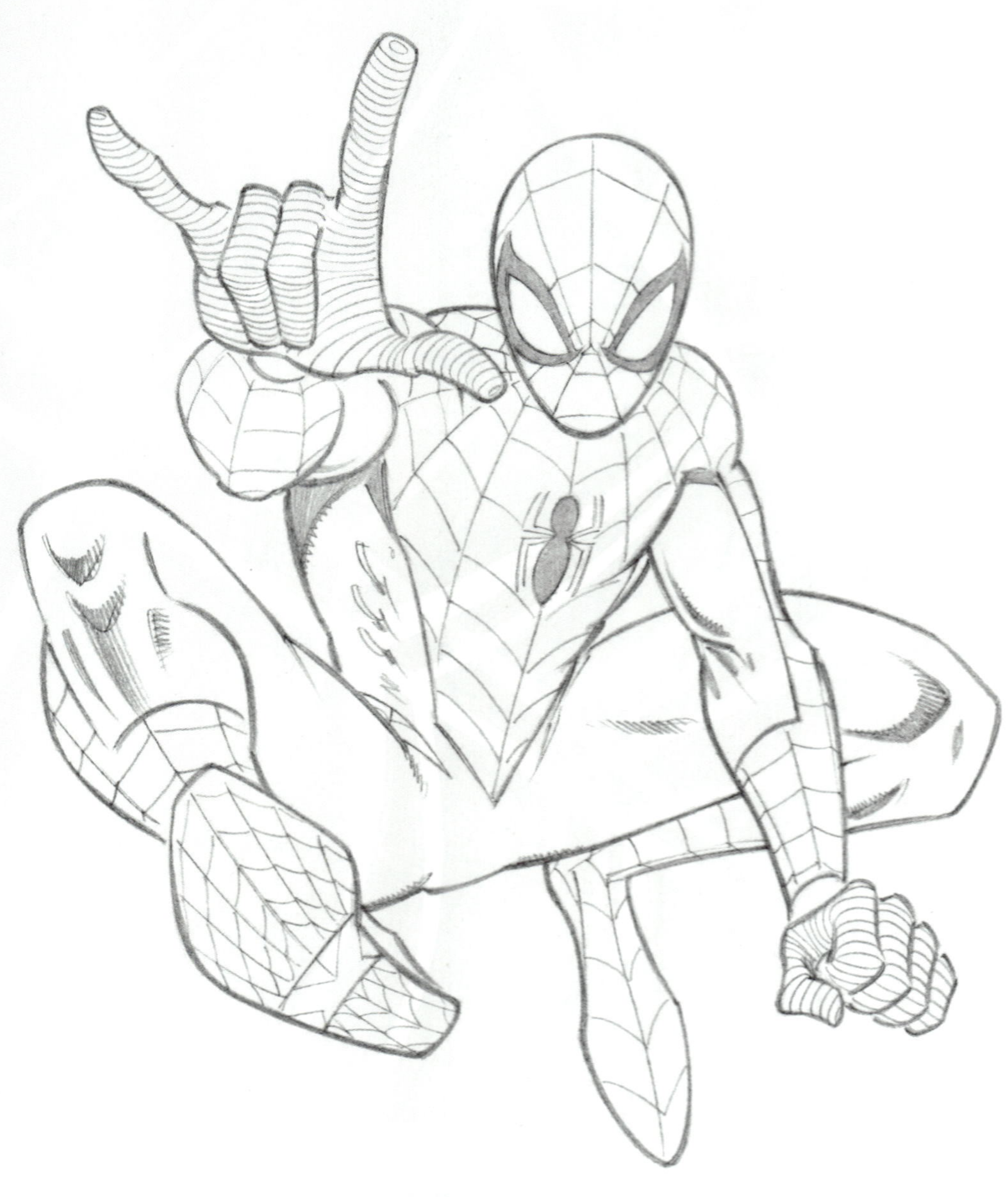

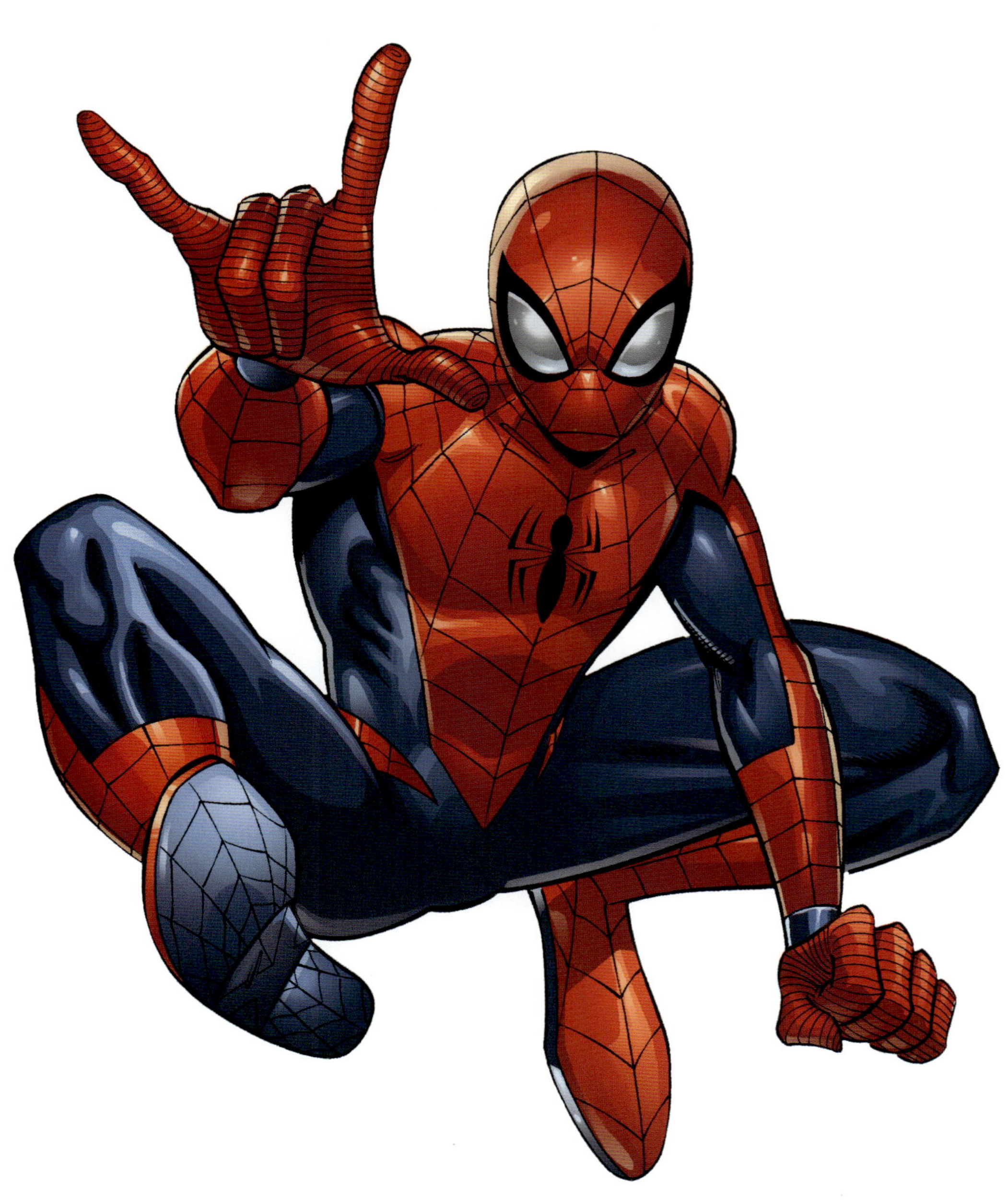

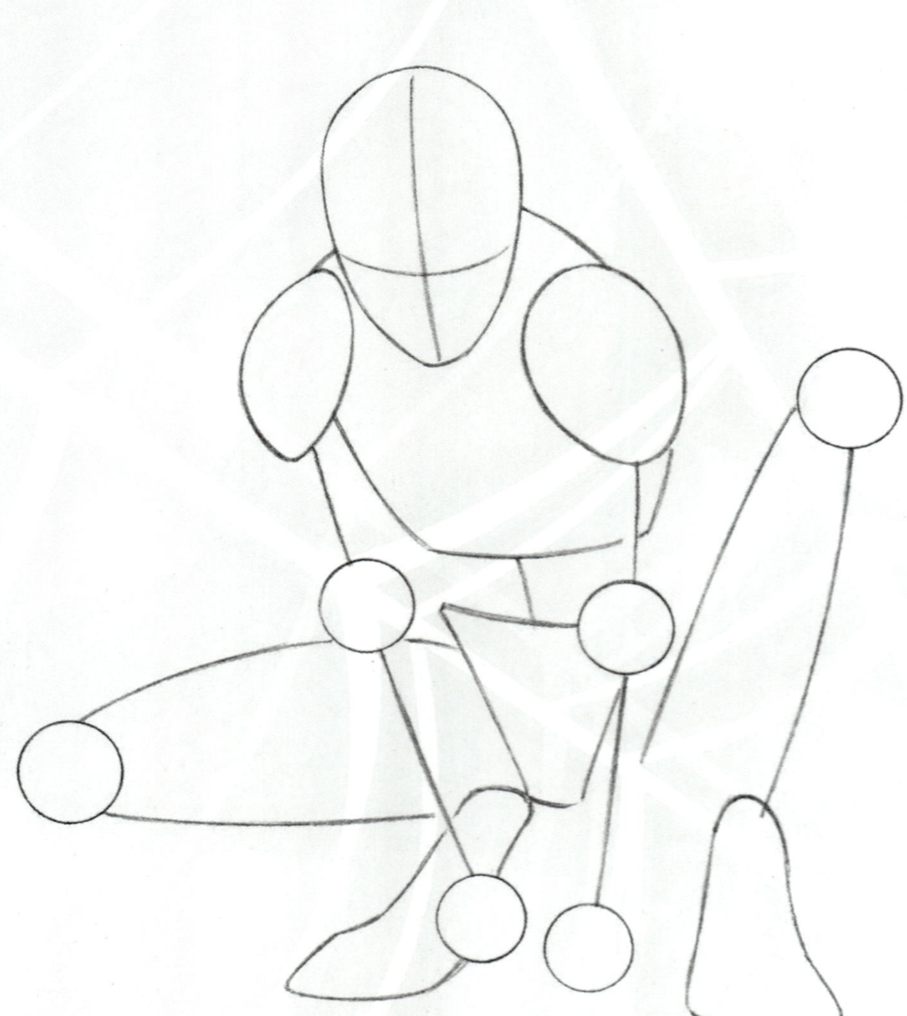

STEP 2

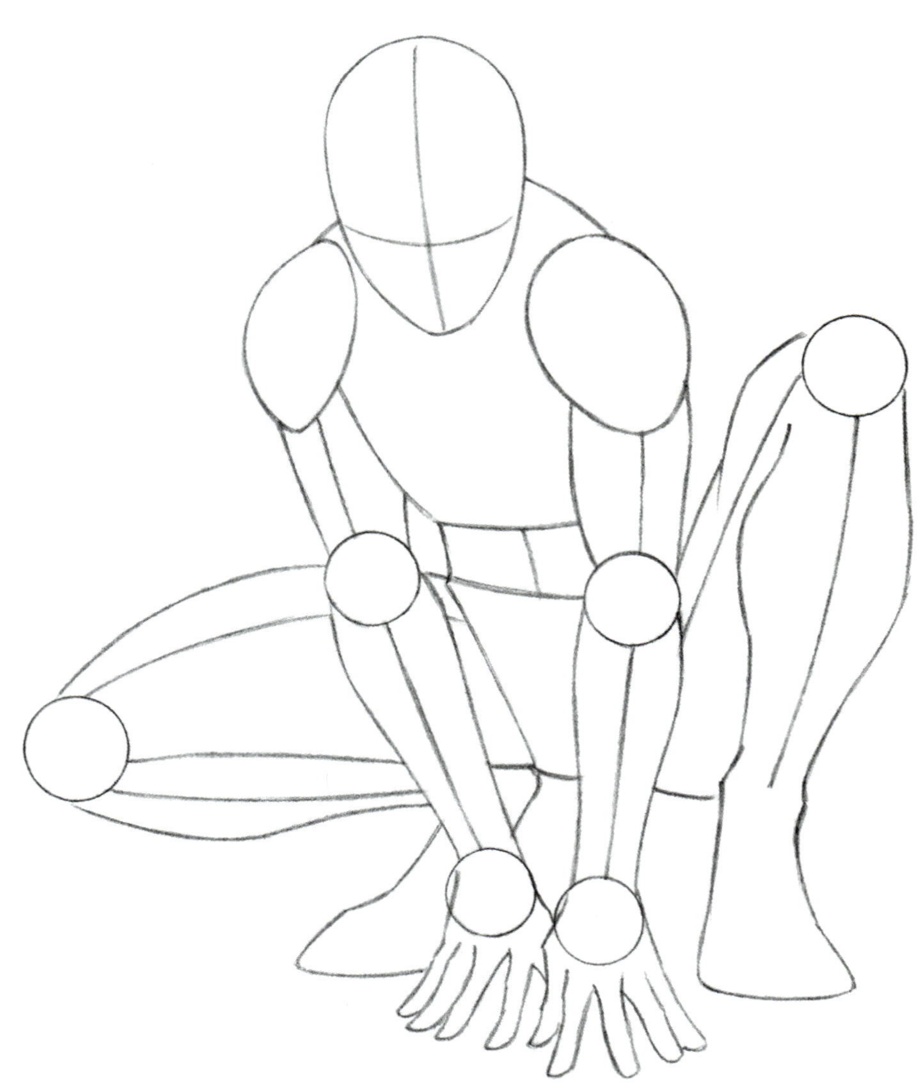

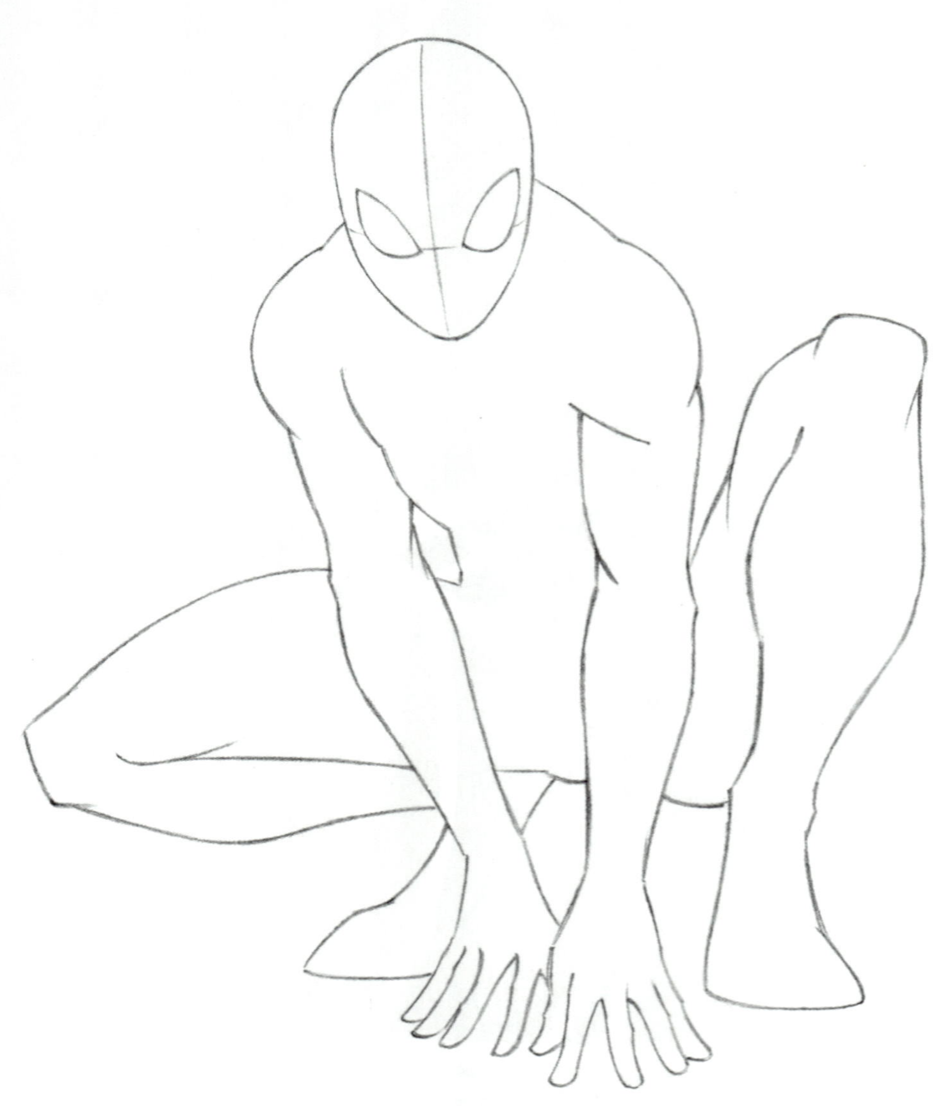

STEP 4

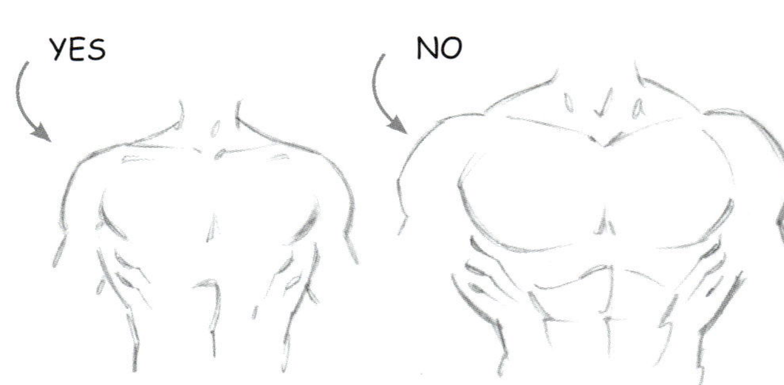

Spider-Man's chest

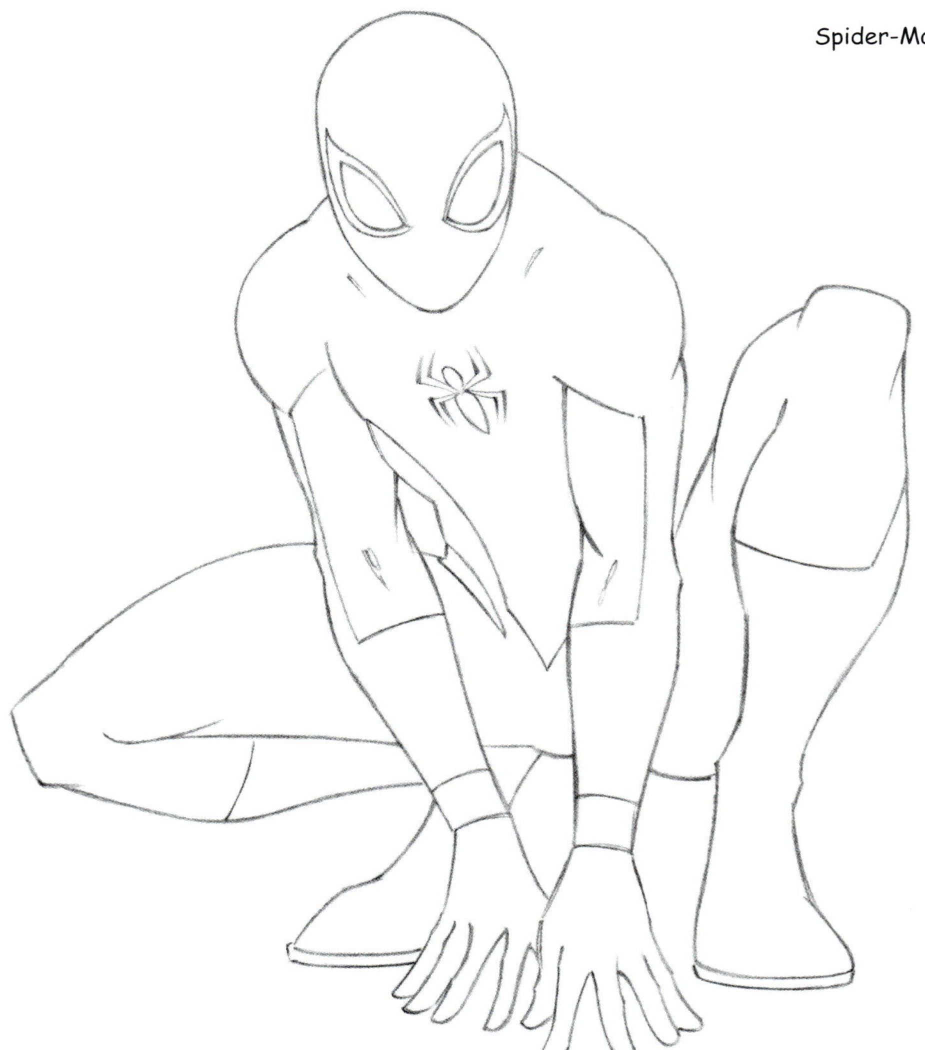

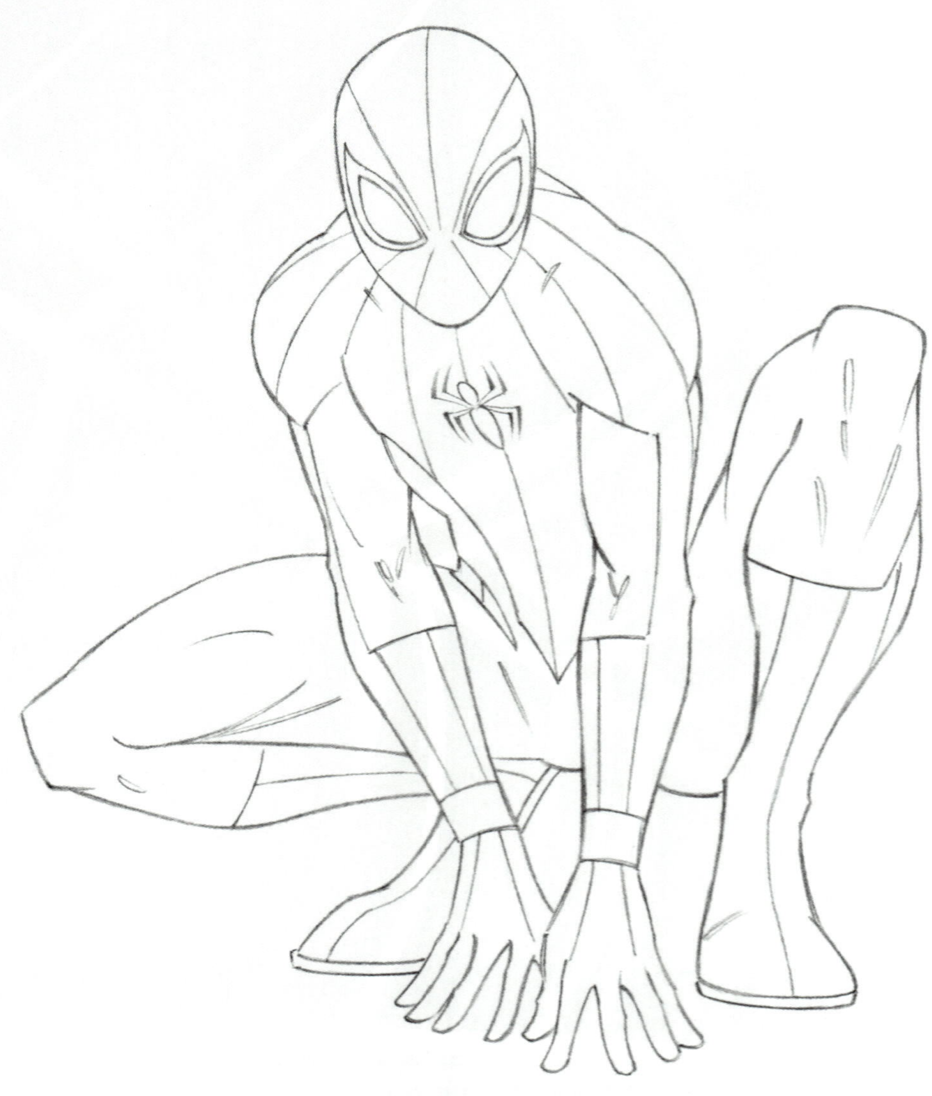

STEP 6

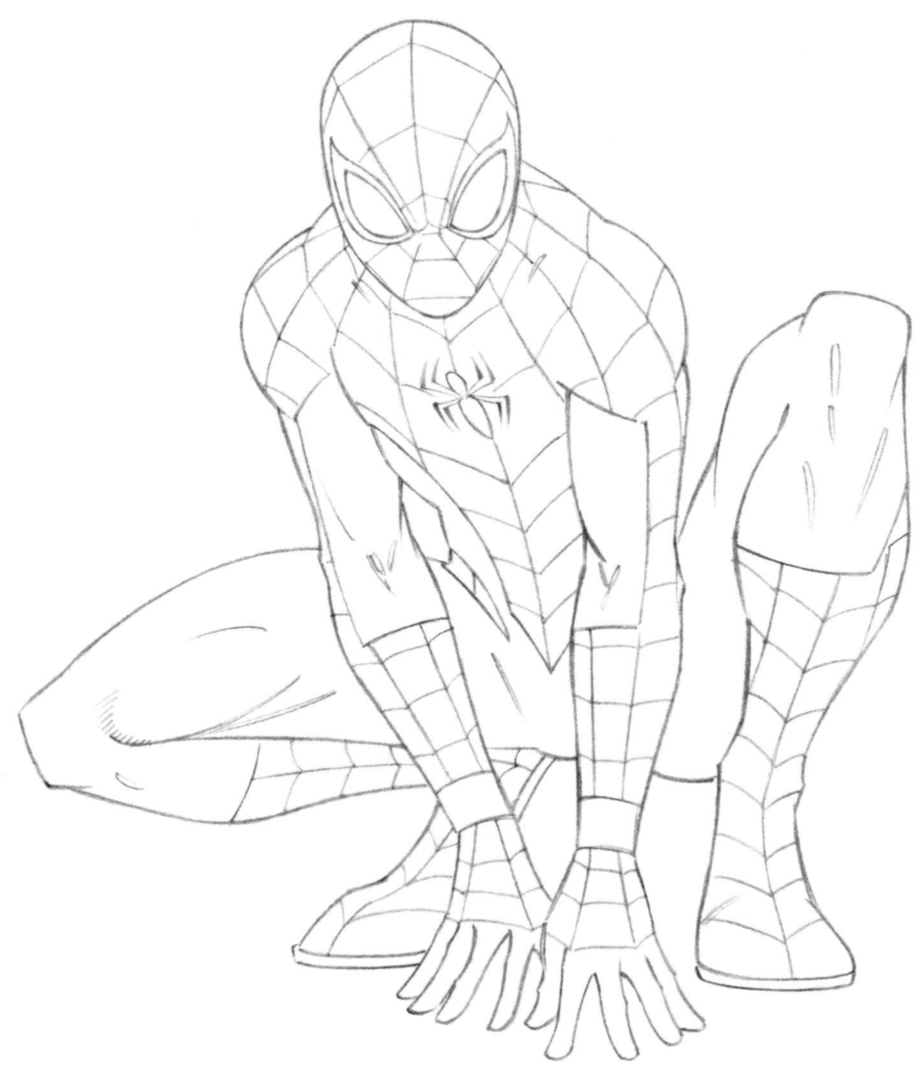

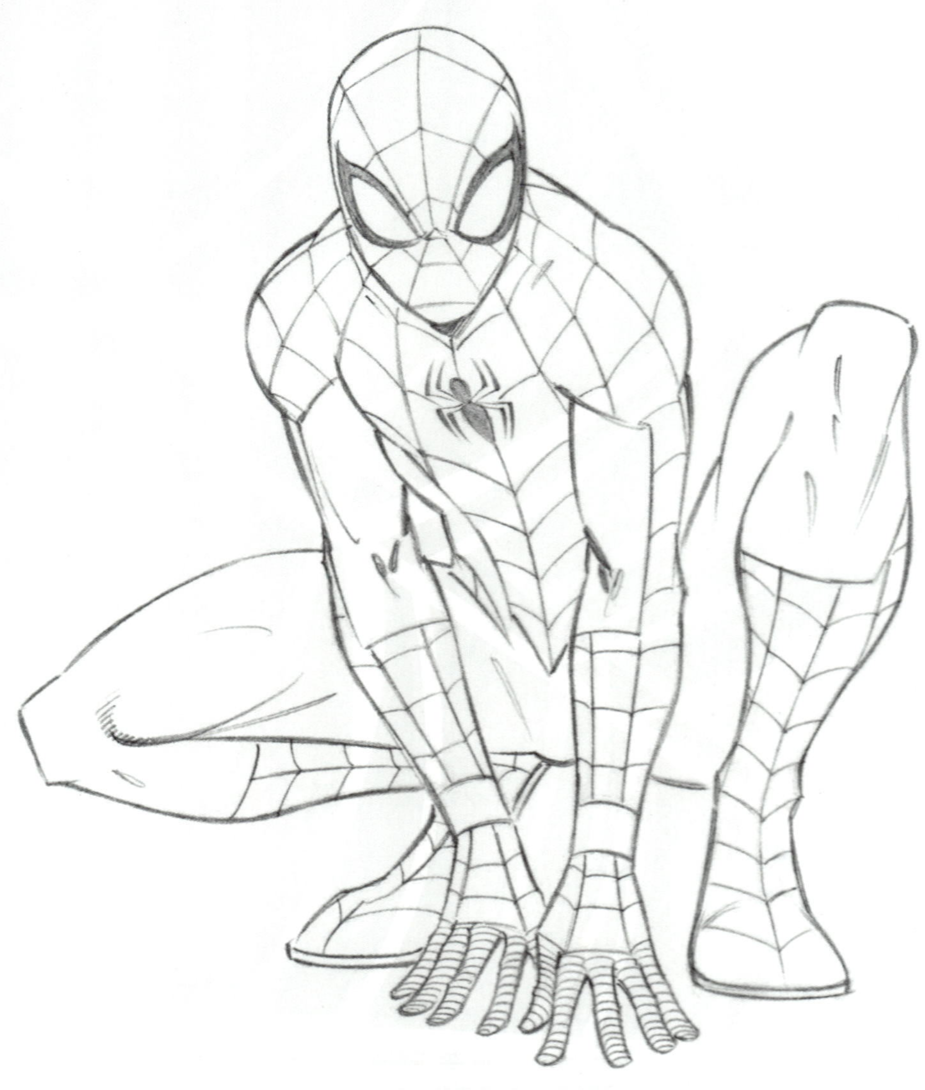

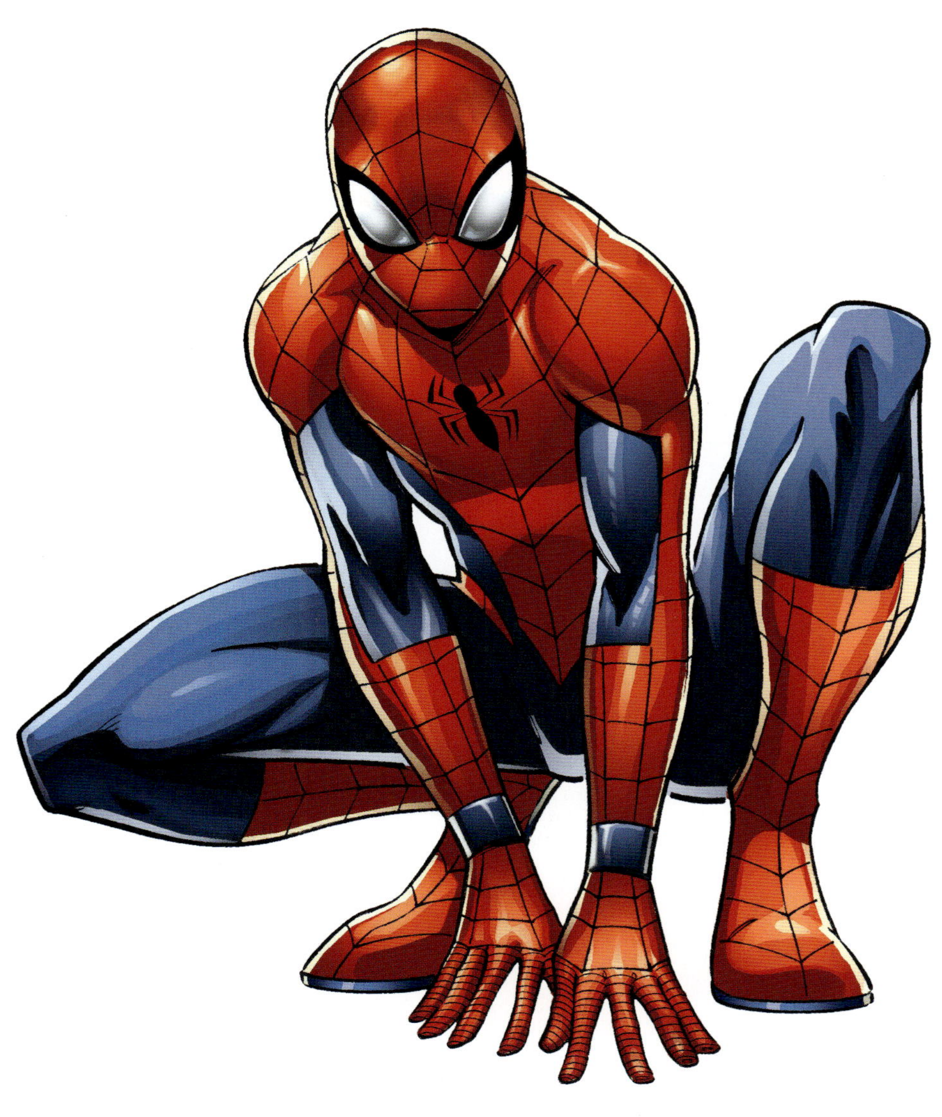

SPIDER-MAN

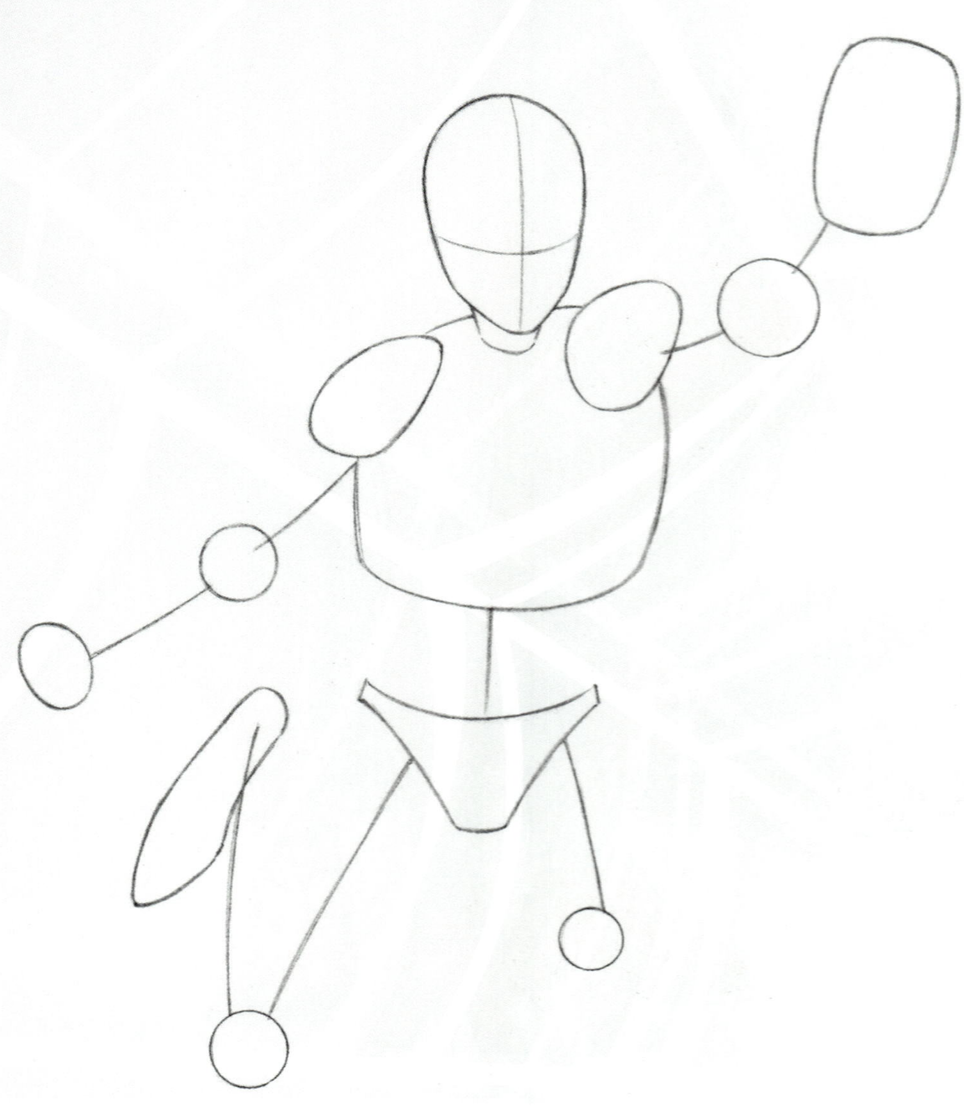

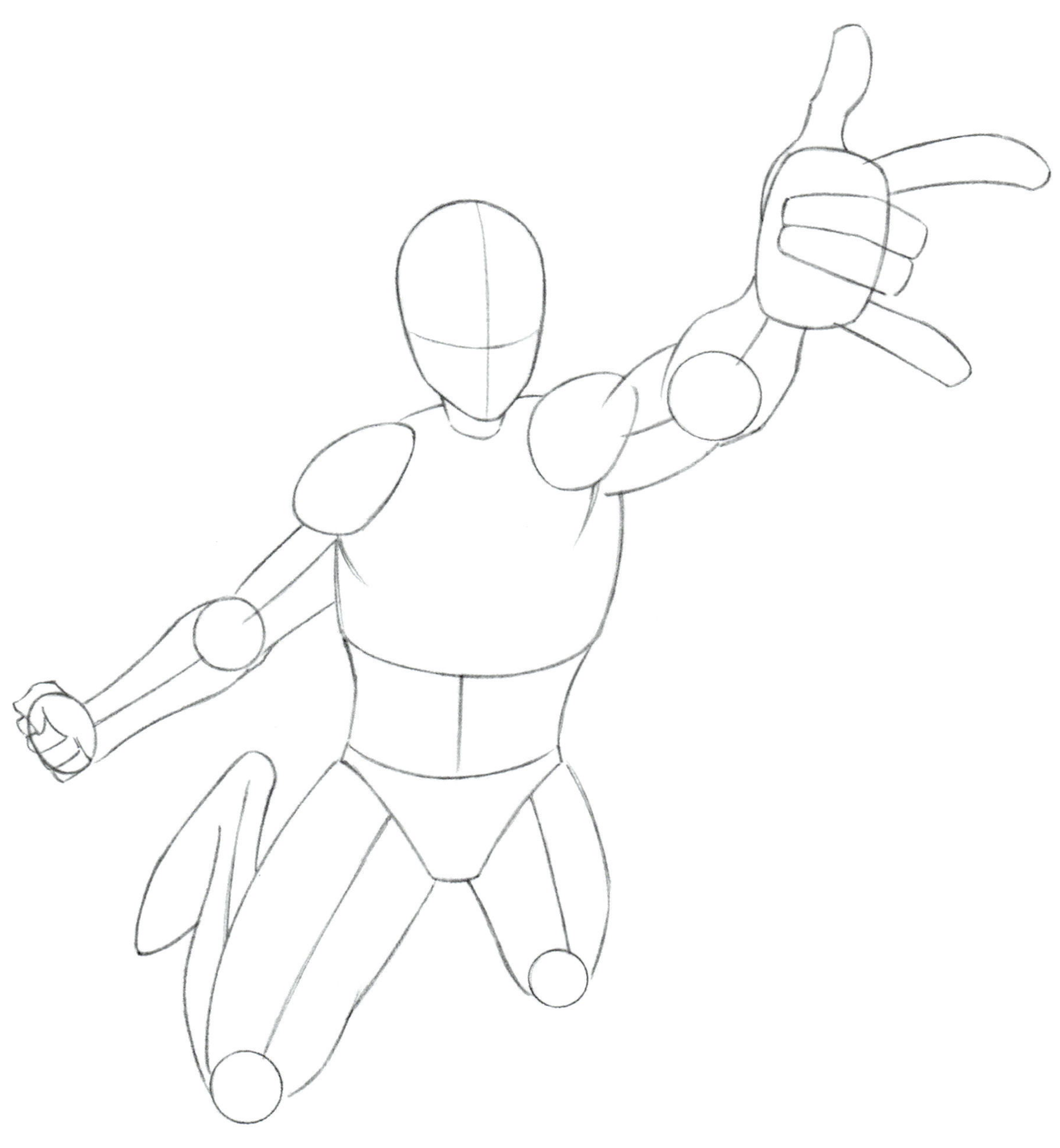

The *Amazing Spider-Man #1* cover art was by **Jack Kirby** and **Steve Ditko**.

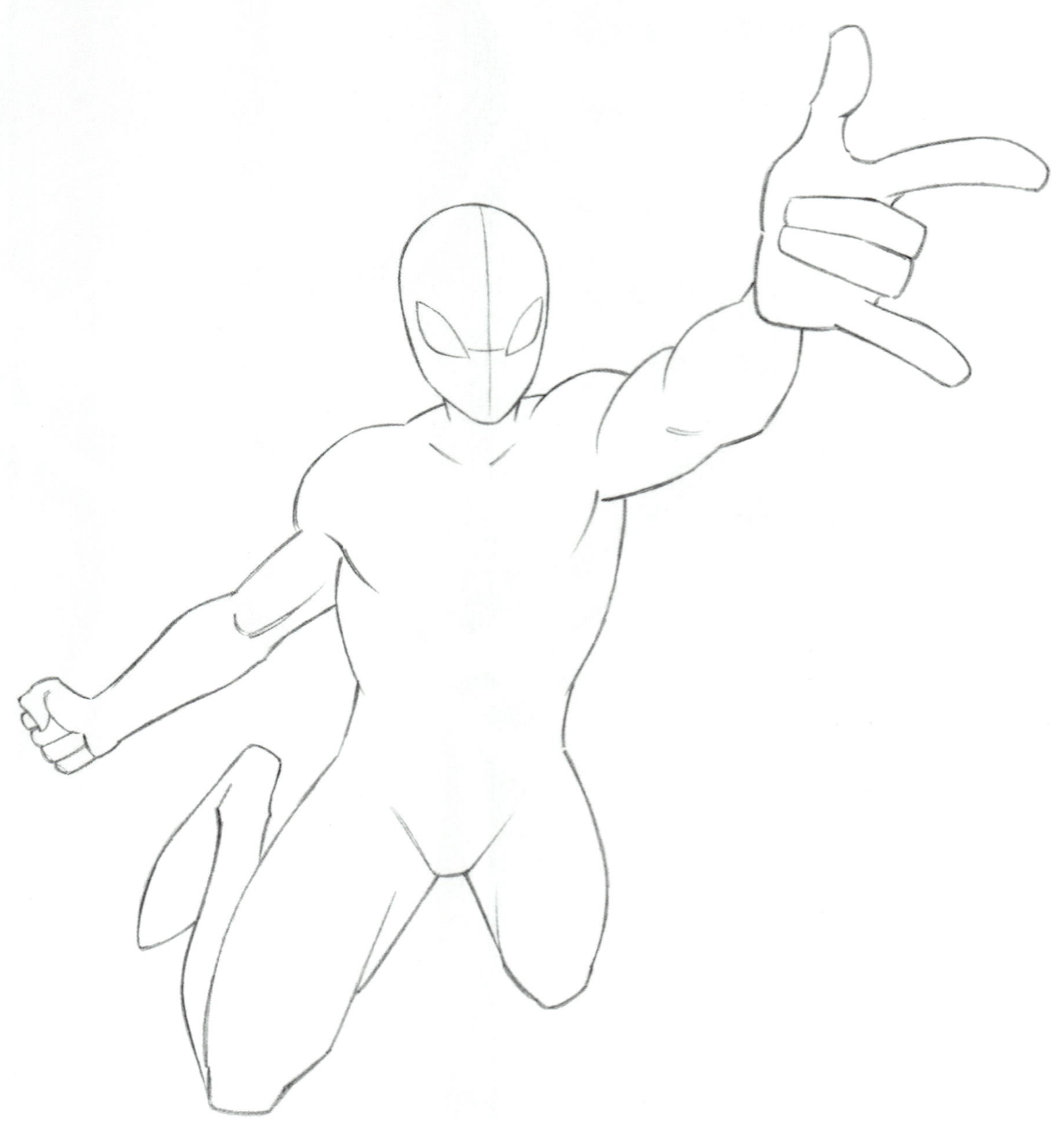

STEP 4

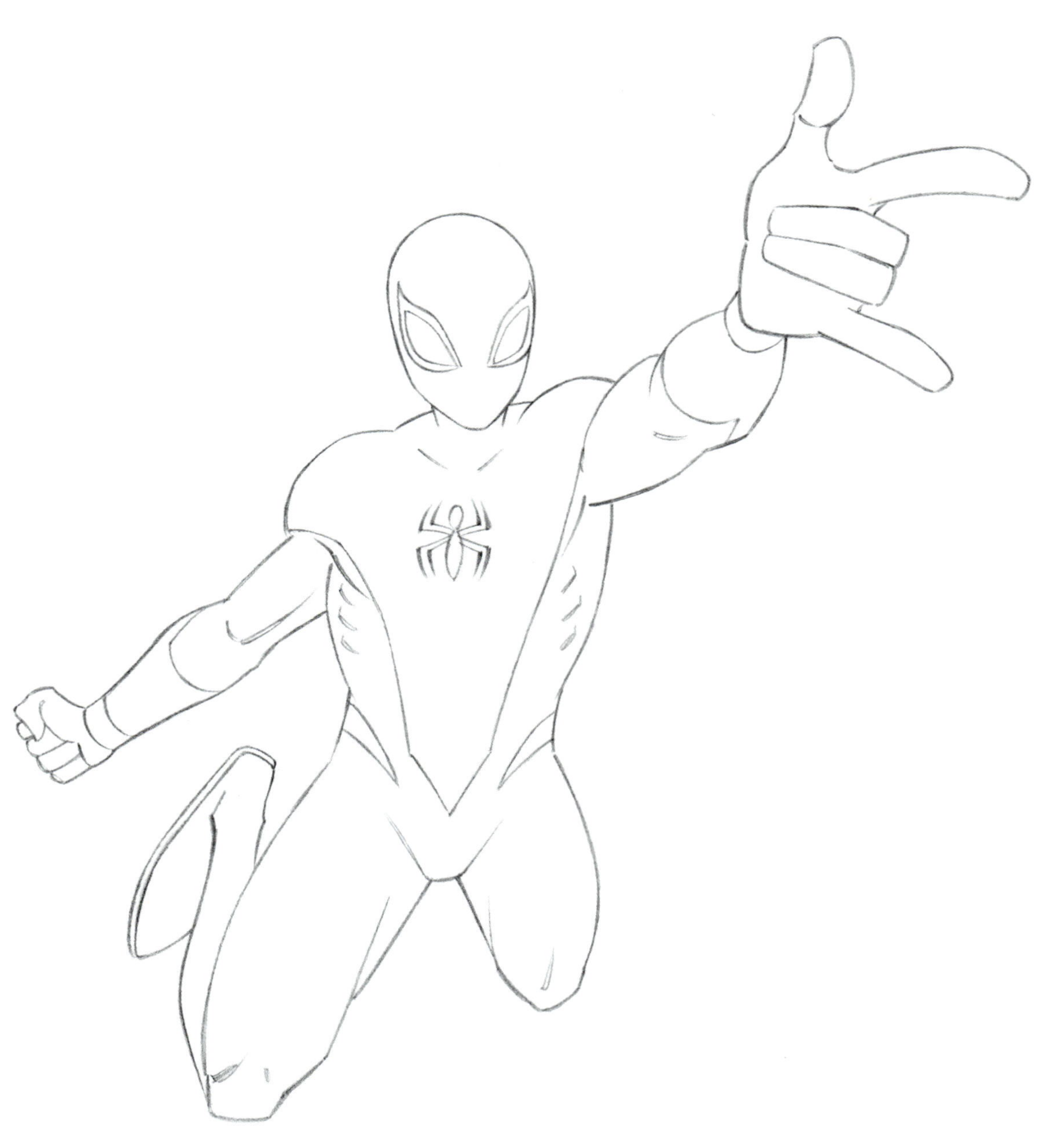

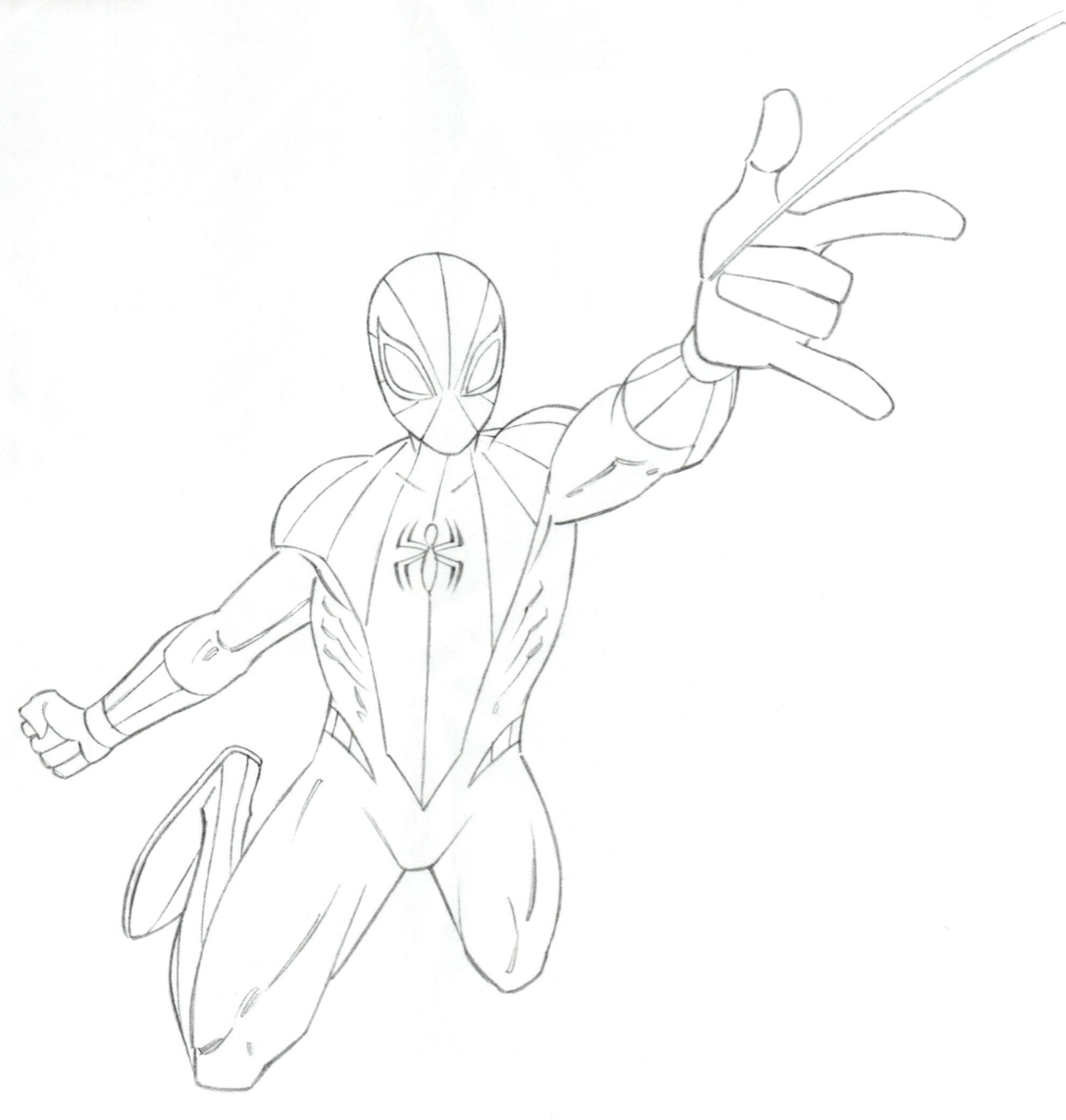

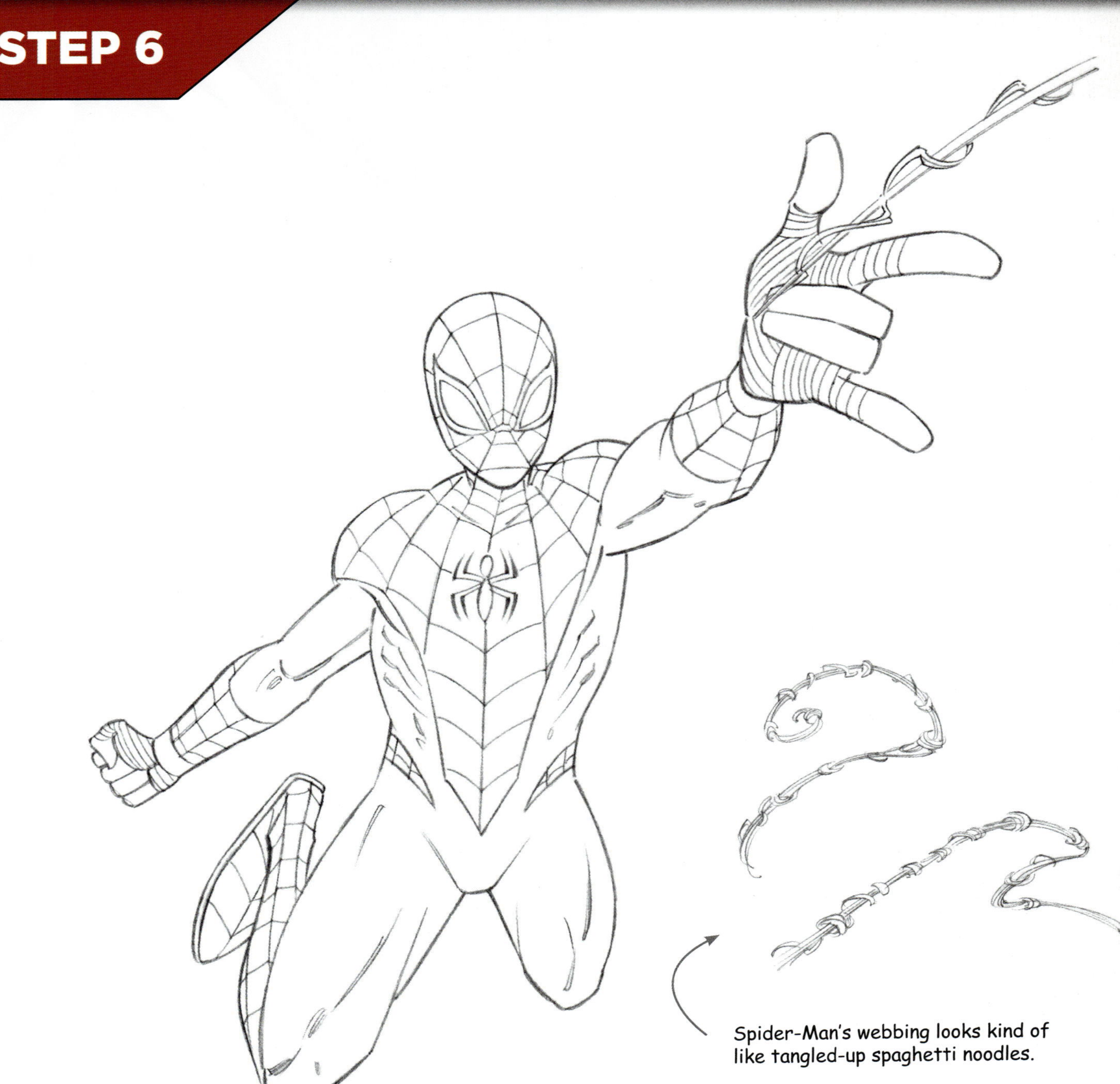

Spider-Man's webbing looks kind of like tangled-up spaghetti noodles.

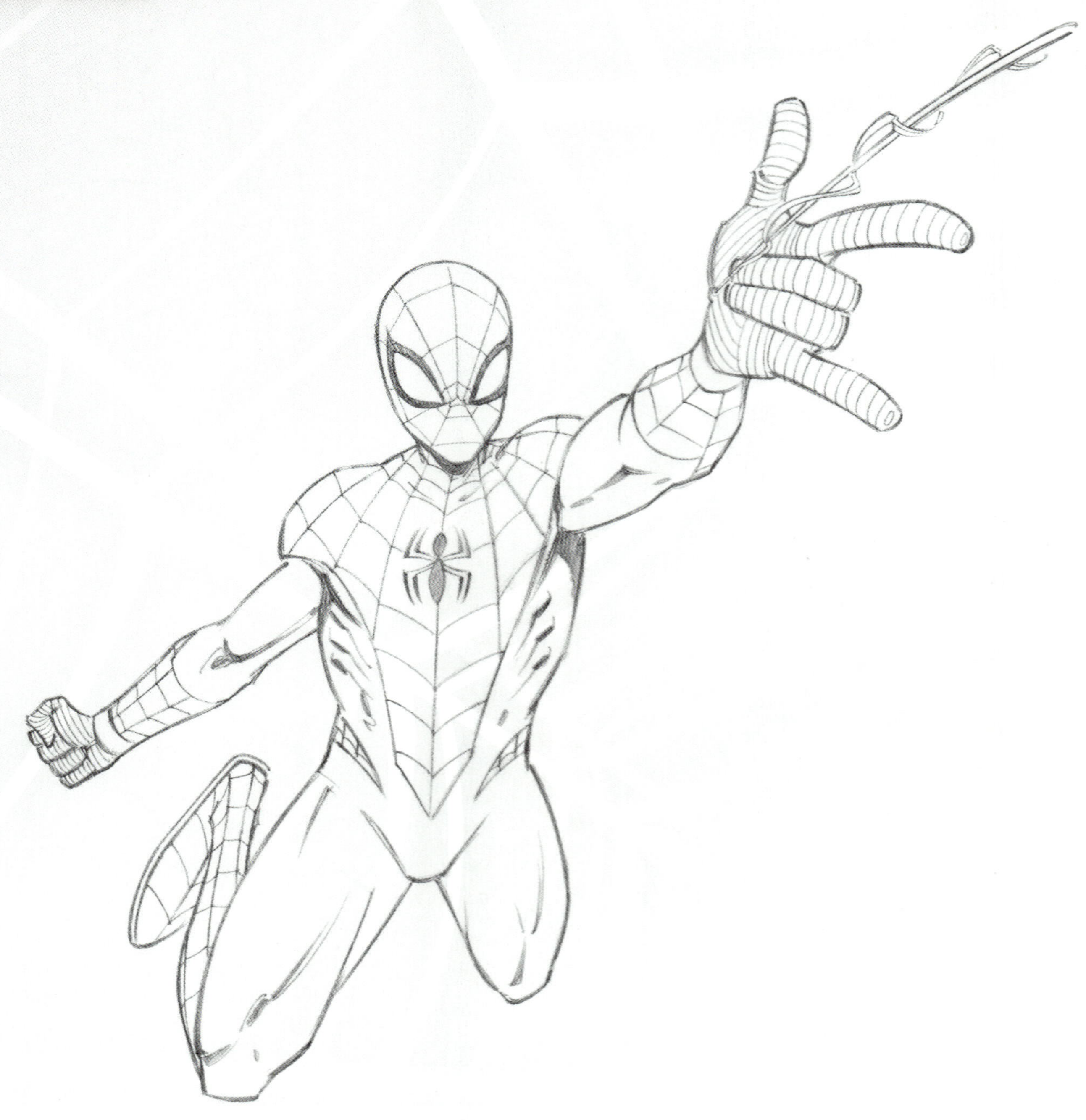

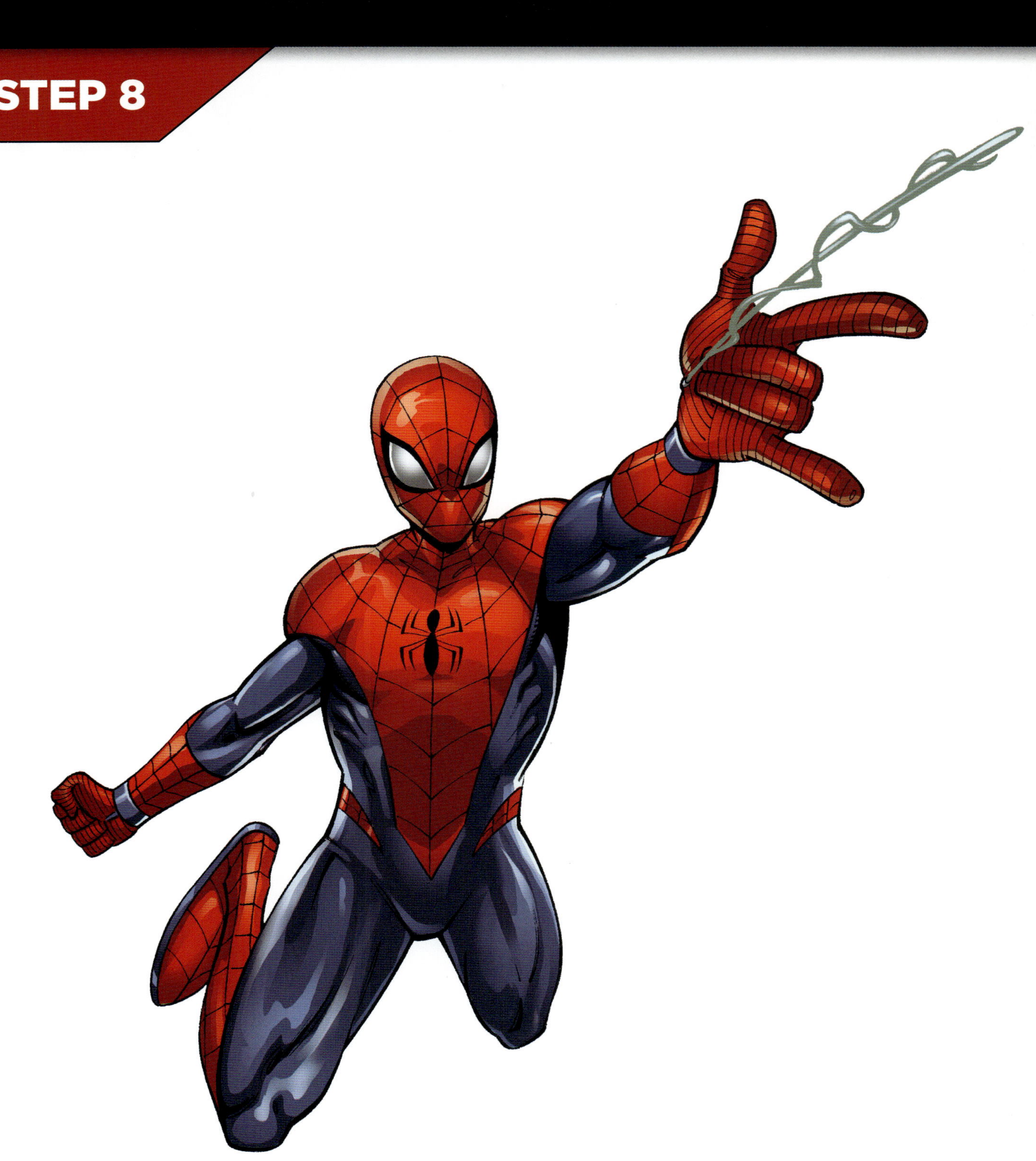

THE GREEN GOBLIN

The father of Peter Parker's best friend, Harry, businessman Norman Osborn moonlights as the unstable Green Goblin and causes Spider-Man more tragedy than any other foe. Norman Osborn is co-owner of Osborn Industries, which specializes in chemical manufacturing and research and development. Osborn becomes the Green Goblin after testing a strength-enhancing serum on himself. He emerges smarter and superhumanly strong, but at the cost of his sanity.

STEP 1

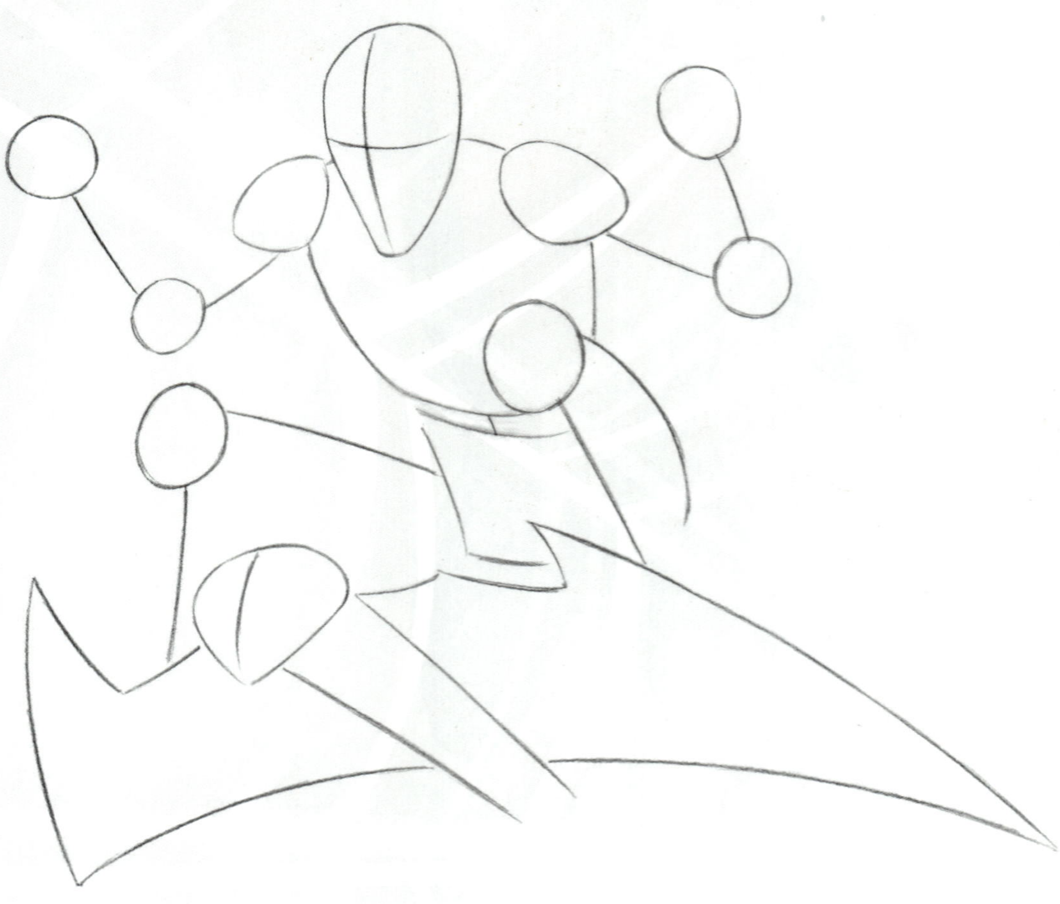

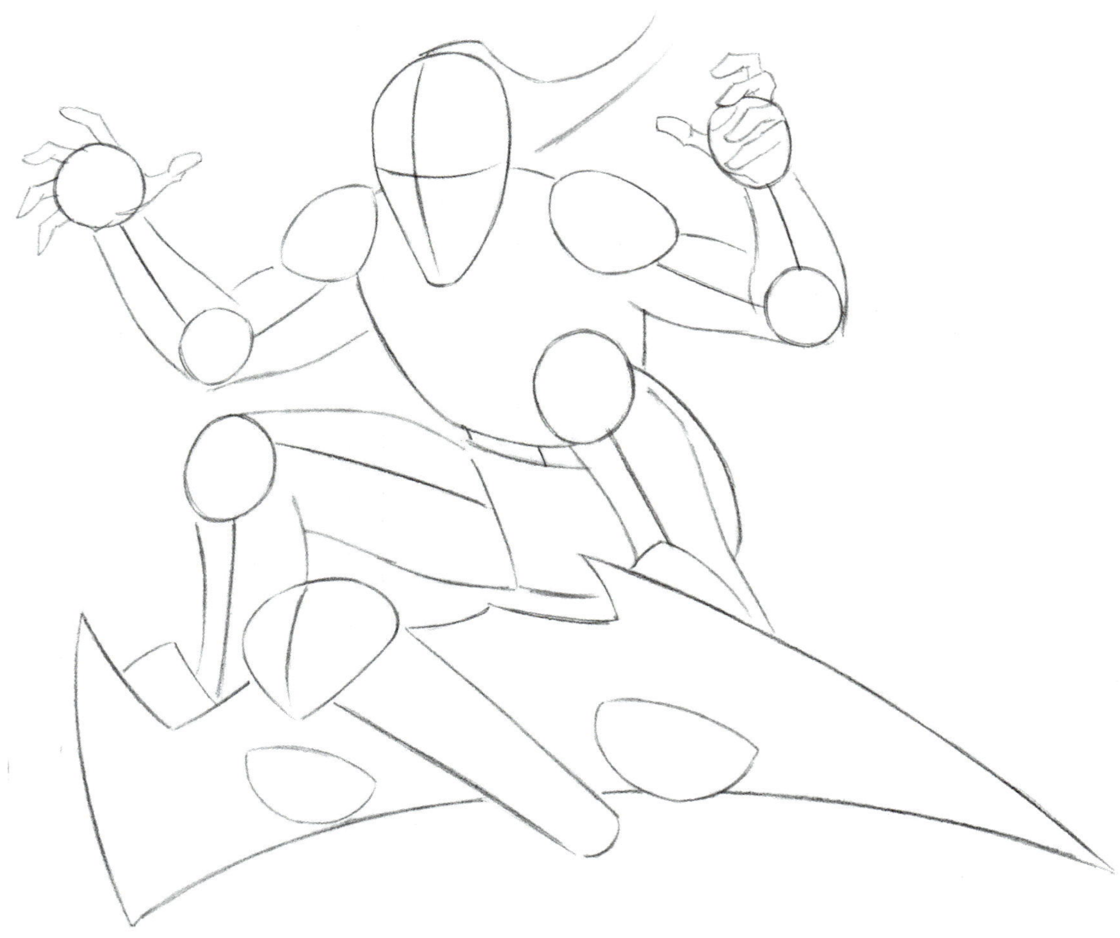

Spider-Man's arch enemy, the Green Goblin, fights using his Goblin Glider, bombs, flying "razor bats," laser-emitting gloves, and gas that nullifies Spider-Man's spider-sense.

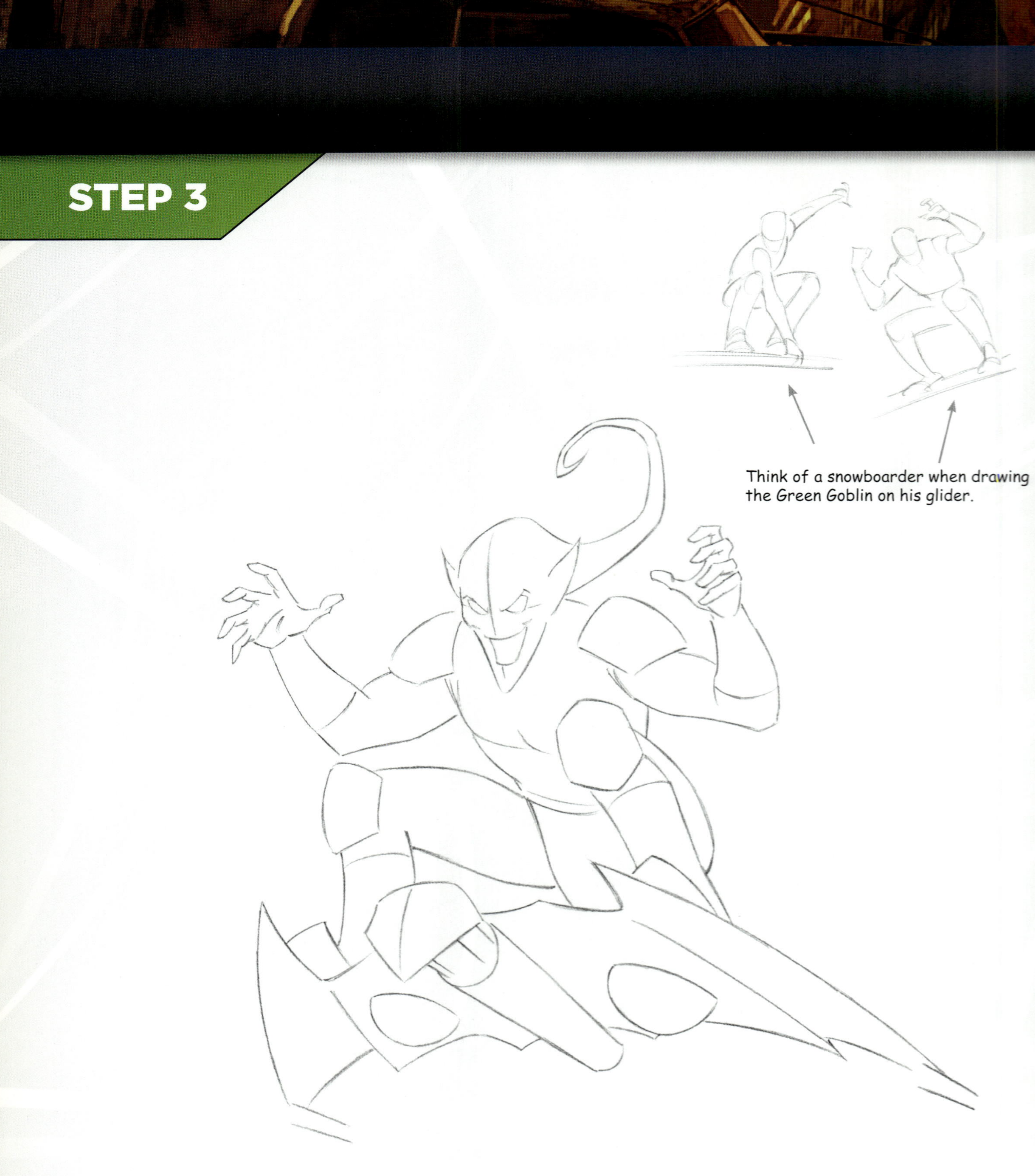

Think of a snowboarder when drawing the Green Goblin on his glider.

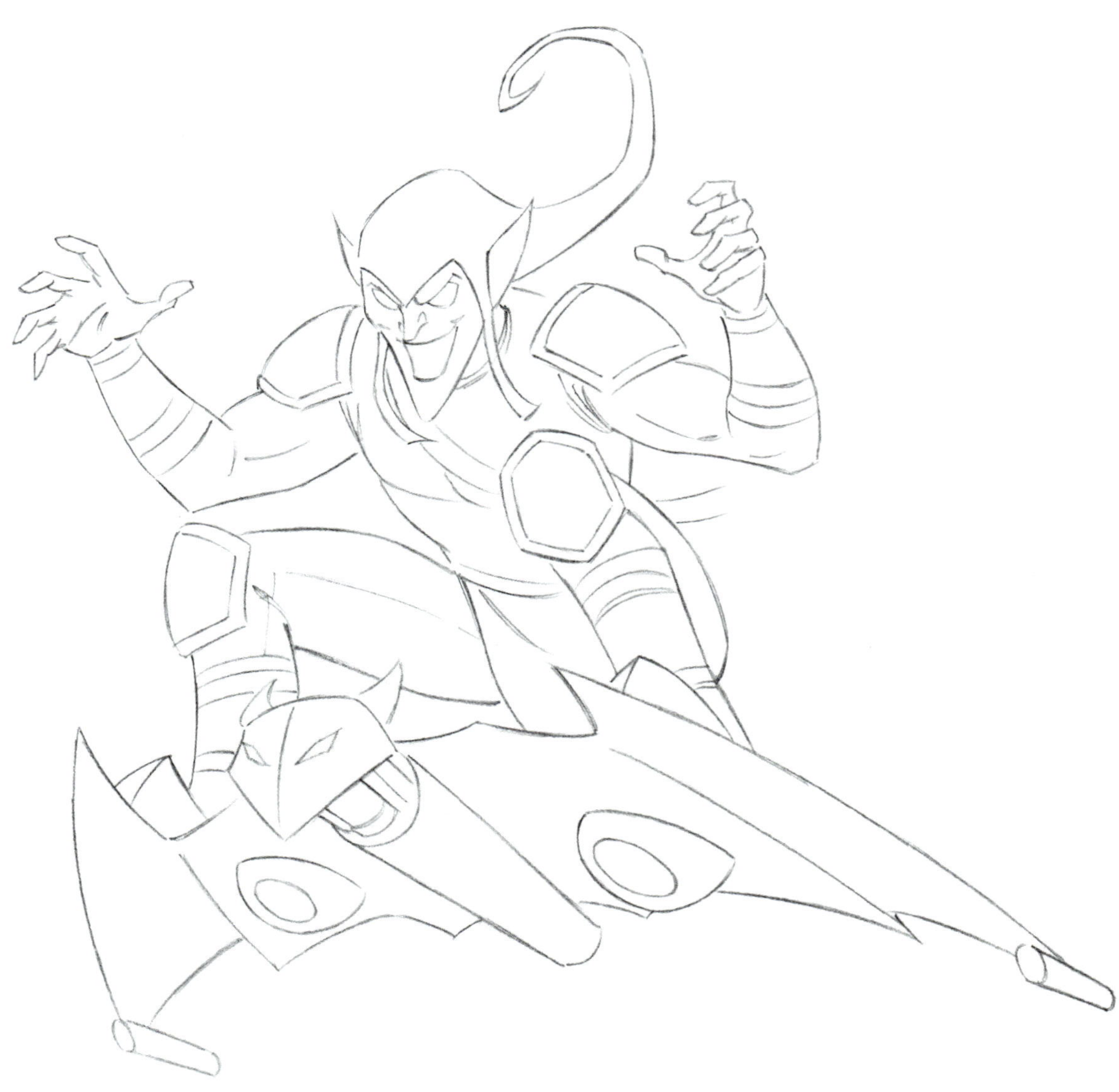

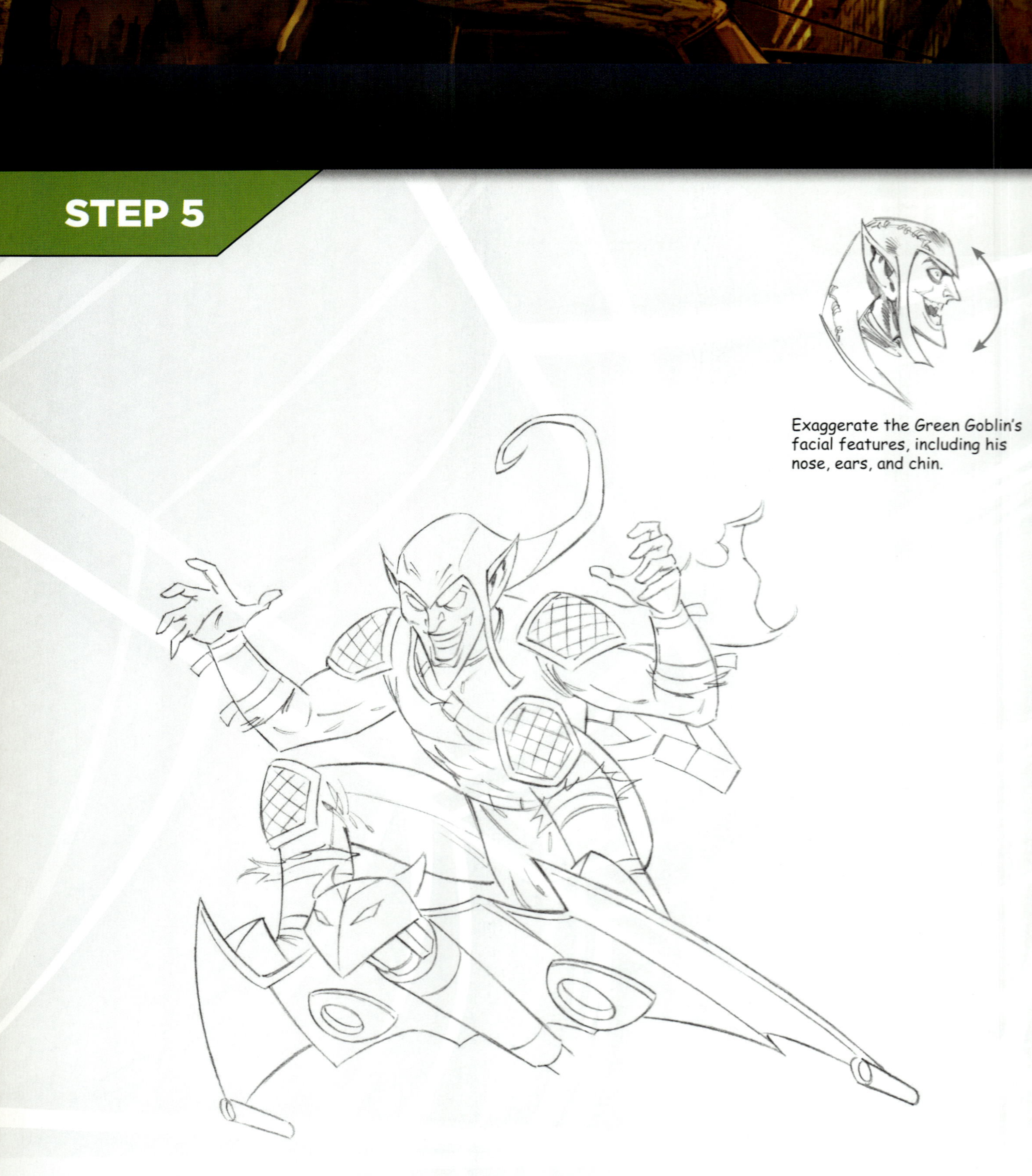

Exaggerate the Green Goblin's facial features, including his nose, ears, and chin.

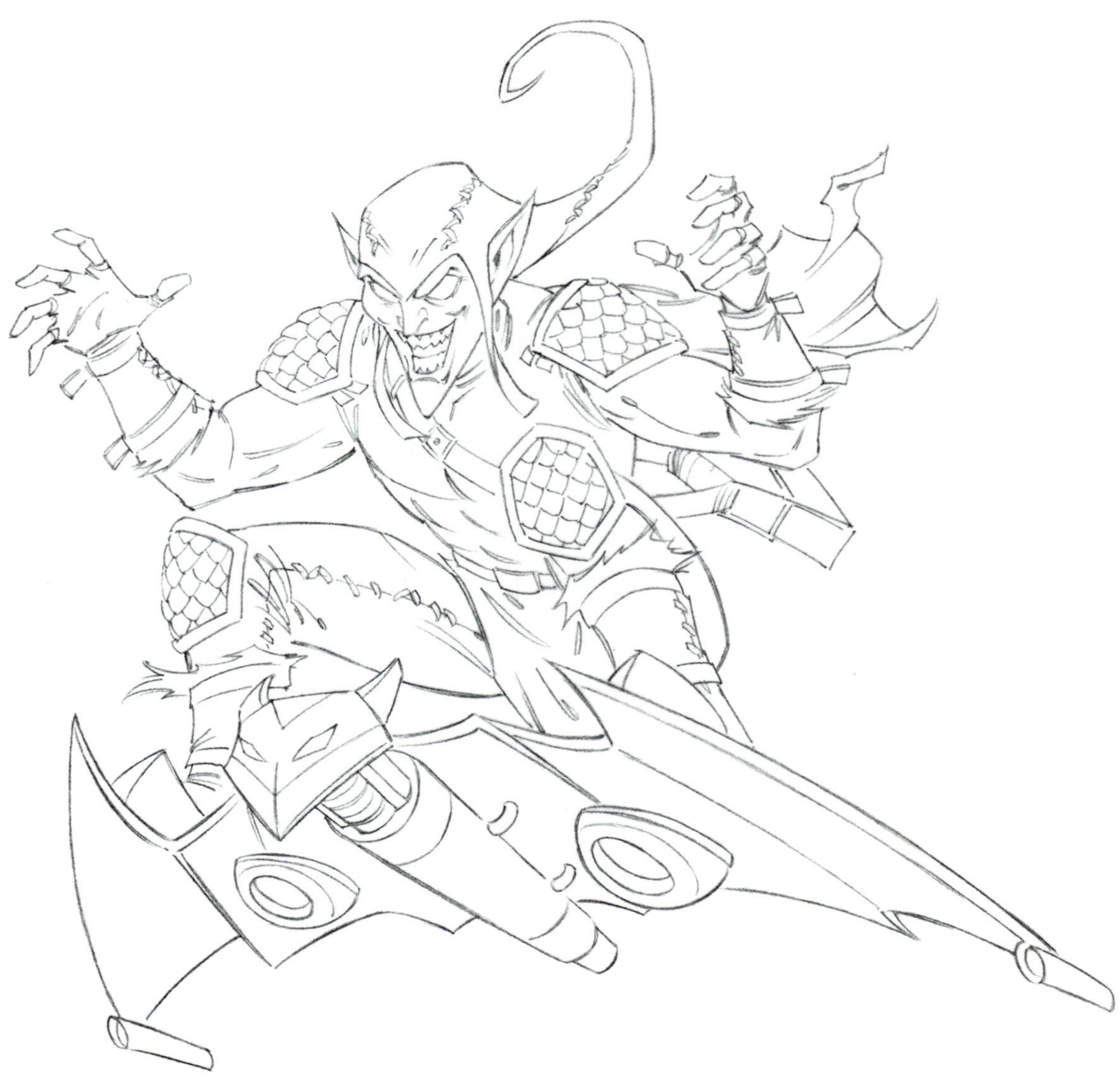

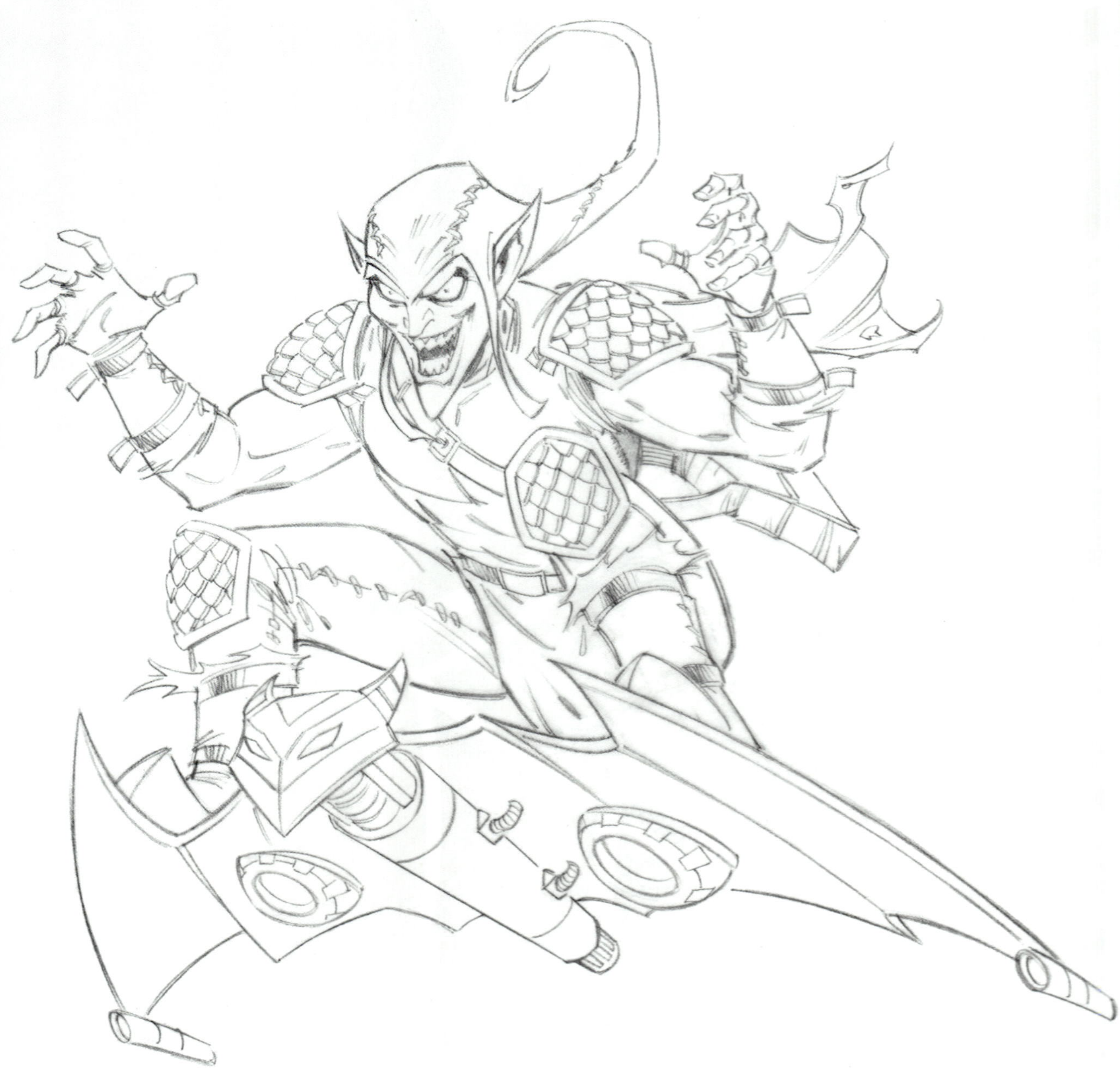

The Green Goblin's first appearance was in *The Amazing Spider-Man* issue #14 in 1964.

STEP 8

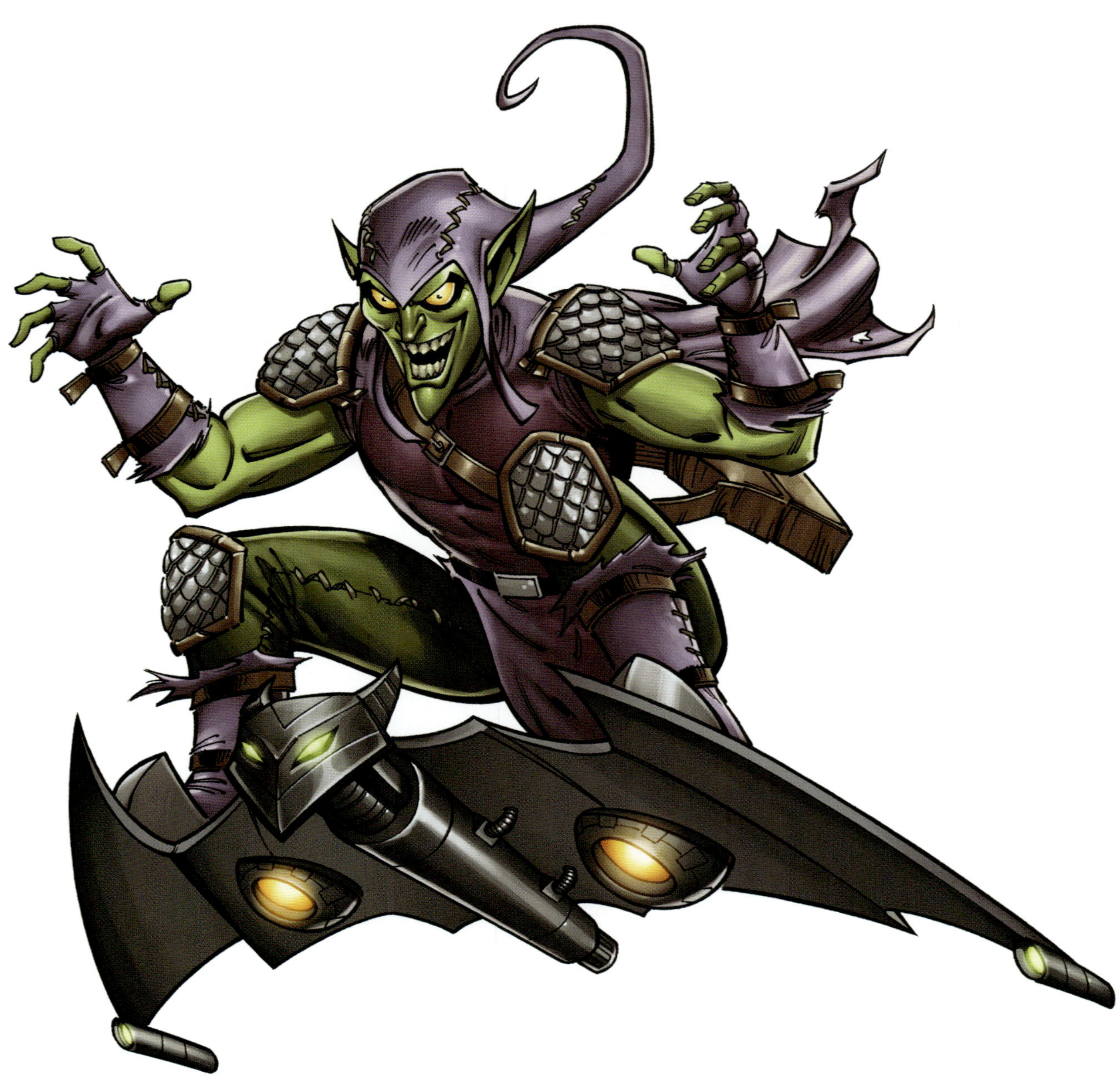

DR. OCTOPUS

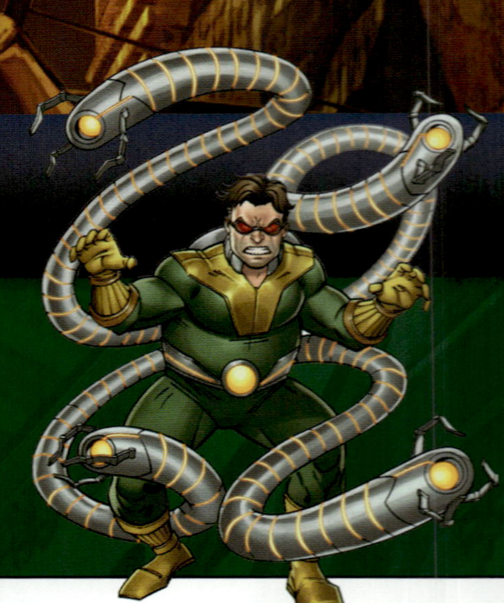

Dr. Otto Octavius holds a Ph.D. in nuclear science and is the world's leading authority on nuclear radiation and its effects on human physiology. He is also a brilliant engineer and inventor. However, after accidental exposure to atomic radiation, Doctor Octopus now telepathically controls four dangerous mechanical arms that are fused to his body.

STEP 1

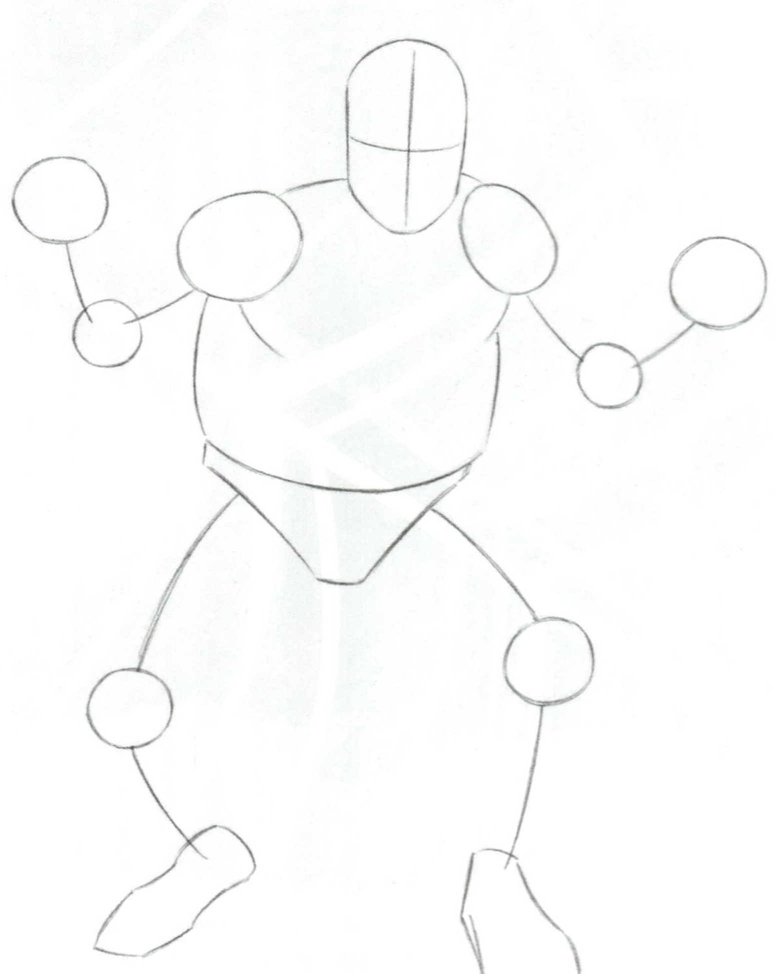

Doc Ock travels quickly, scales walls, and can **stand up to 50 feet** in the air using his mechanical arms as legs. He can also **"feel"** basic **sensations** with them.

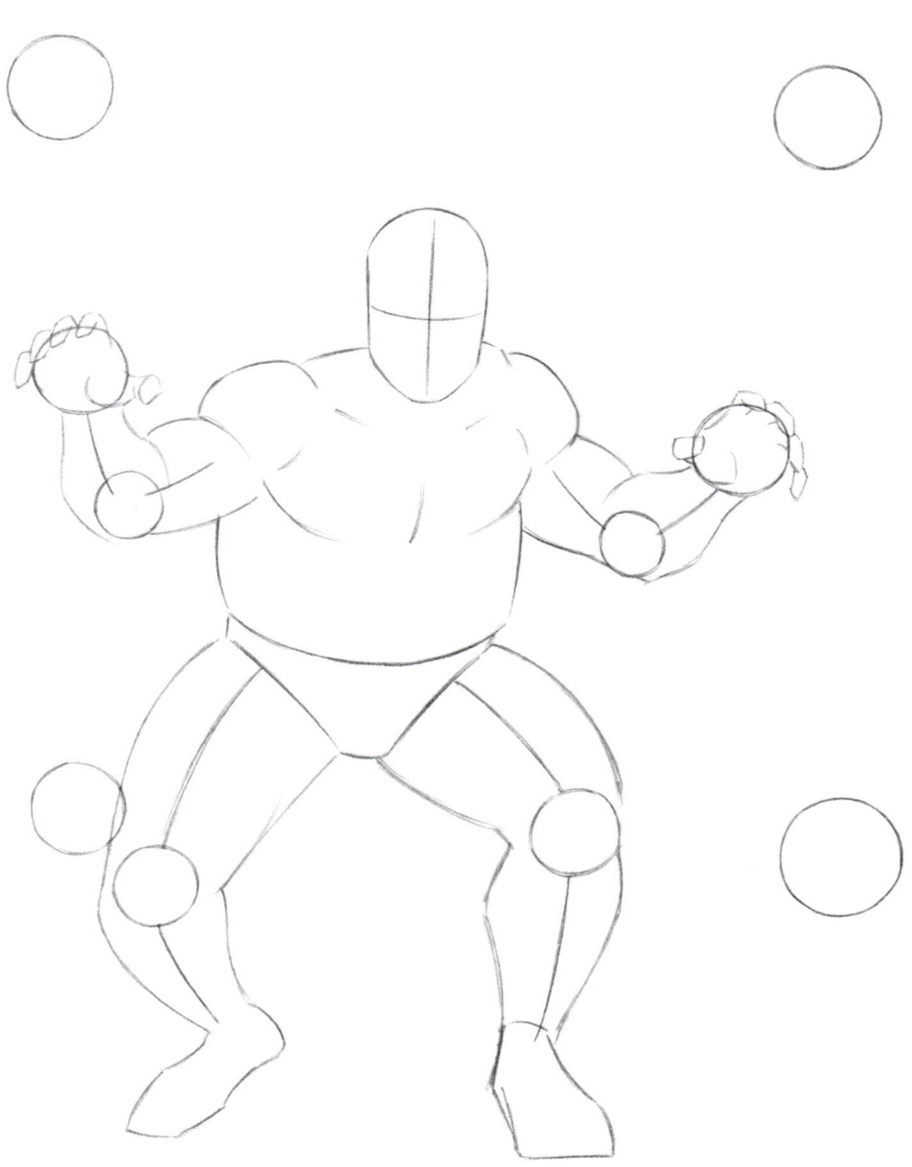

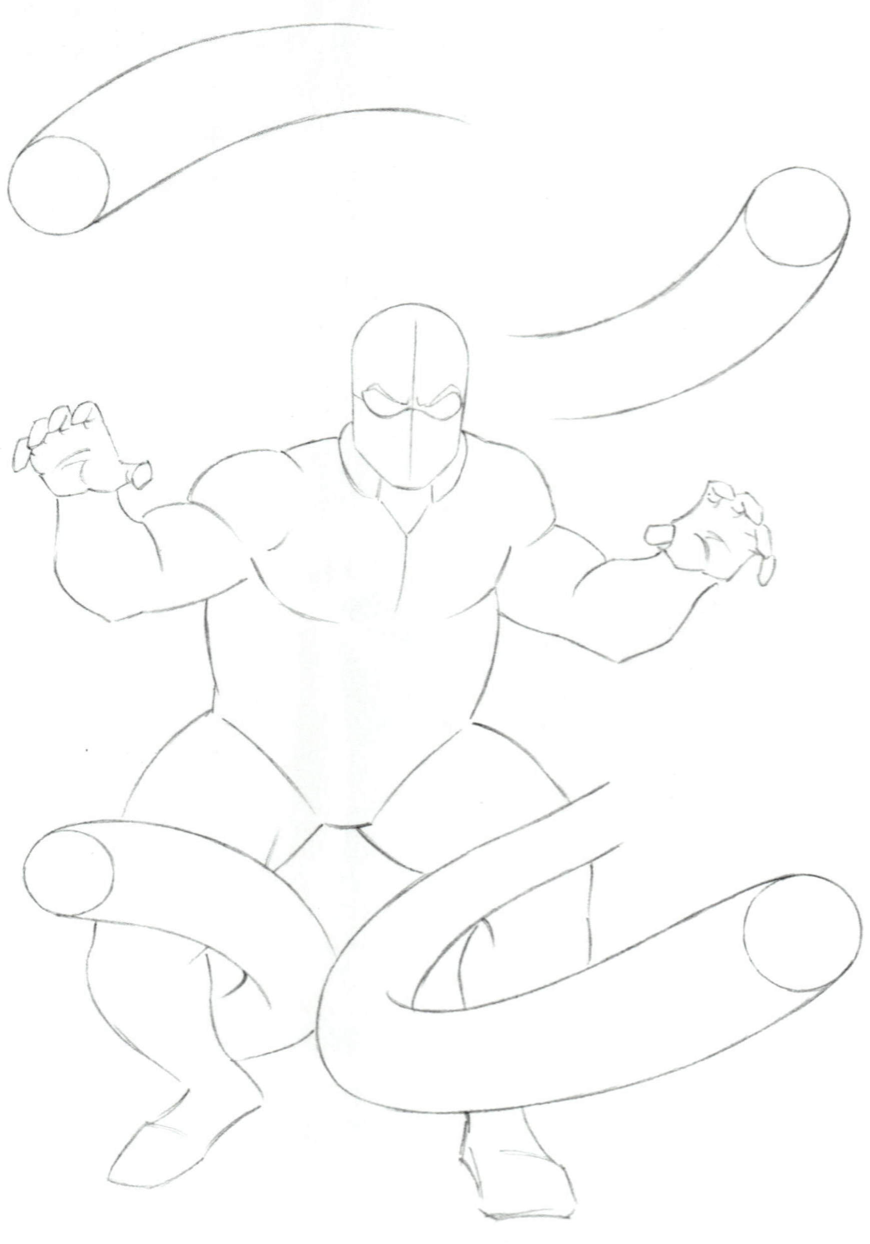

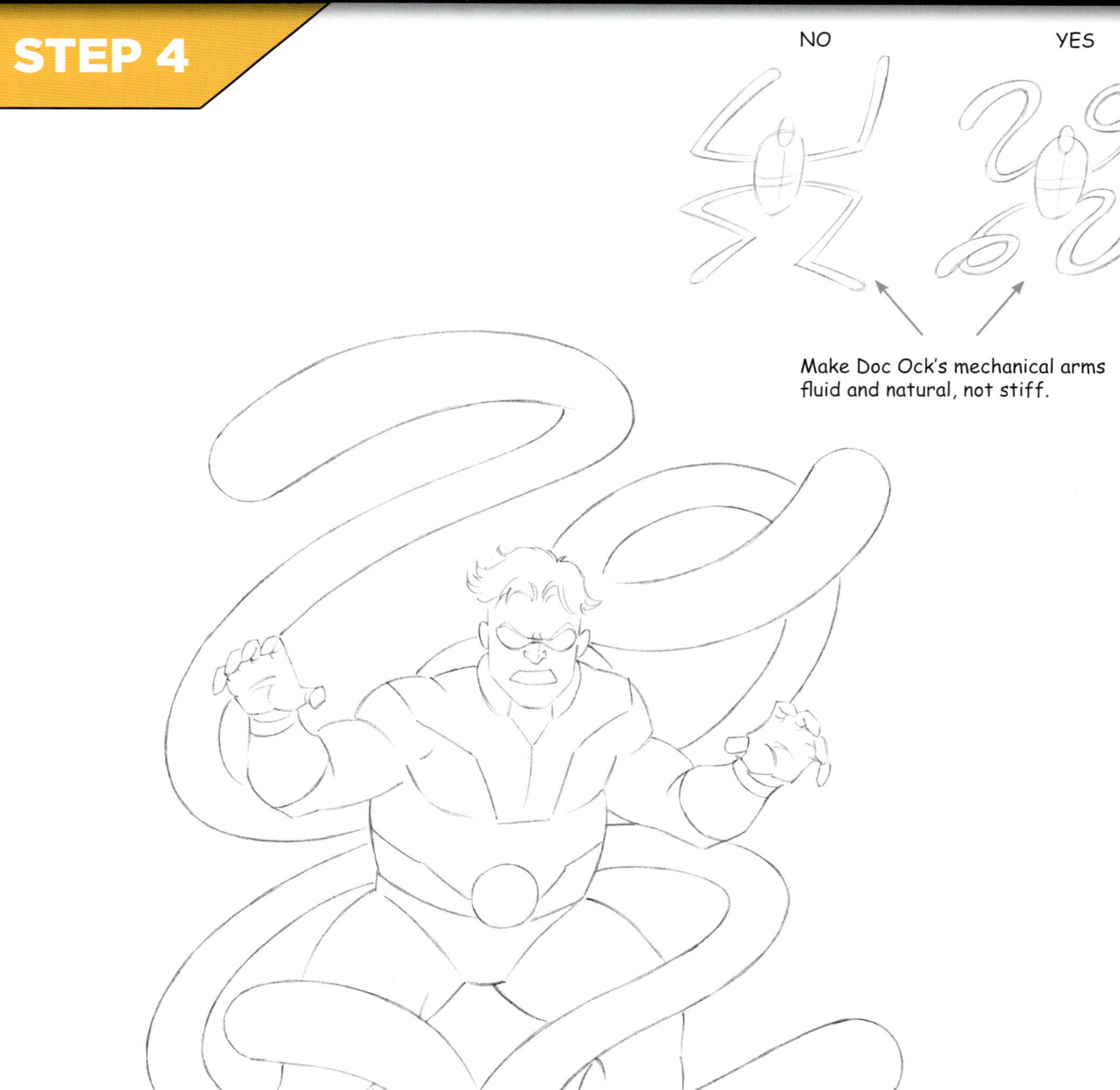

Make Doc Ock's mechanical arms fluid and natural, not stiff.

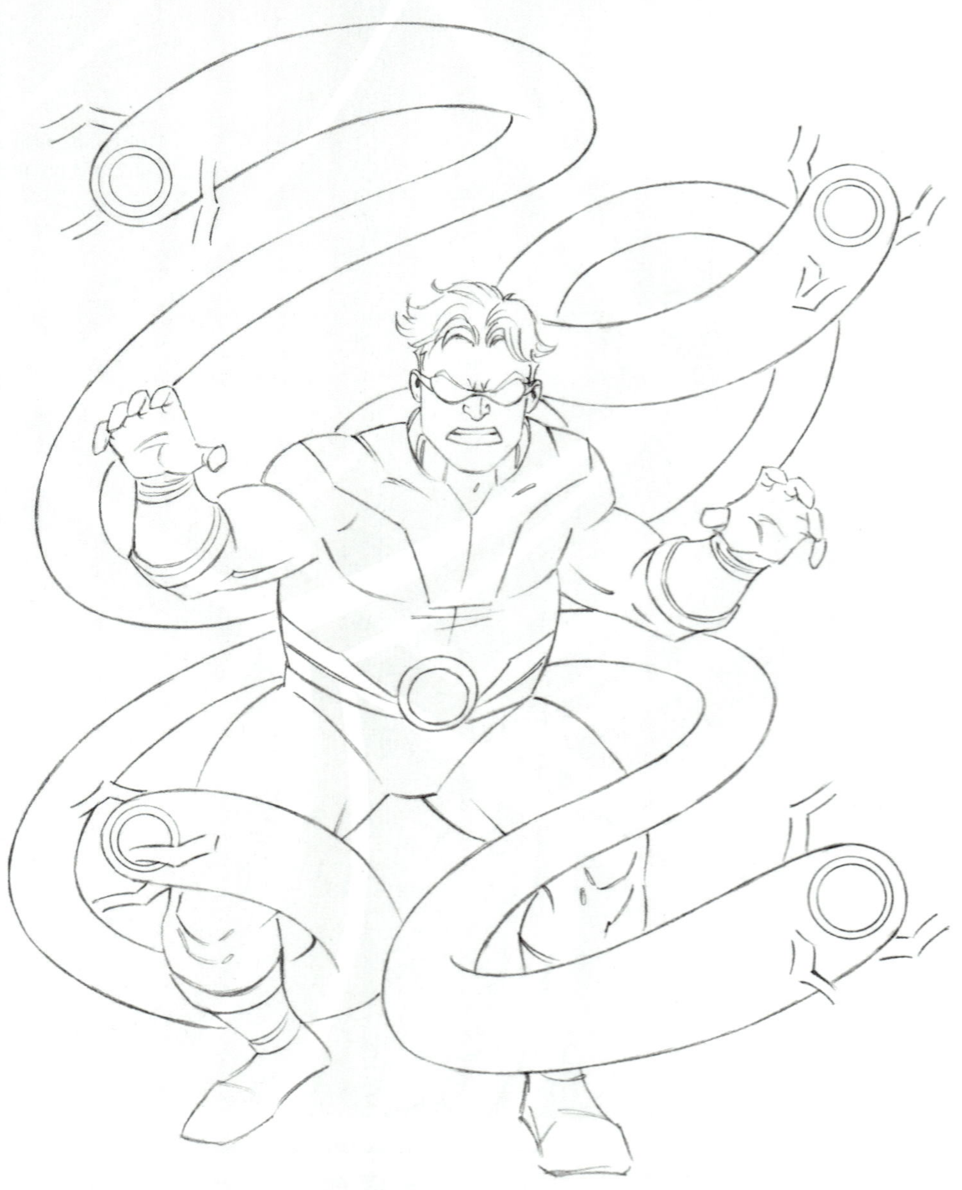

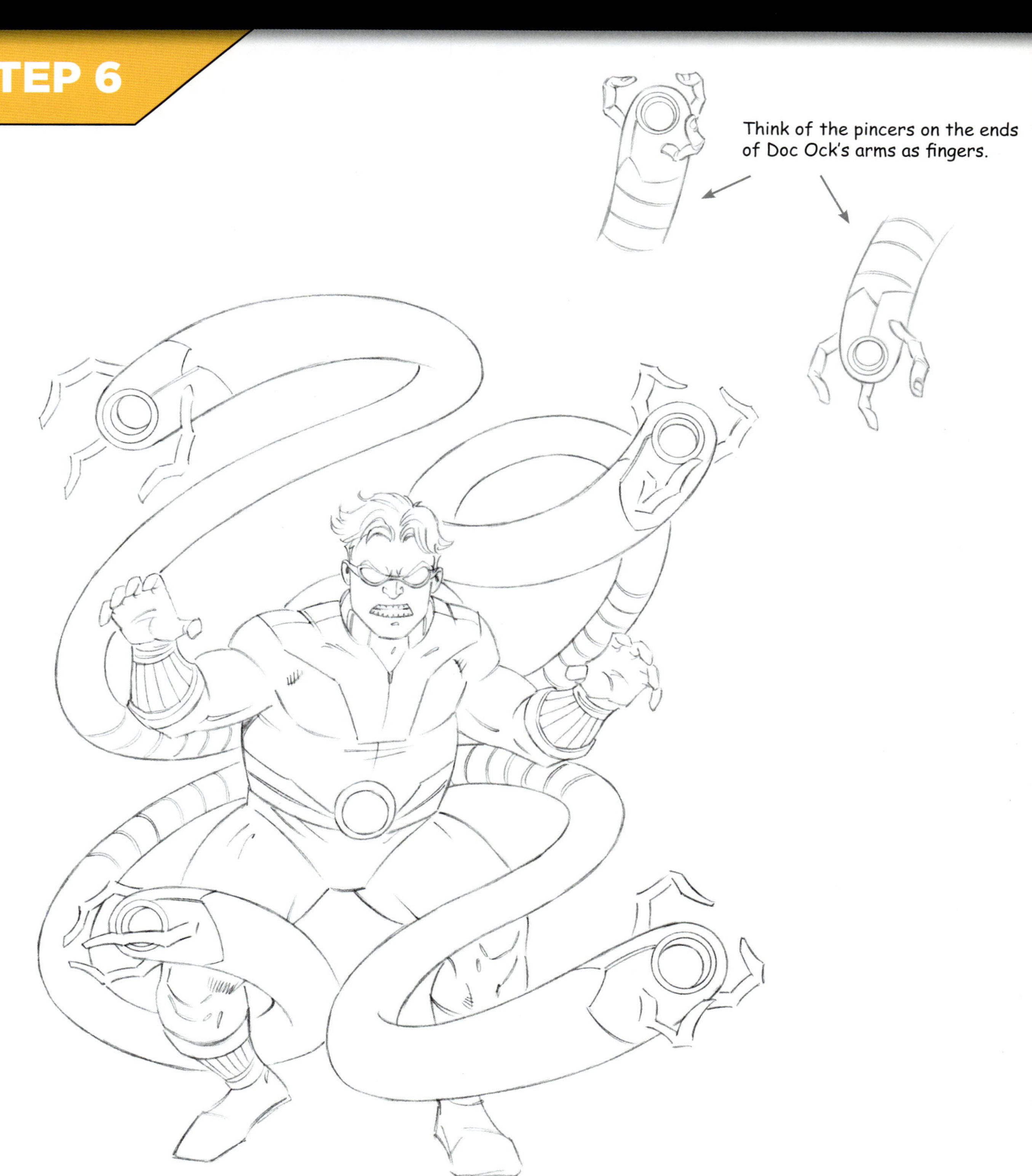

Think of the pincers on the ends of Doc Ock's arms as fingers.

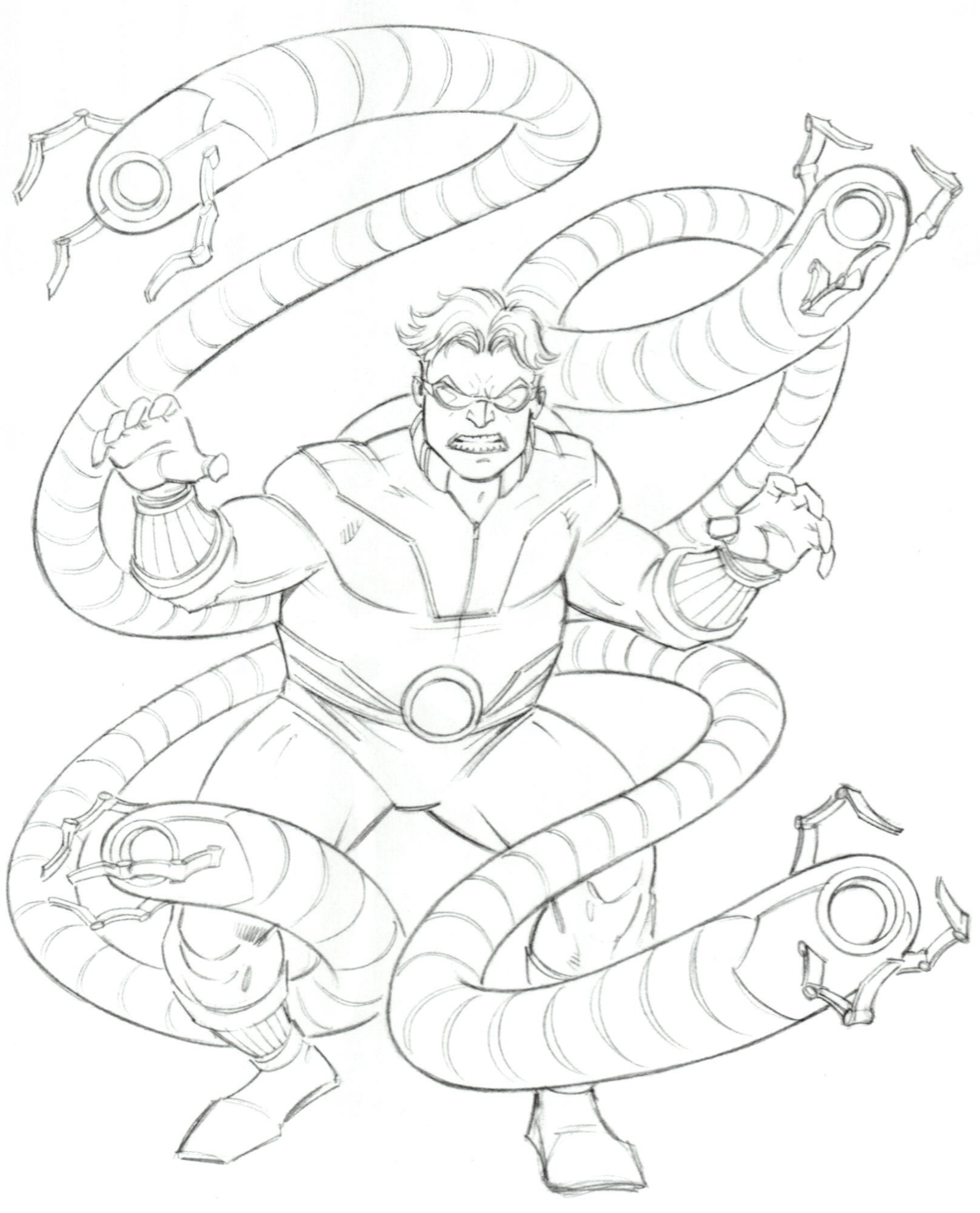

The first appearance of **Doctor Octopus** was in the third issue of *The Amazing Spider-Man* in July 1963.

STEP 8

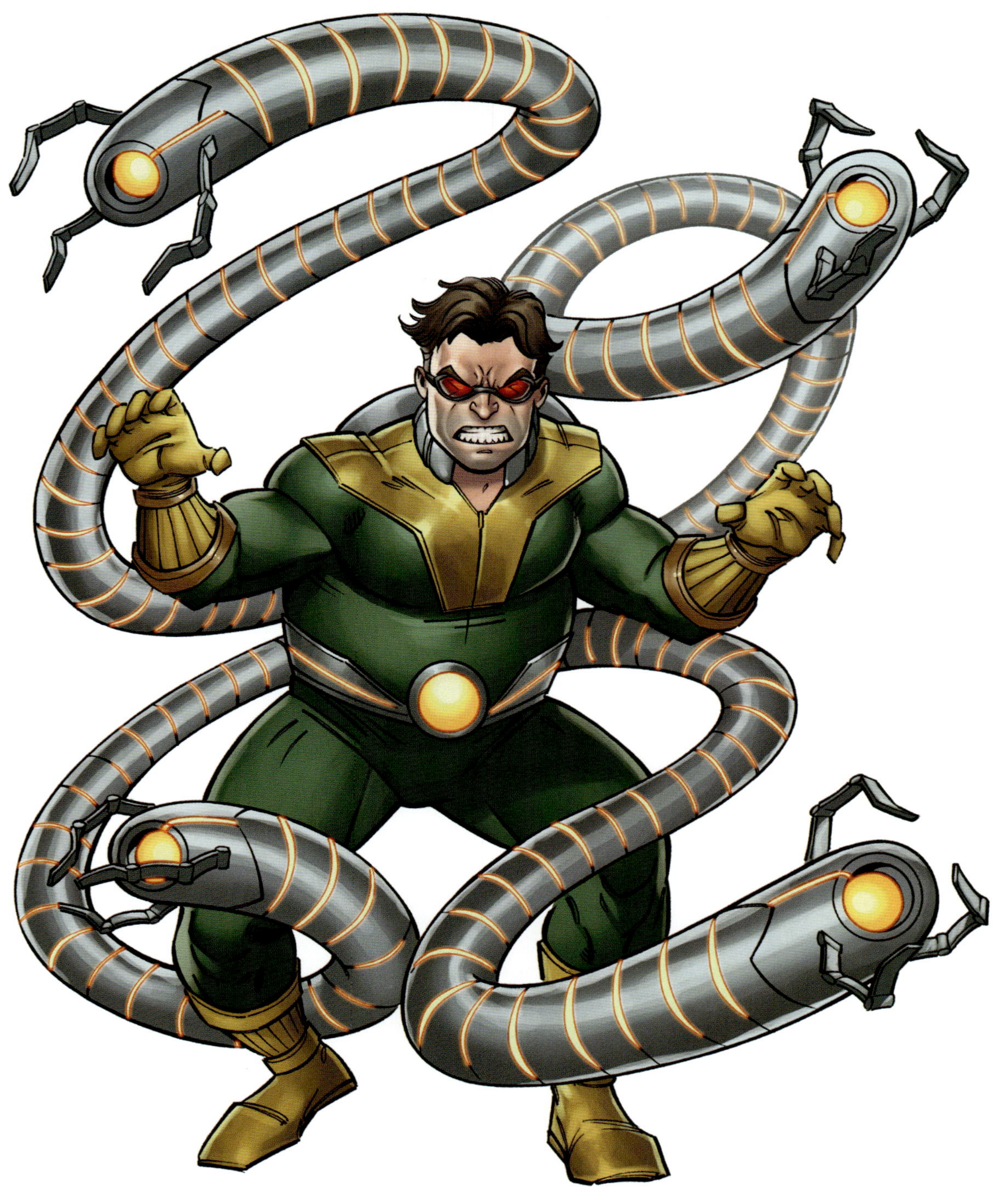

LIZARD

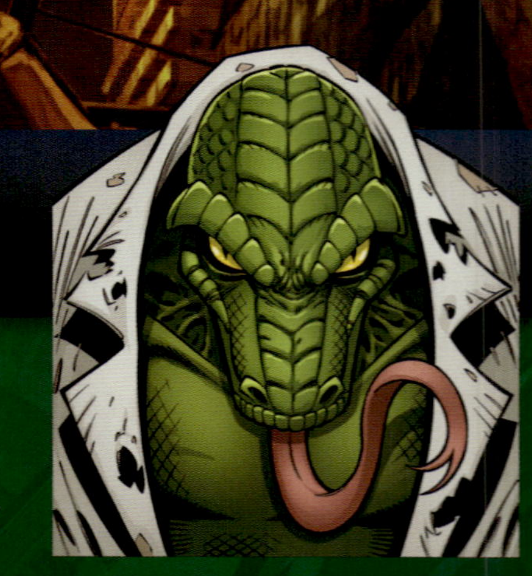

Dr. Curtis Connors, a world-renowned herpetologist and gifted surgeon, becomes obsessed with uncovering the secrets of reptilian regeneration so he can grow back his arm after it is amputated. After developing a serum that includes reptilian DNA, he tests it on himself. His arm does indeed grow back, but there is one side effect: Connors is subsequently transformed into a reptilian monster!

STEP 1

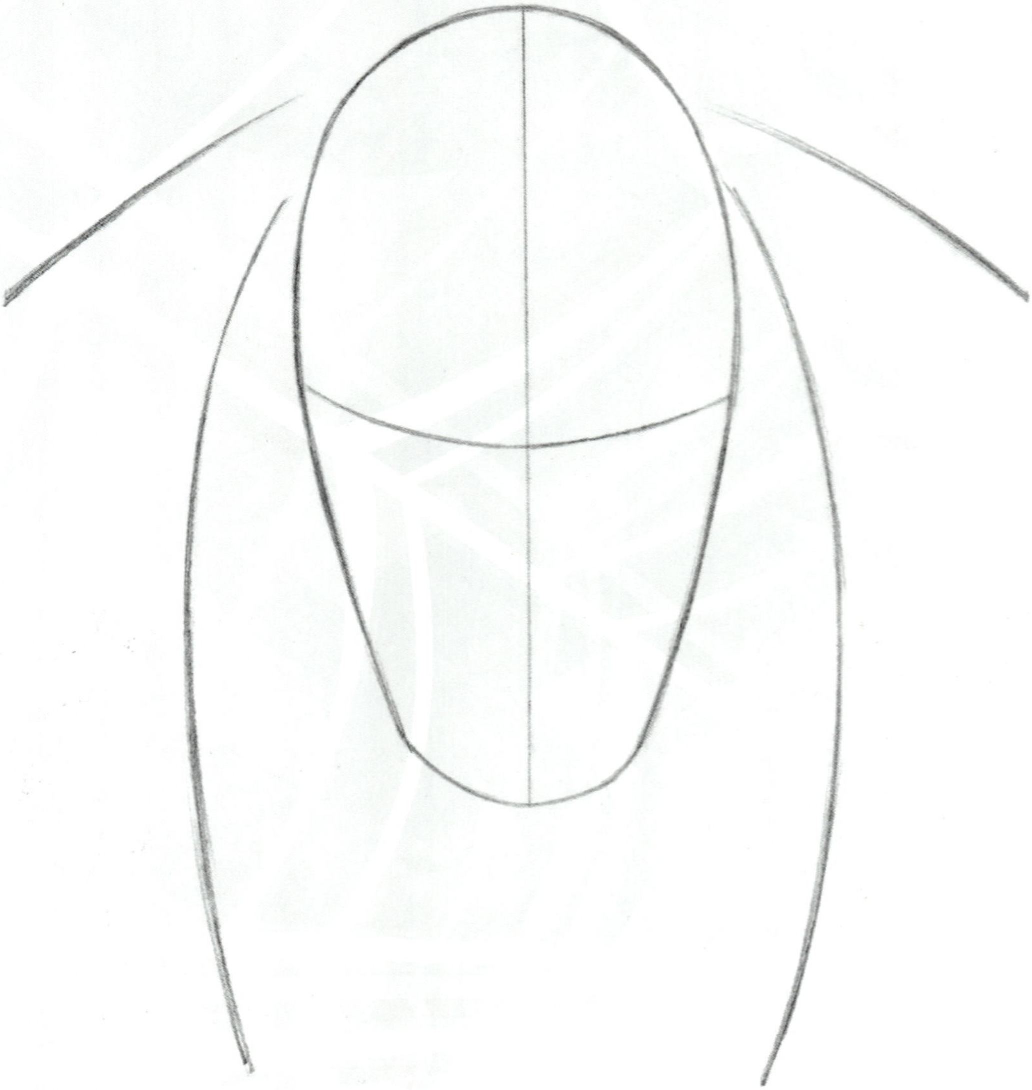

Curt Connors **lost his arm** while working **as a surgeon in a war zone**. He went to war to treat wounded GIs, but after he was **injured in a blast**, he himself came home wounded.

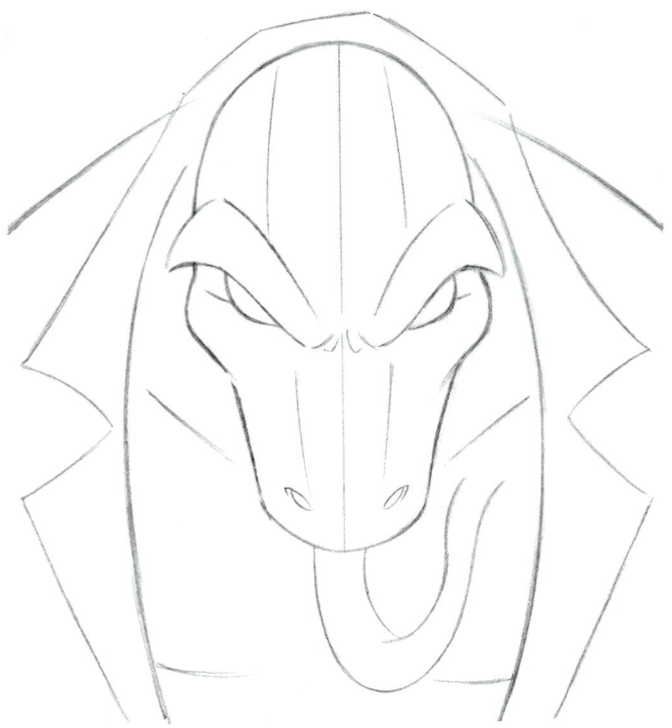

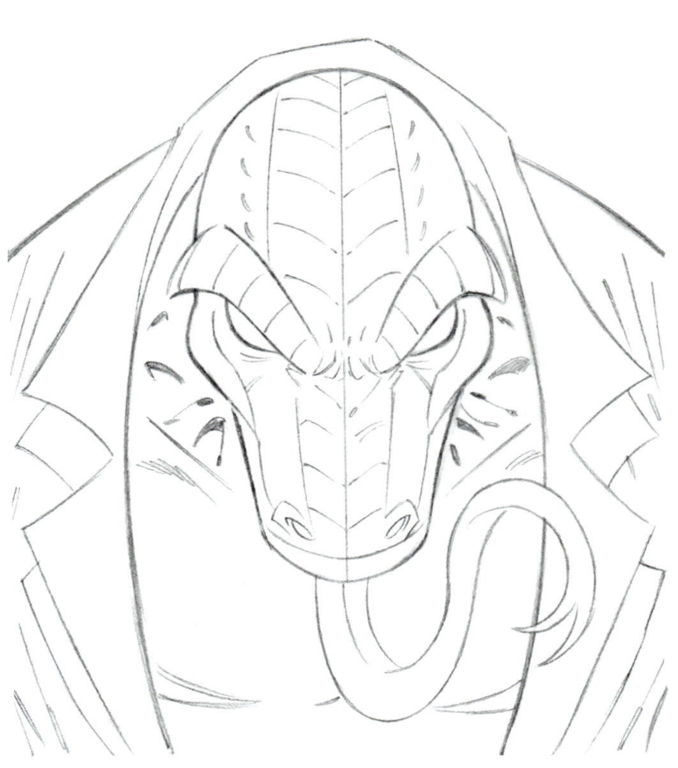

STEP 3

Note the look of Lizard's
overlapping scales.

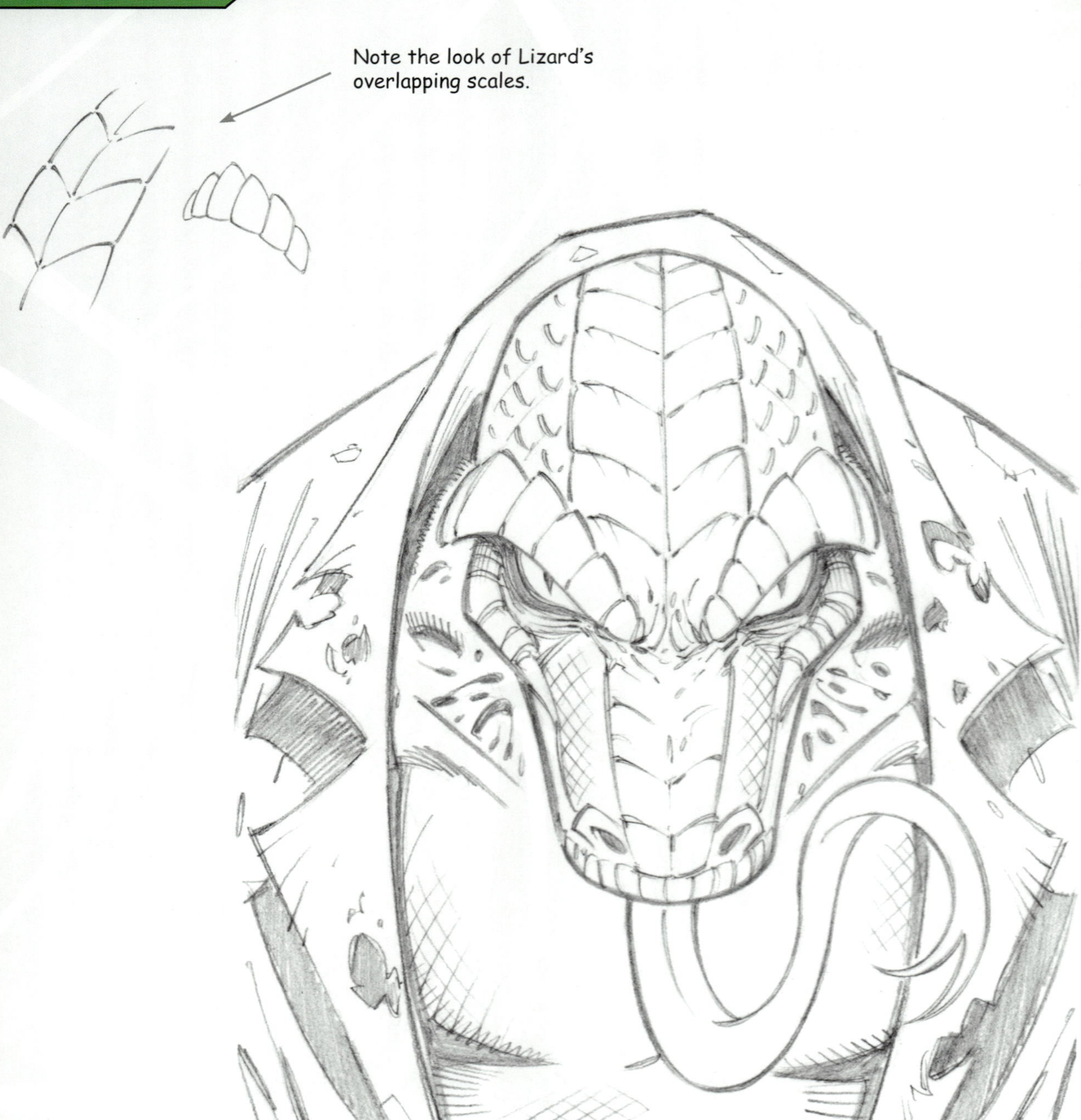

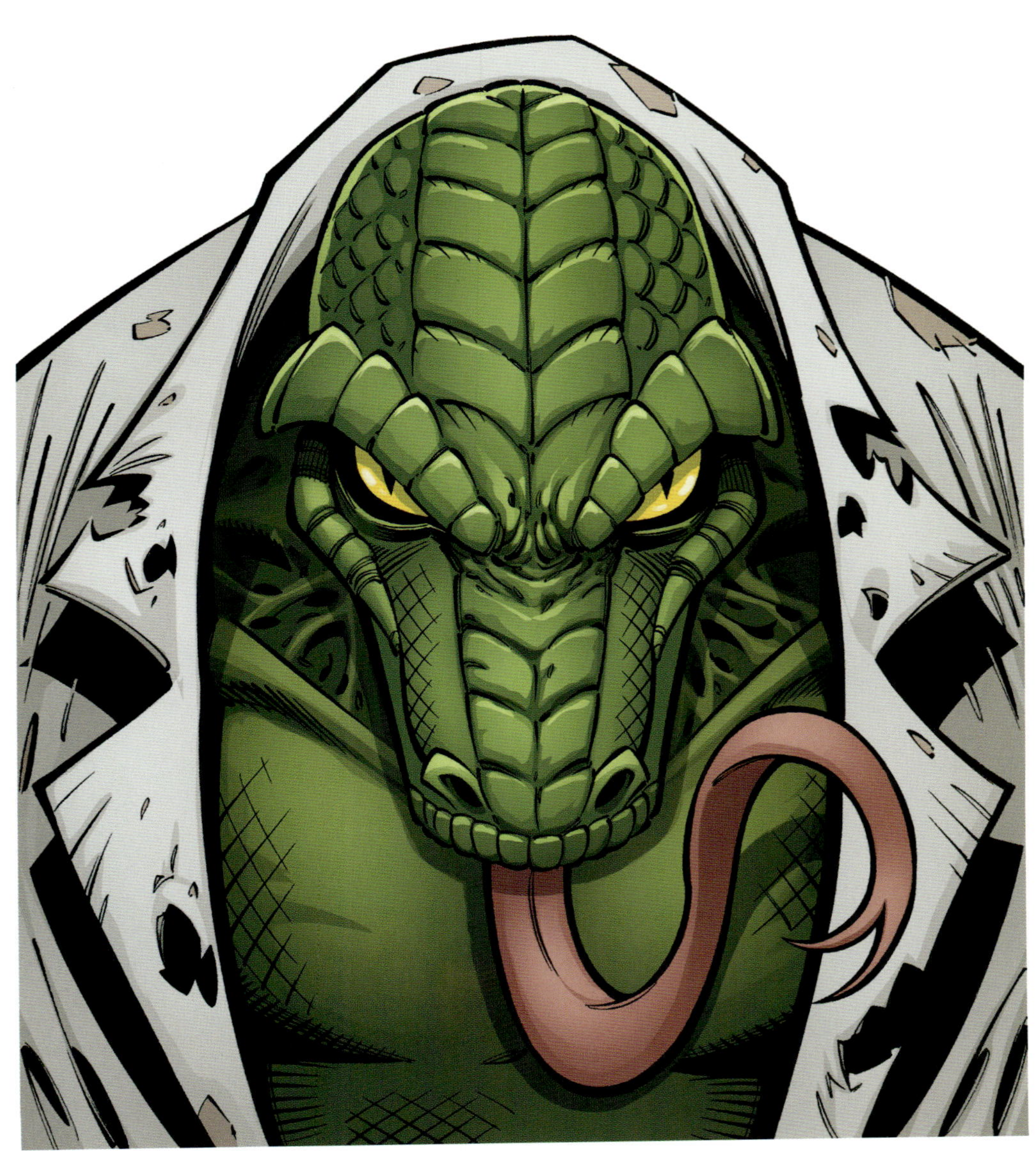

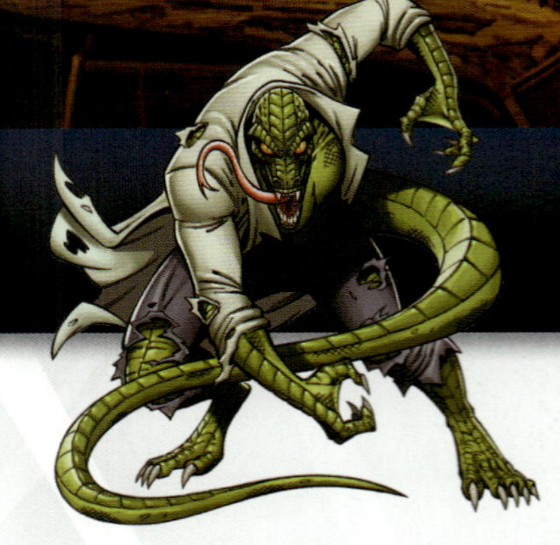

STEP 1

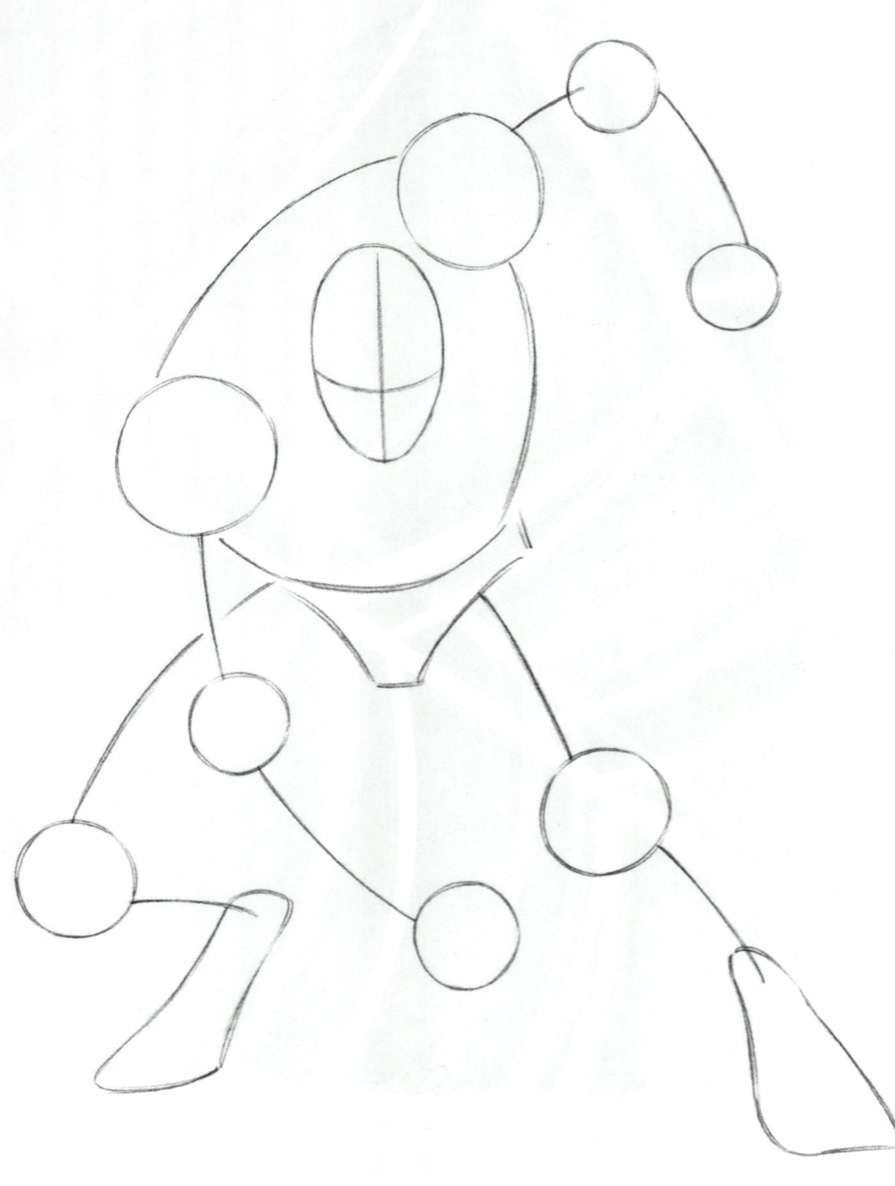

Lizard has the ability to **regenerate** lost or damaged areas of his body, can **telepathically control nearby reptiles,** and can **excrete pheromones** that cause humans to behave violently.

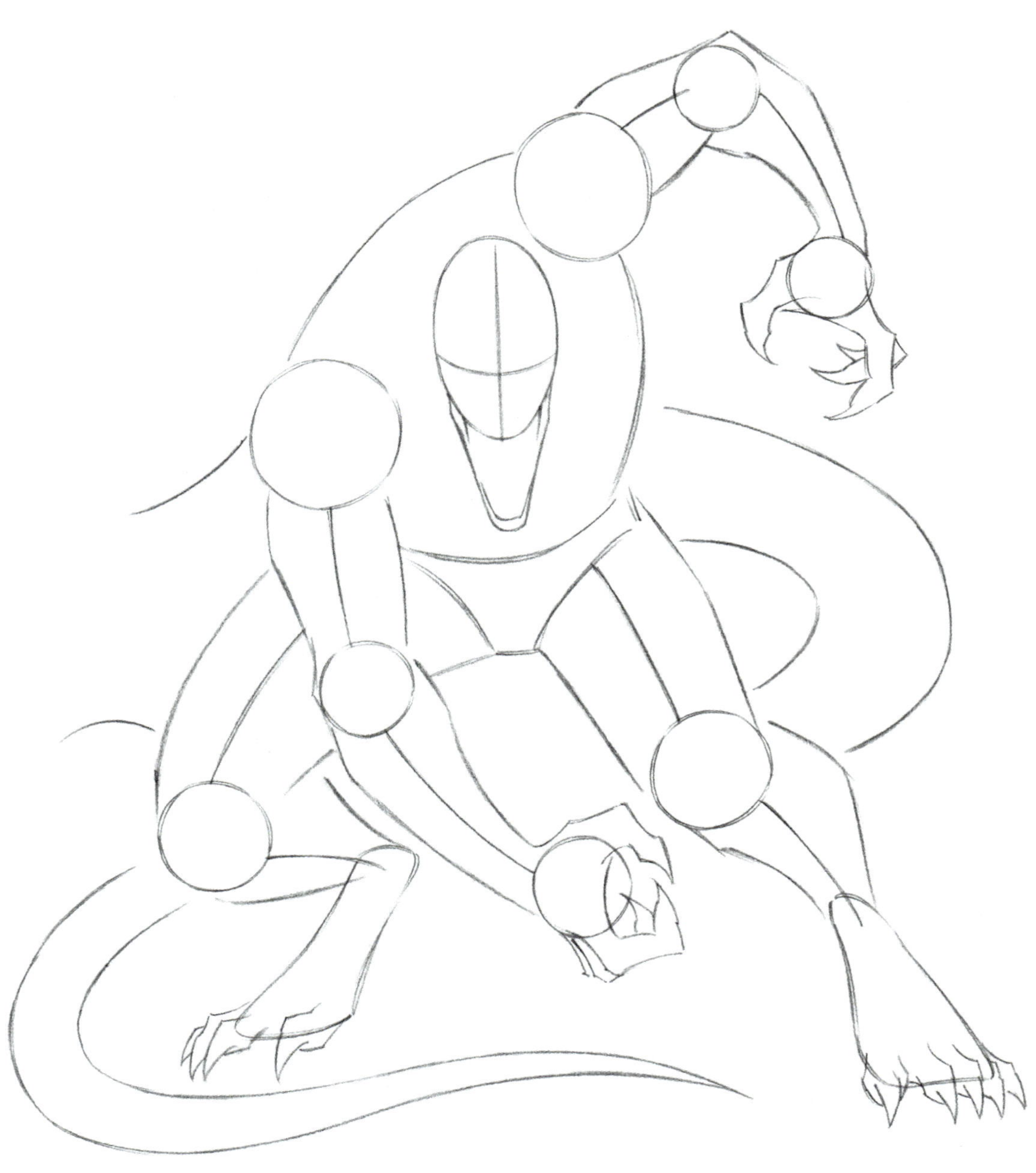

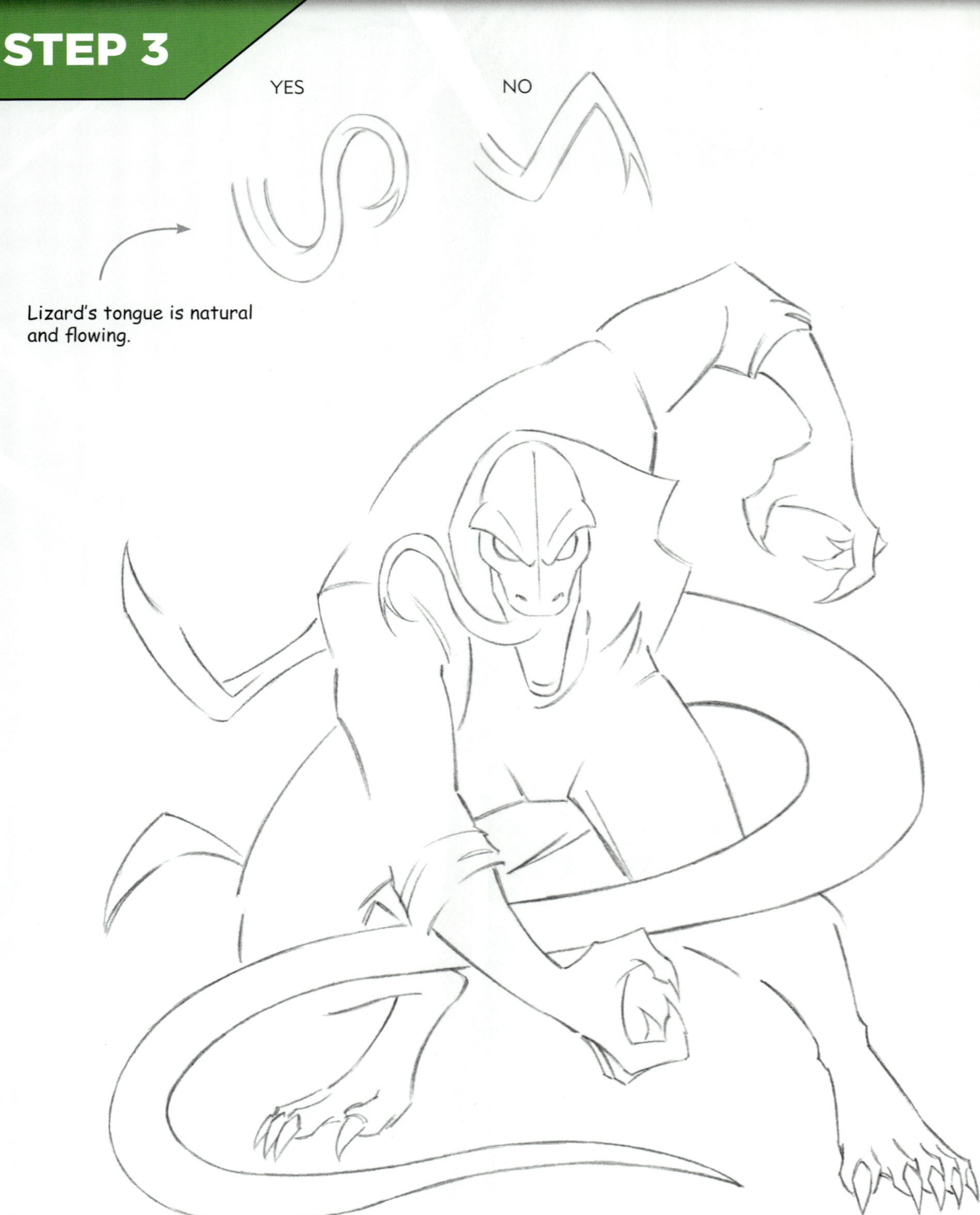

YES
NO
Lizard's tongue is natural
and flowing.

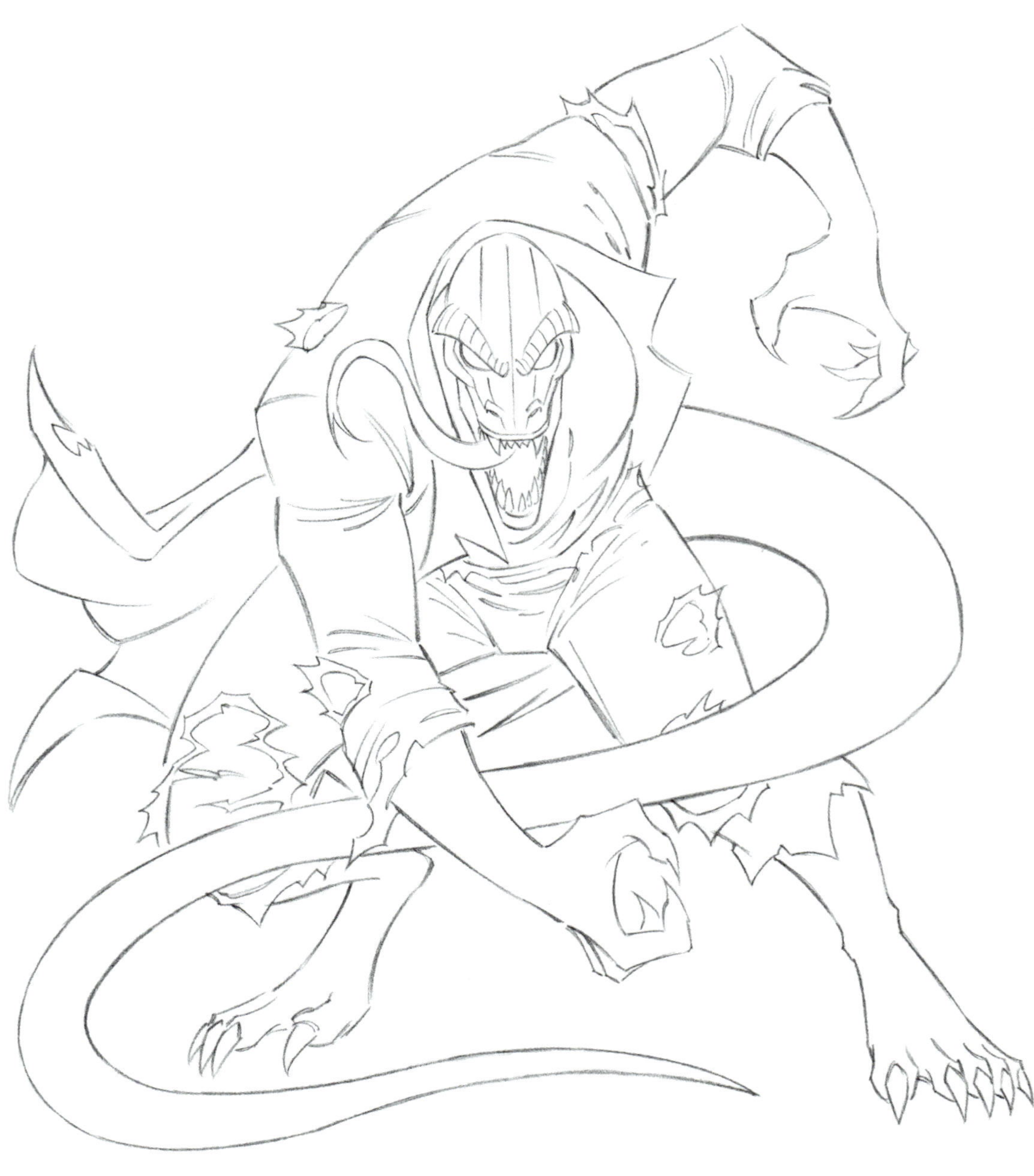

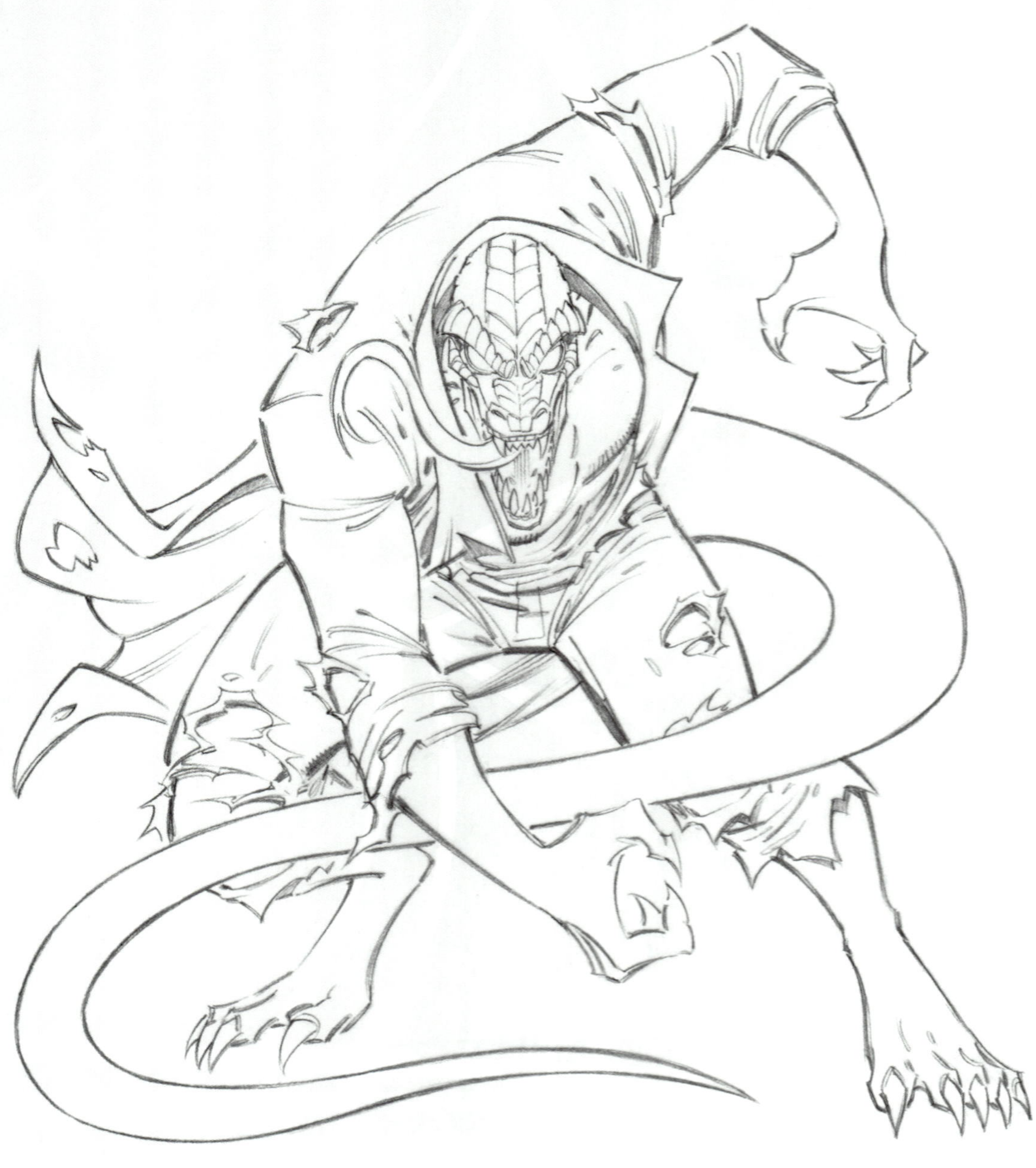

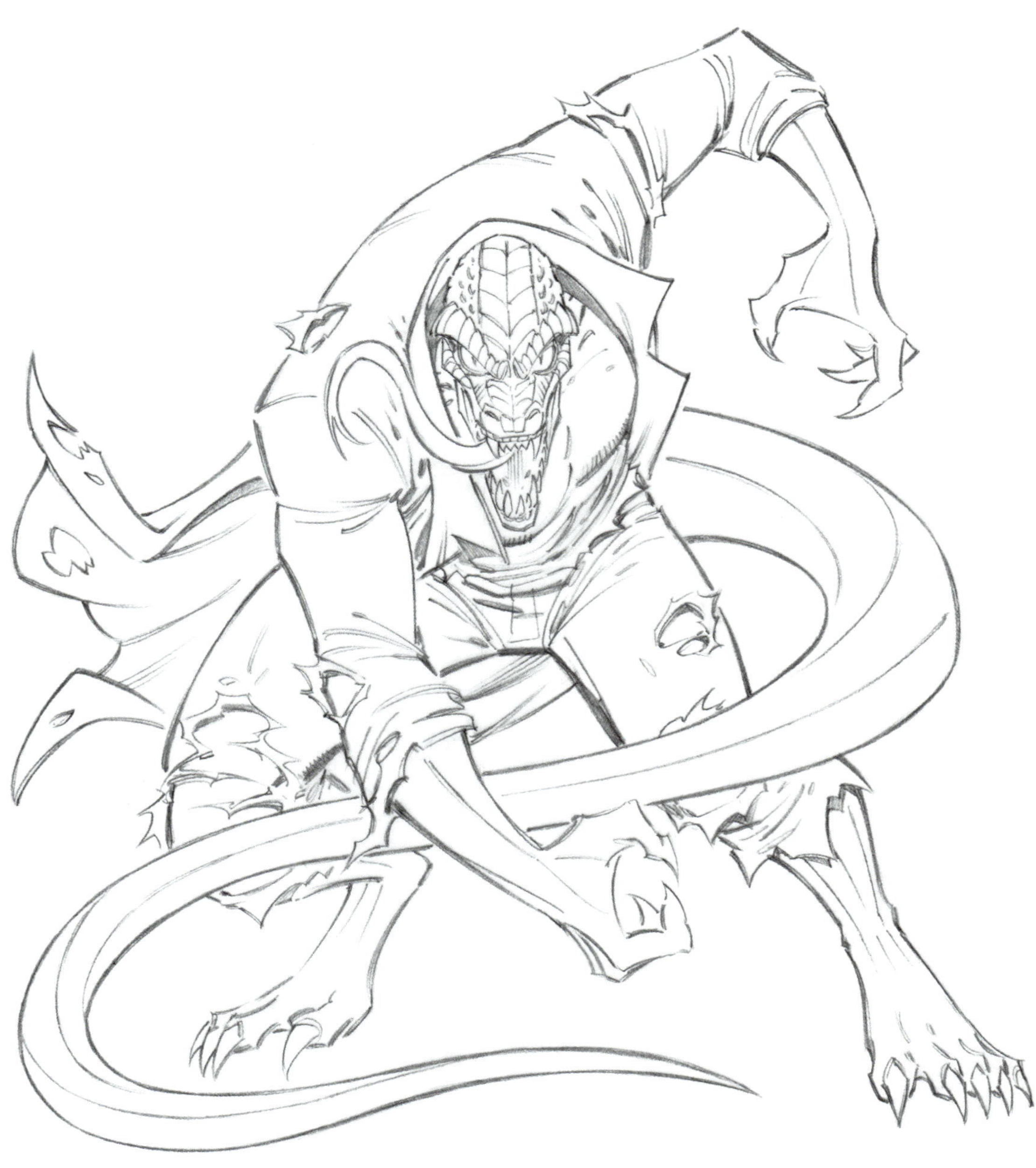

Crosshatching scales with shadow.

Basic crosshatching scales

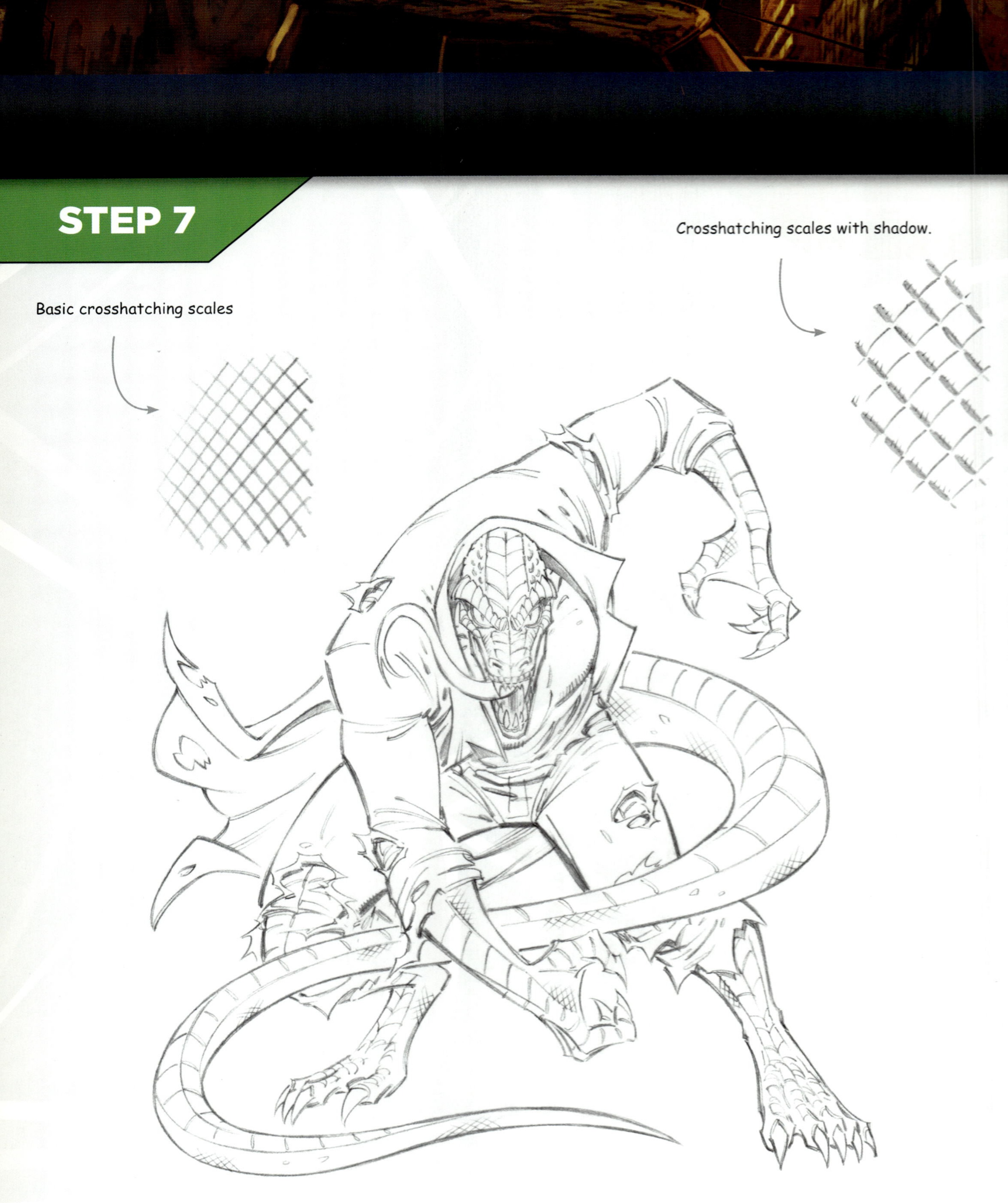

Lizard's first appearance was in issue #6 of *The Amazing Spider-Man* in 1963.

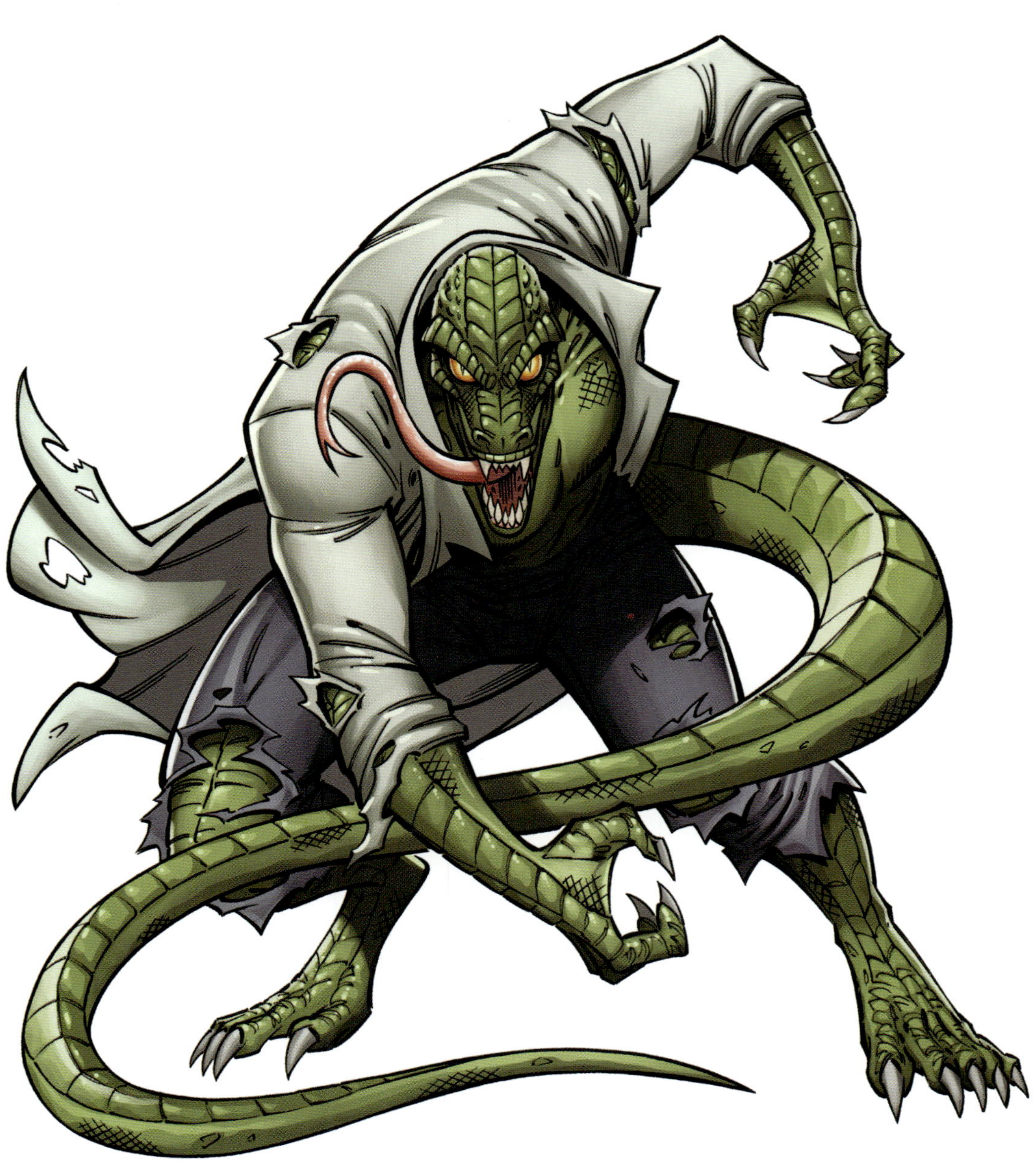

VENOM

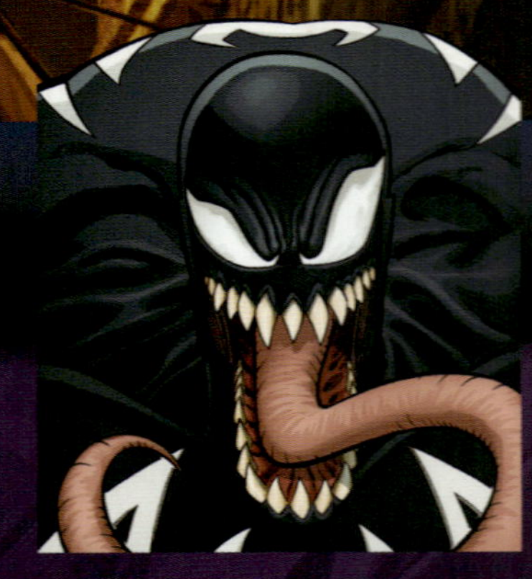

Eddie Brock, former *Daily Globe* journalist, finds his personal life in shambles and blames Spider-Man for his troubles. Eddie falls victim to a parasitic alien suit, which brings out the worst in its wearer, and is transformed into Venom. Because the symbiote suit had previously attached itself to Spider-Man, Venom's abilities mimic those of Spider-Man.

STEP 1

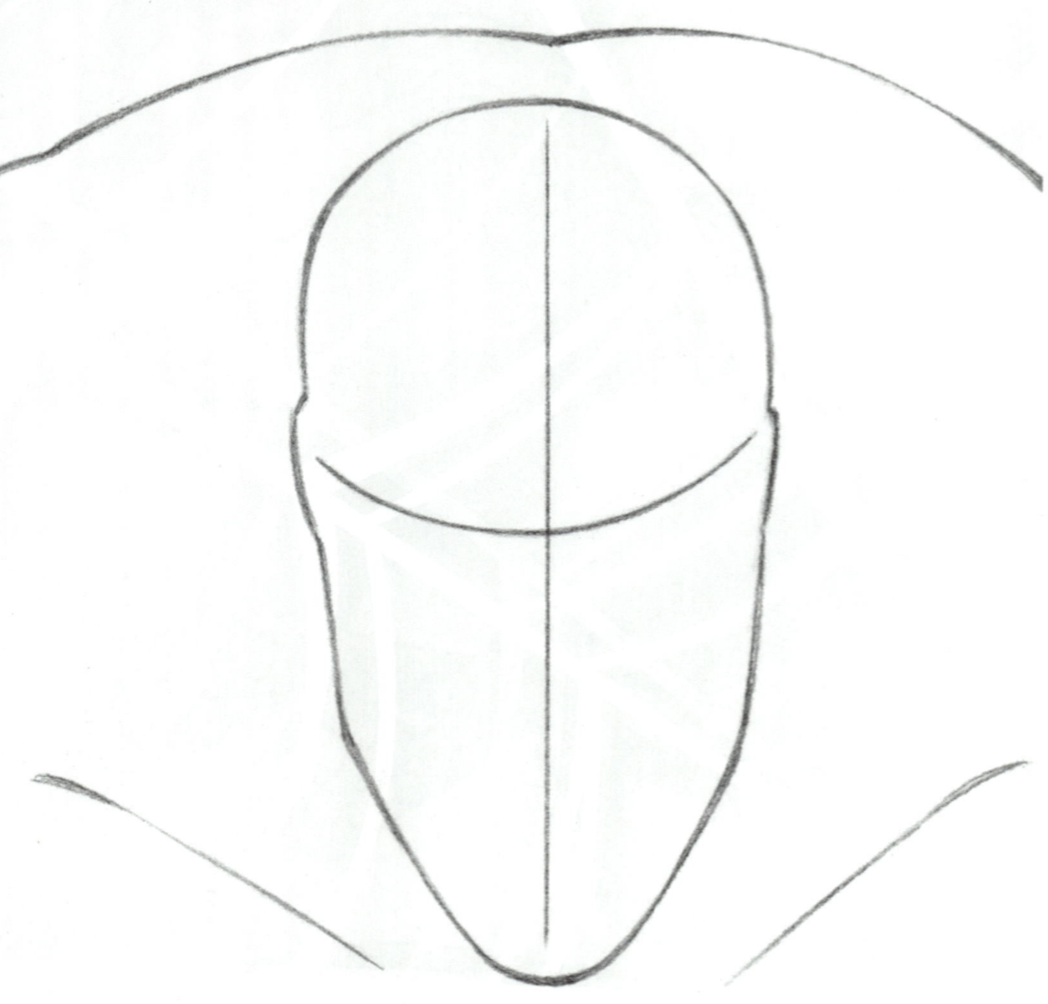

The black and white costume was **a fan idea** originally **intended for Spider-Man.** Marvel used the suit idea but created **a new character** for it.

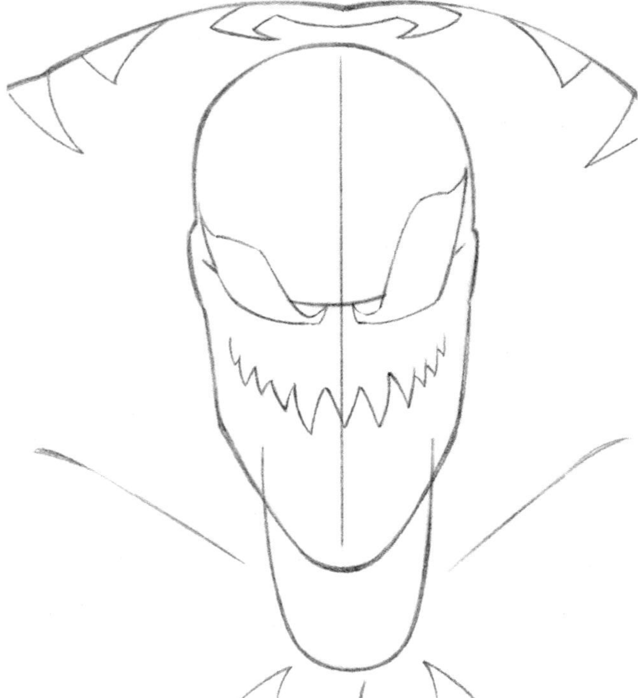

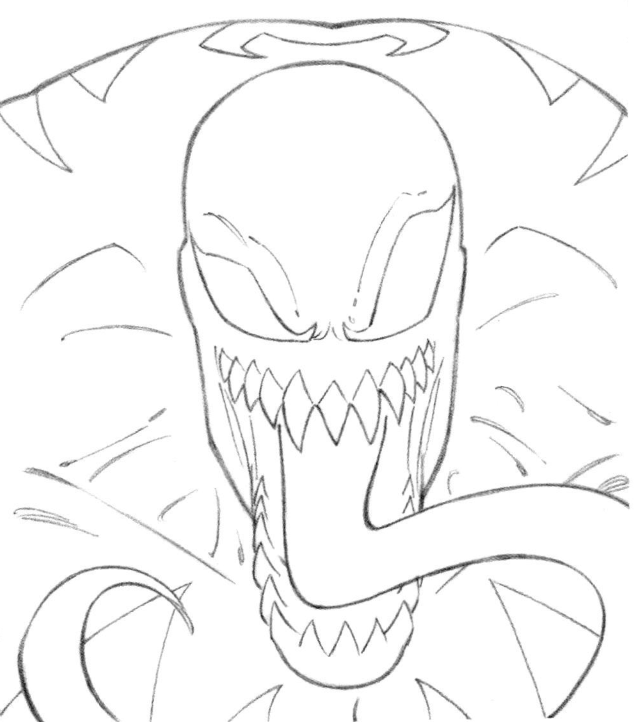

STEP 3

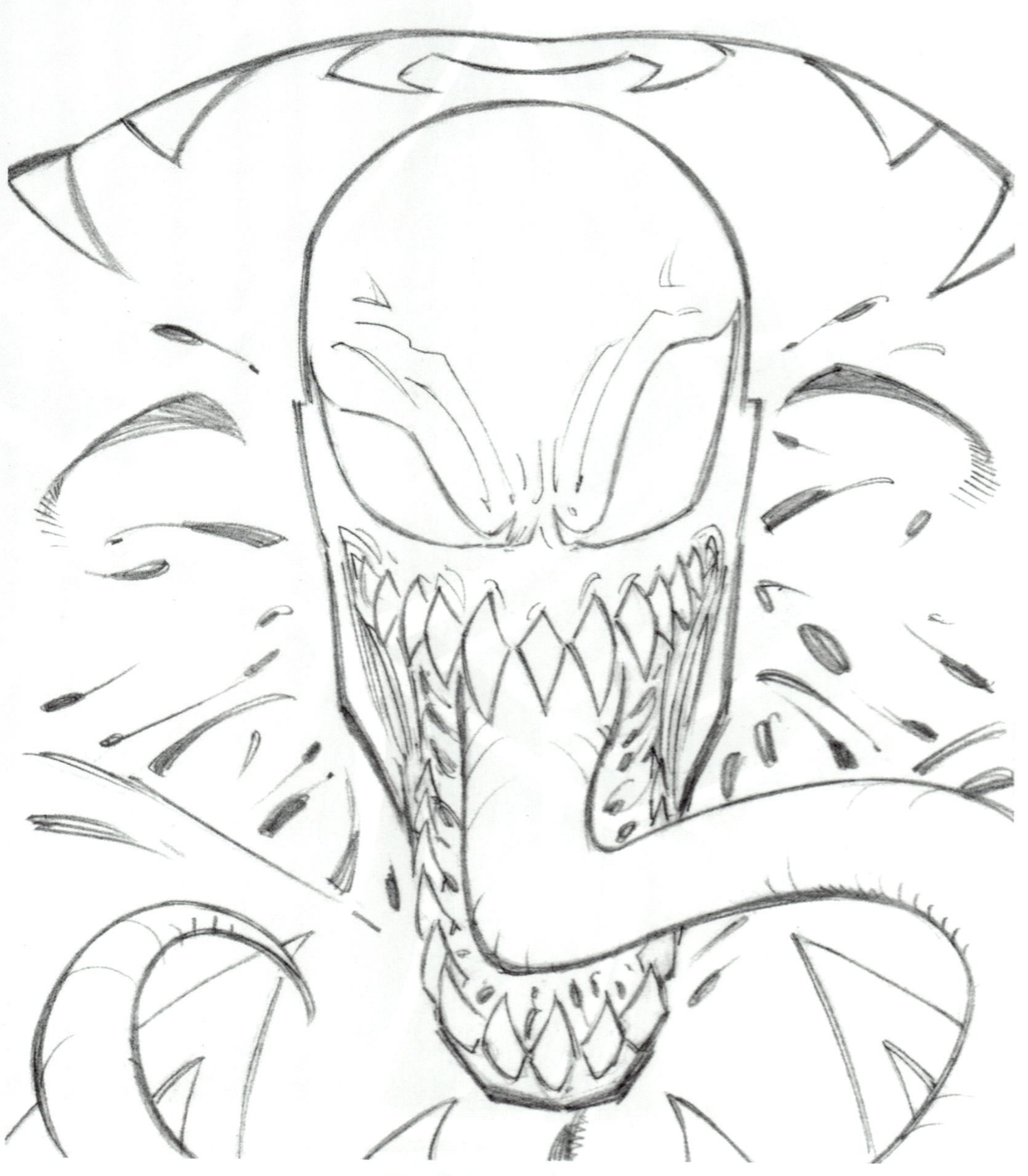

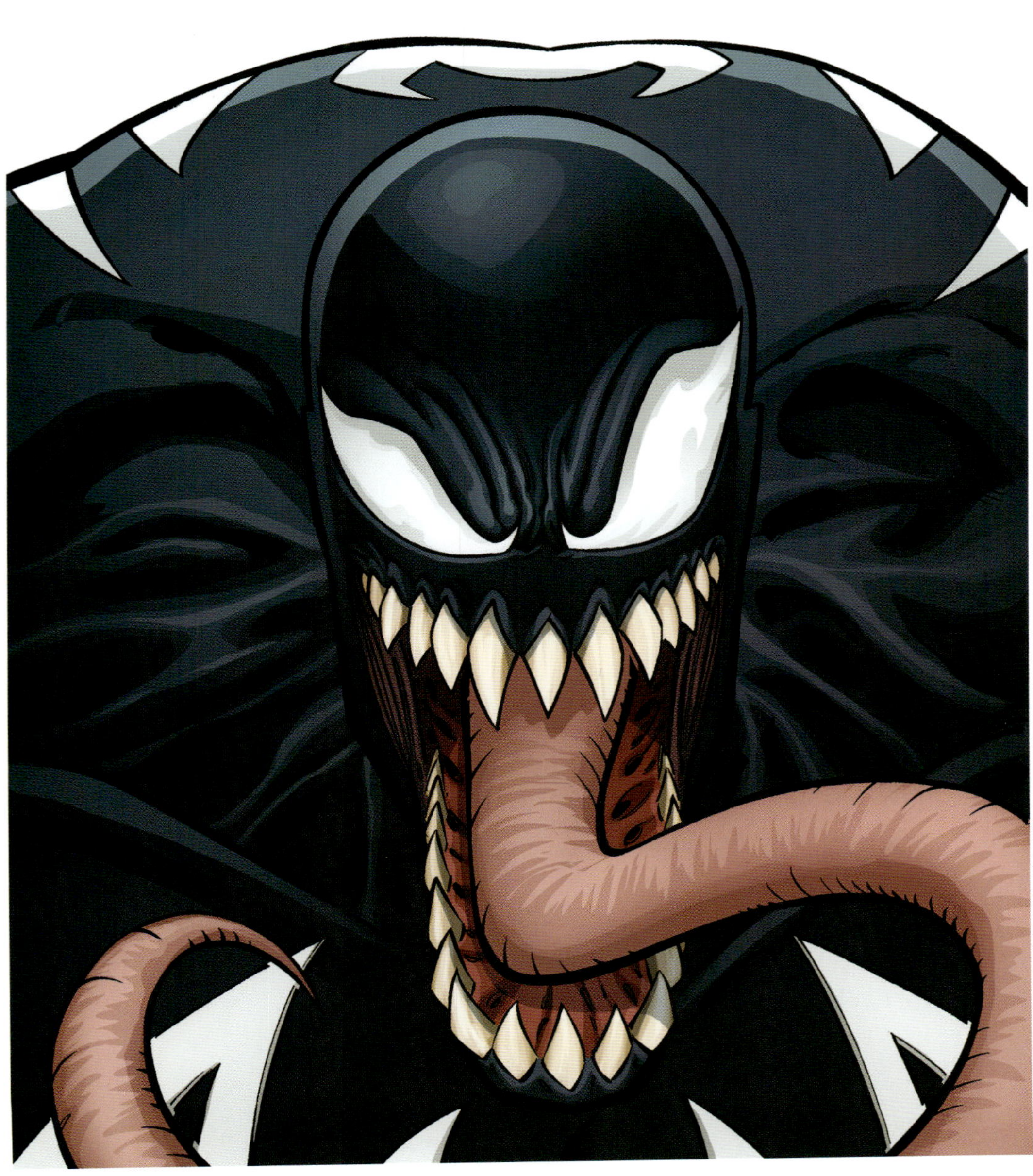

VENOM

STEP 1

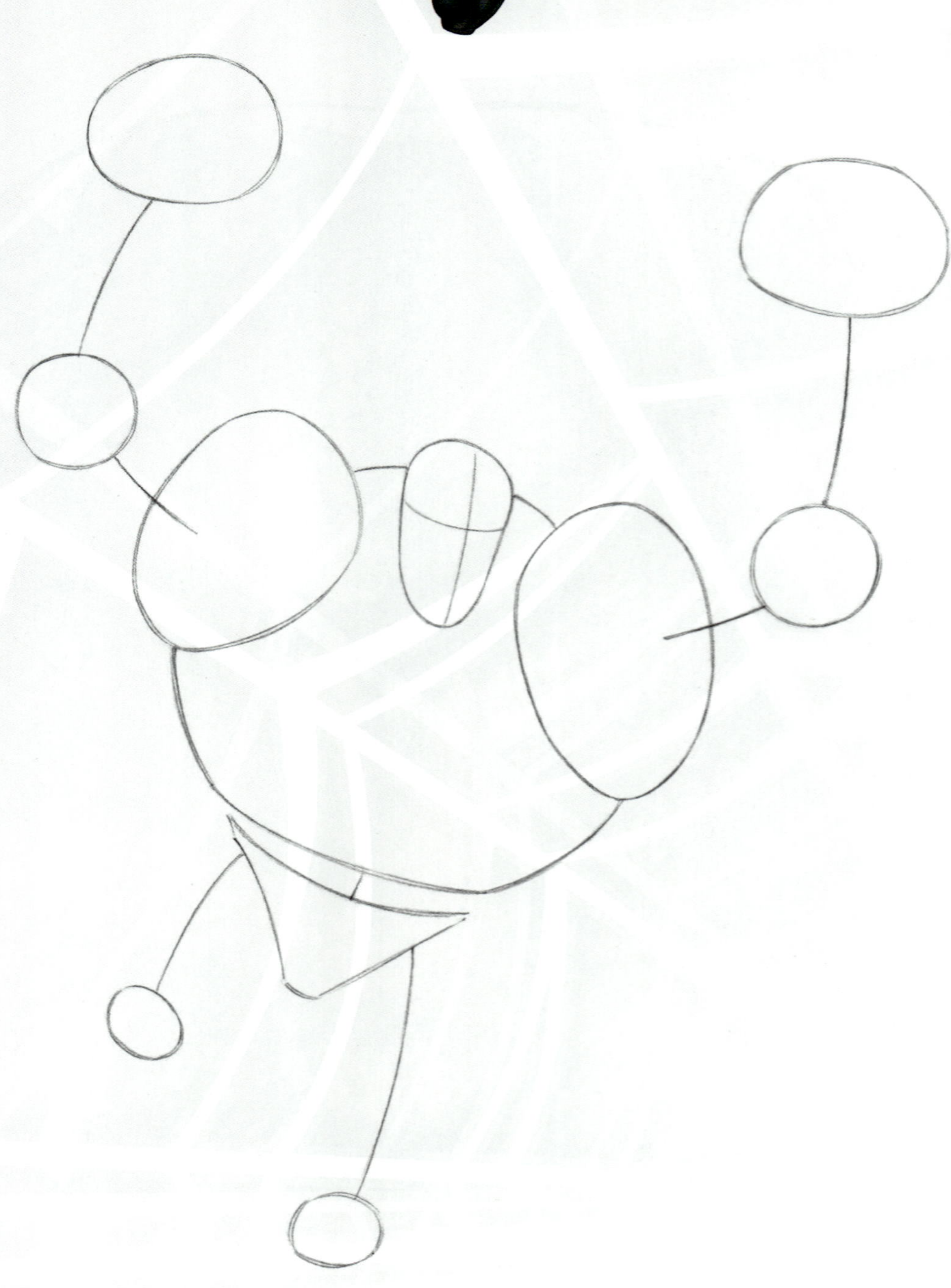

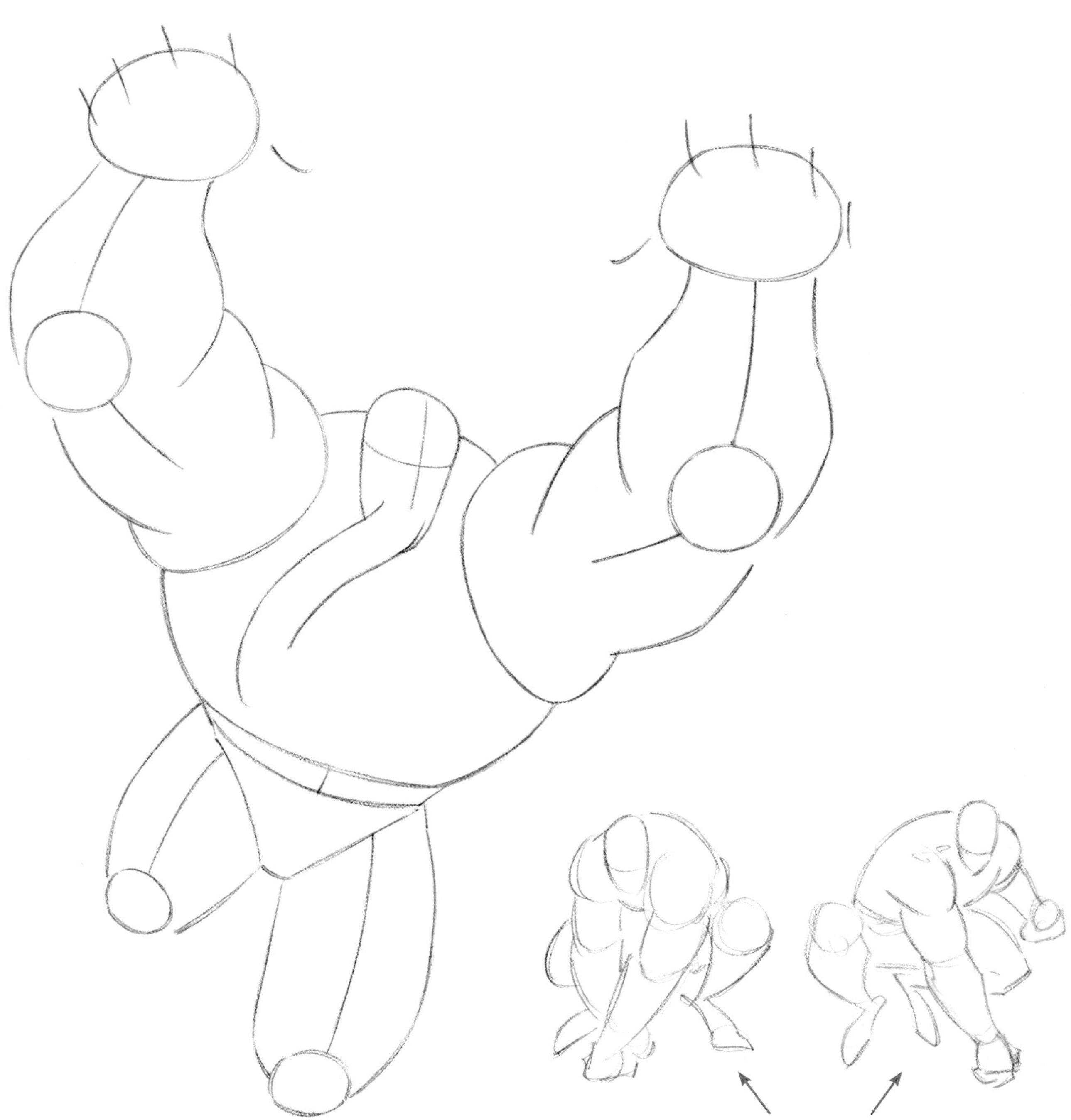

Think of Venom as top-heavy like a gorilla.

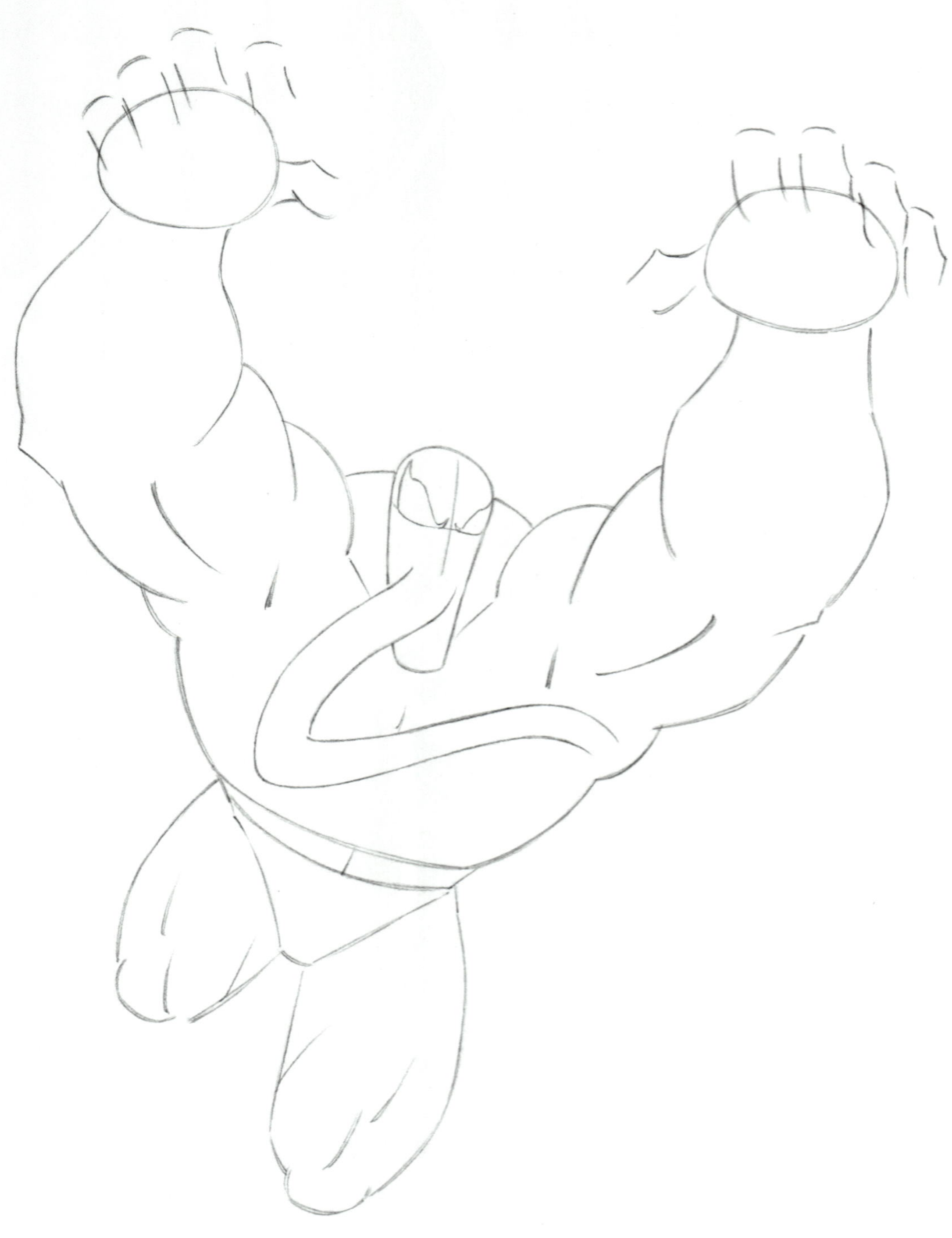

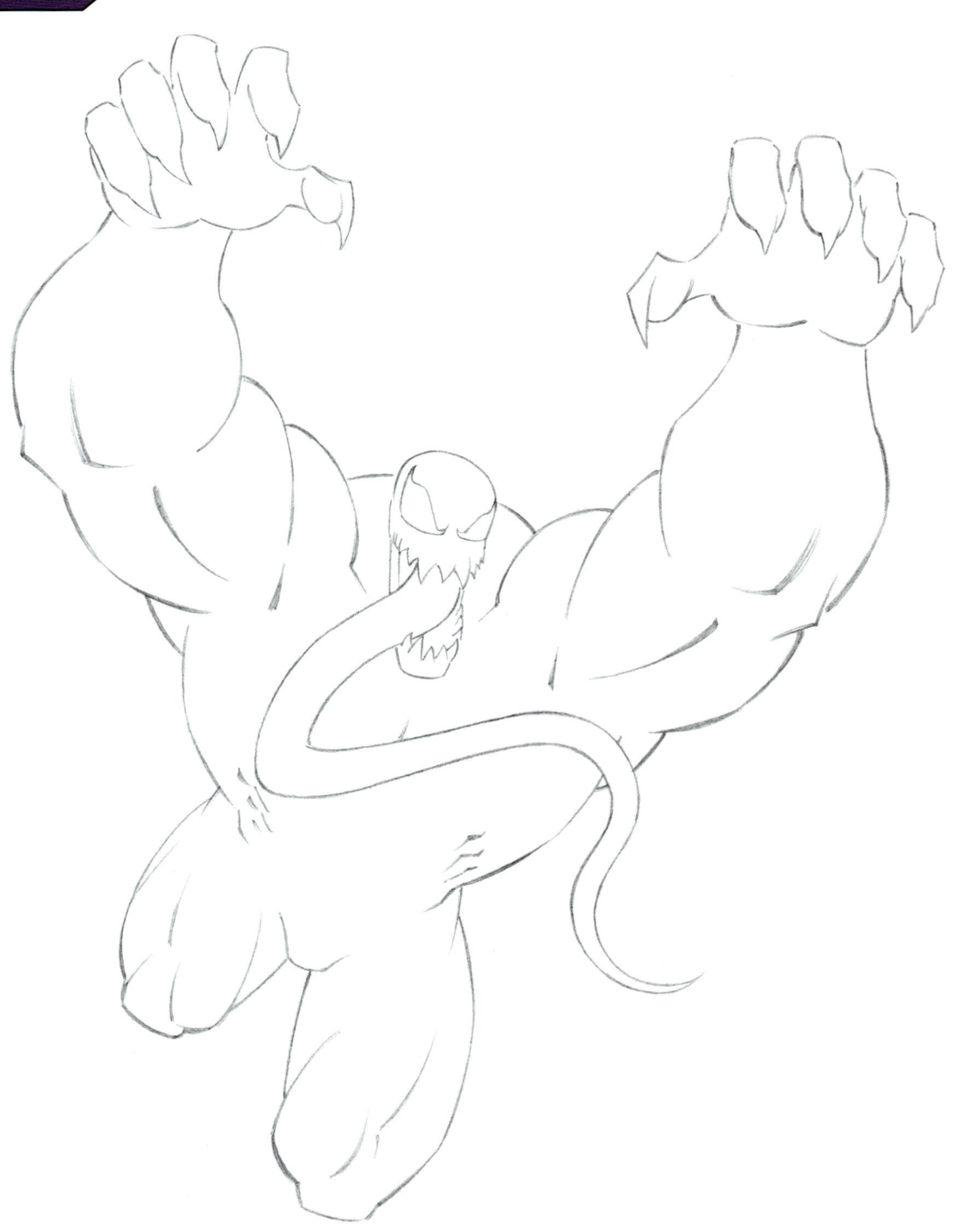

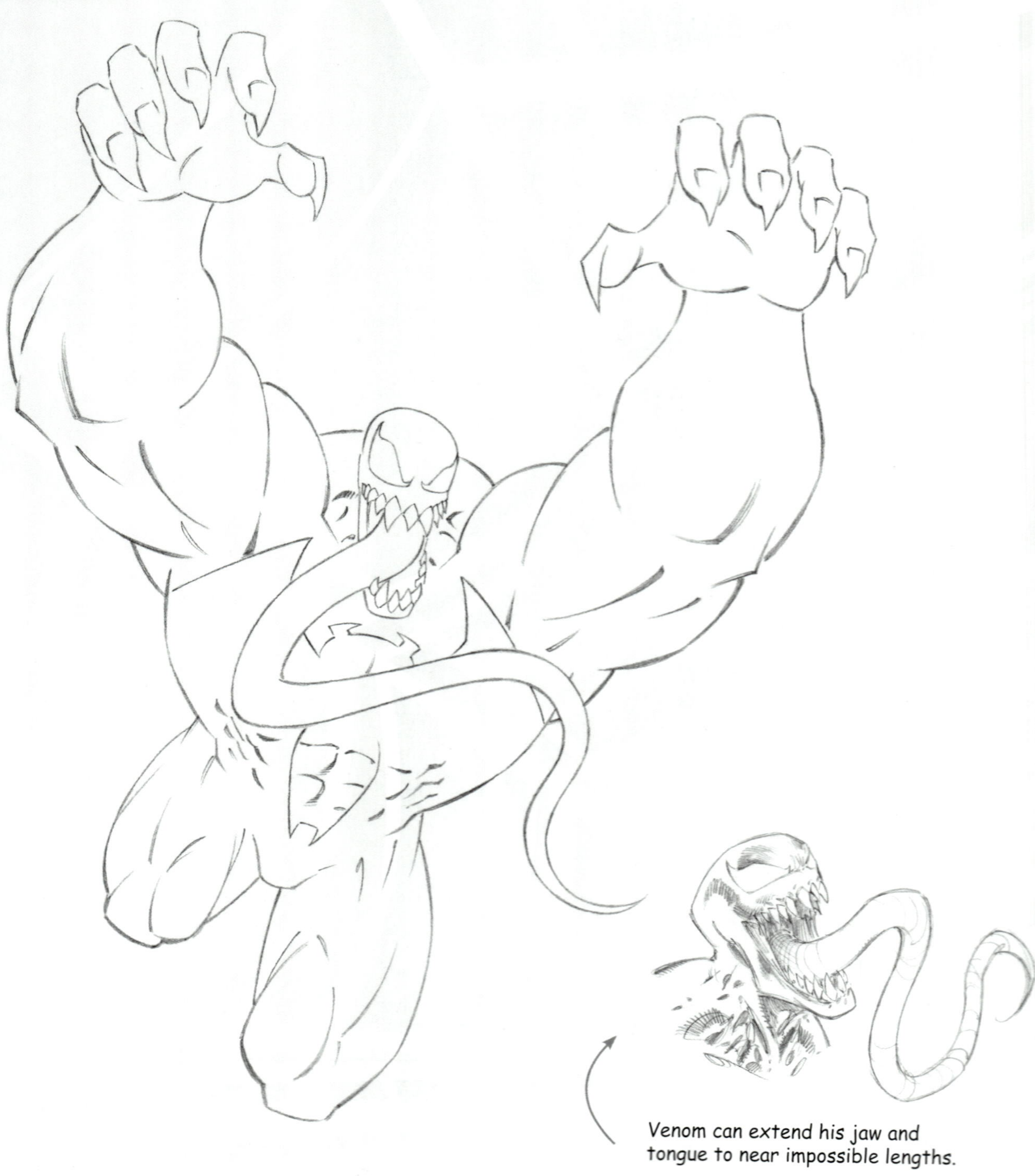

Venom can extend his jaw and
tongue to near impossible lengths.

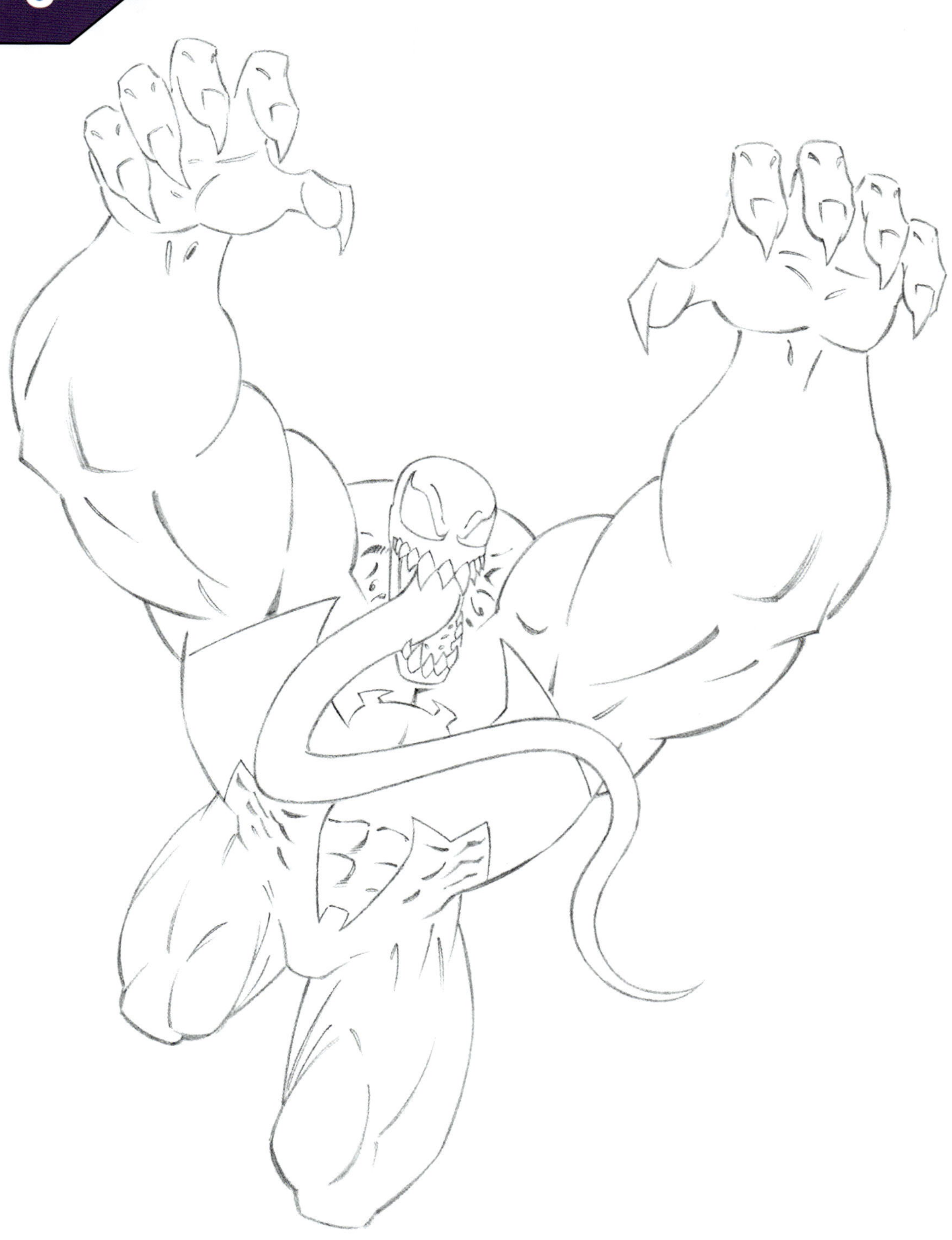

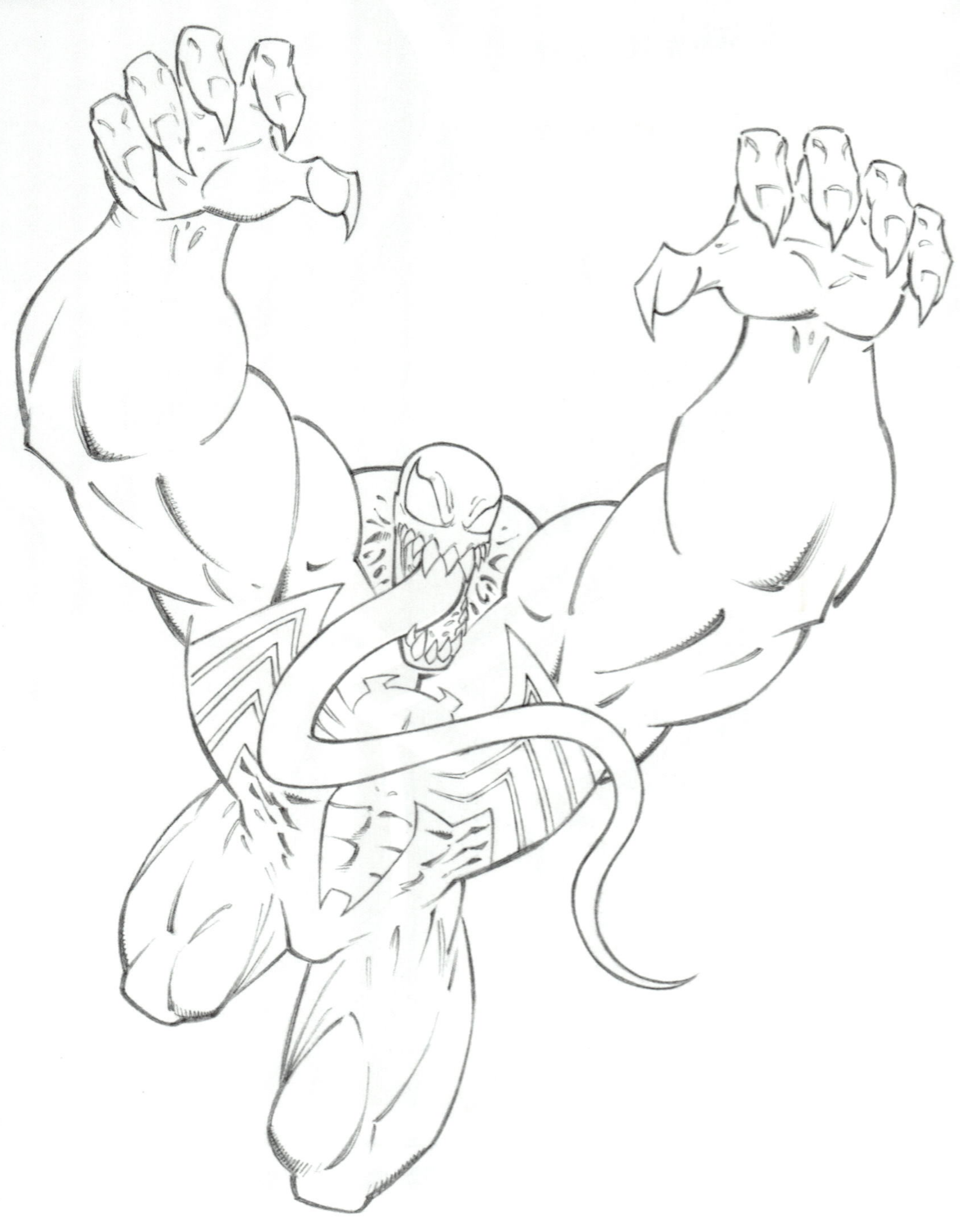

STEP 8

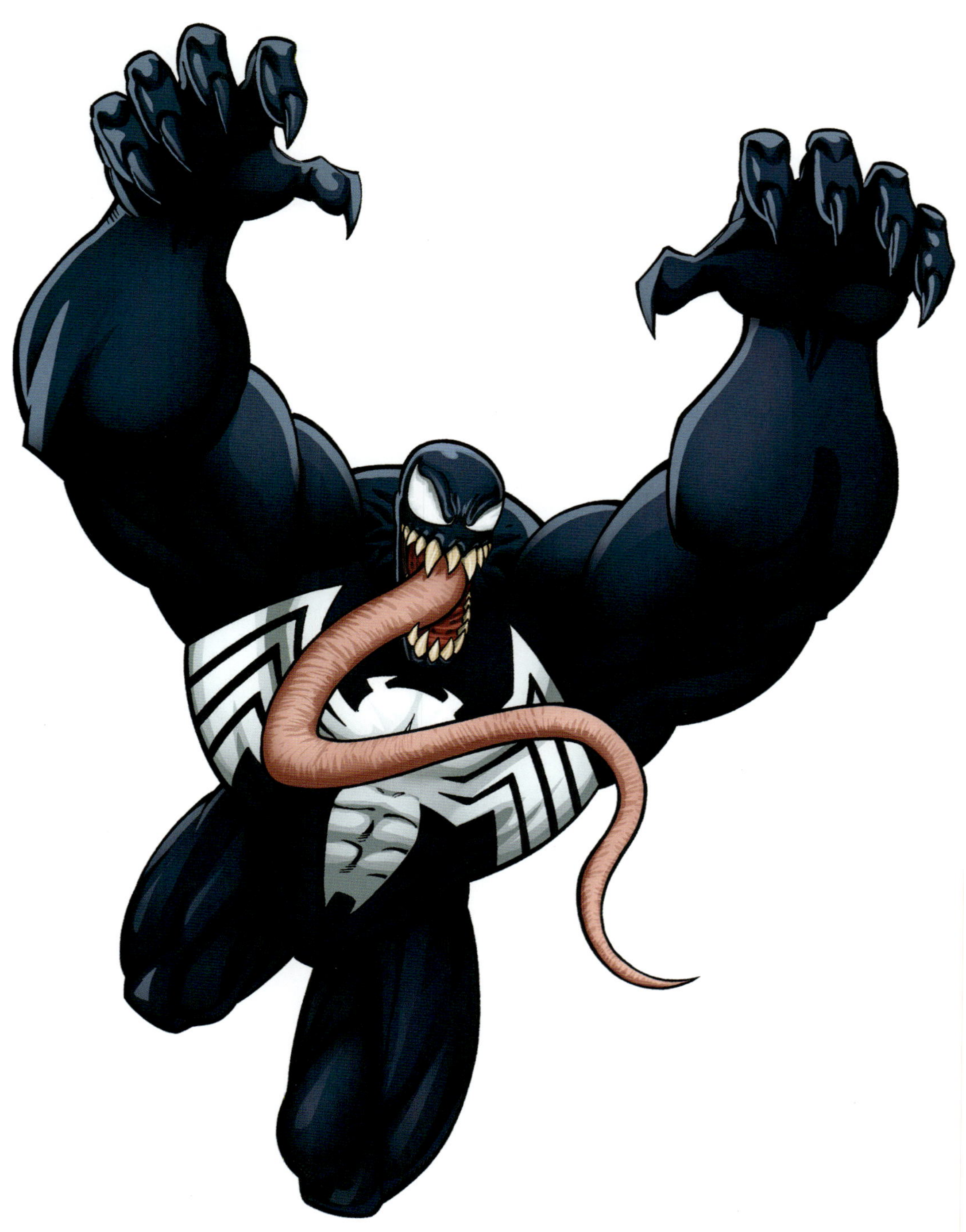

THE VULTURE

Adrian Toomes is a former electronics engineer who employs a special harness of his own design that allows him to fly and endows him with enhanced strength. Obsessed with gaining back his youth, Toomes is quite old, though spry, and a remorseless killer. On several occasions, he restores his youth for a short period, but the effect wears off within hours.

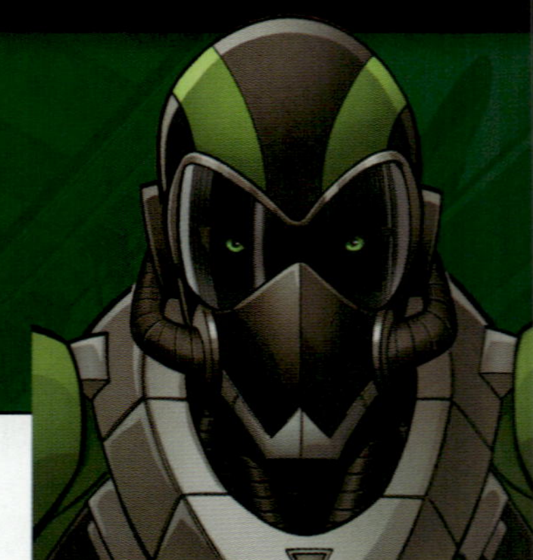

STEP 1

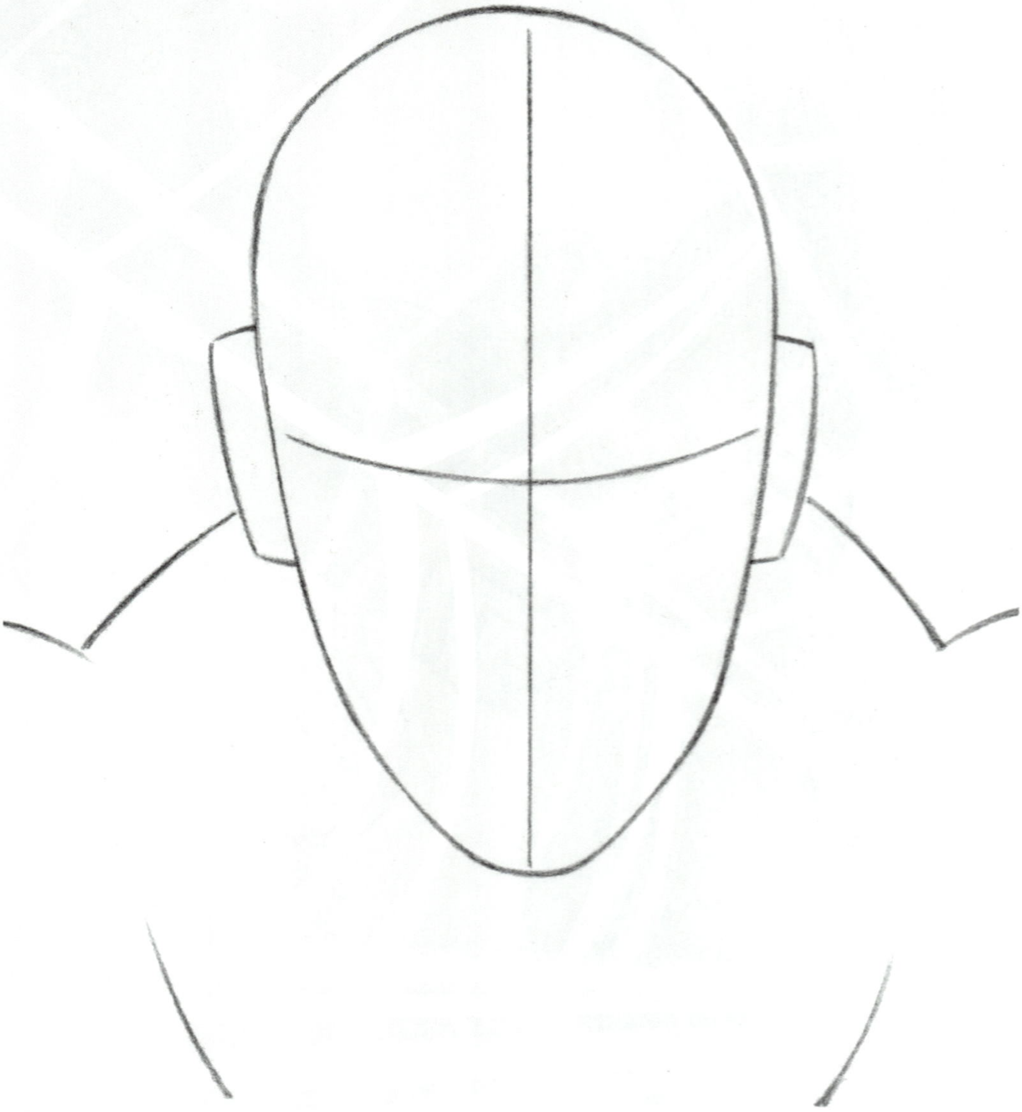

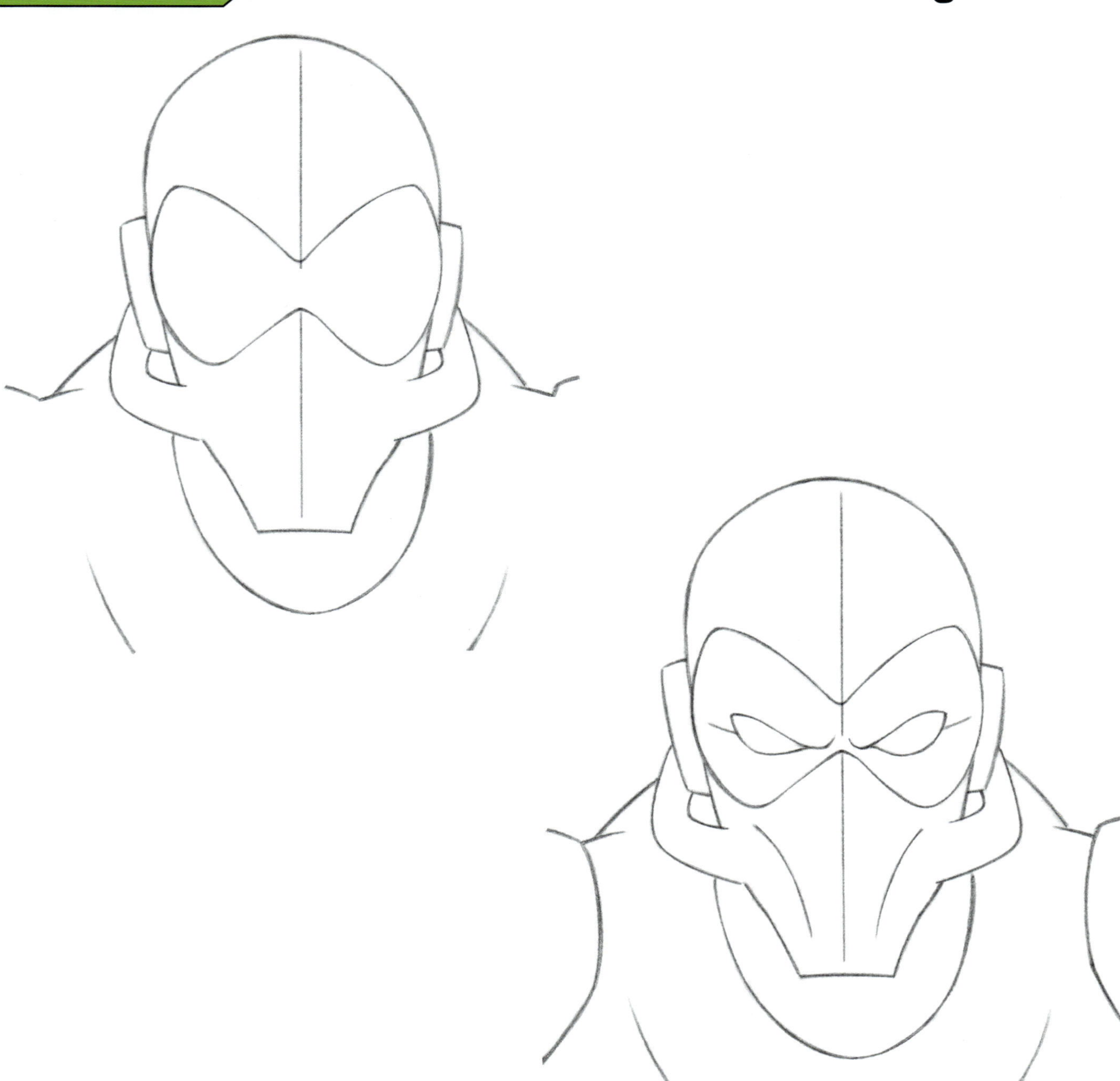

STEP 2
At one point, the **Vulture stole Spider-Man's youth**, leaving the Vulture young and Spider-Man elderly. Luckily for Spider-Man, **the effect wore off** after a couple of hours.
STEP 3

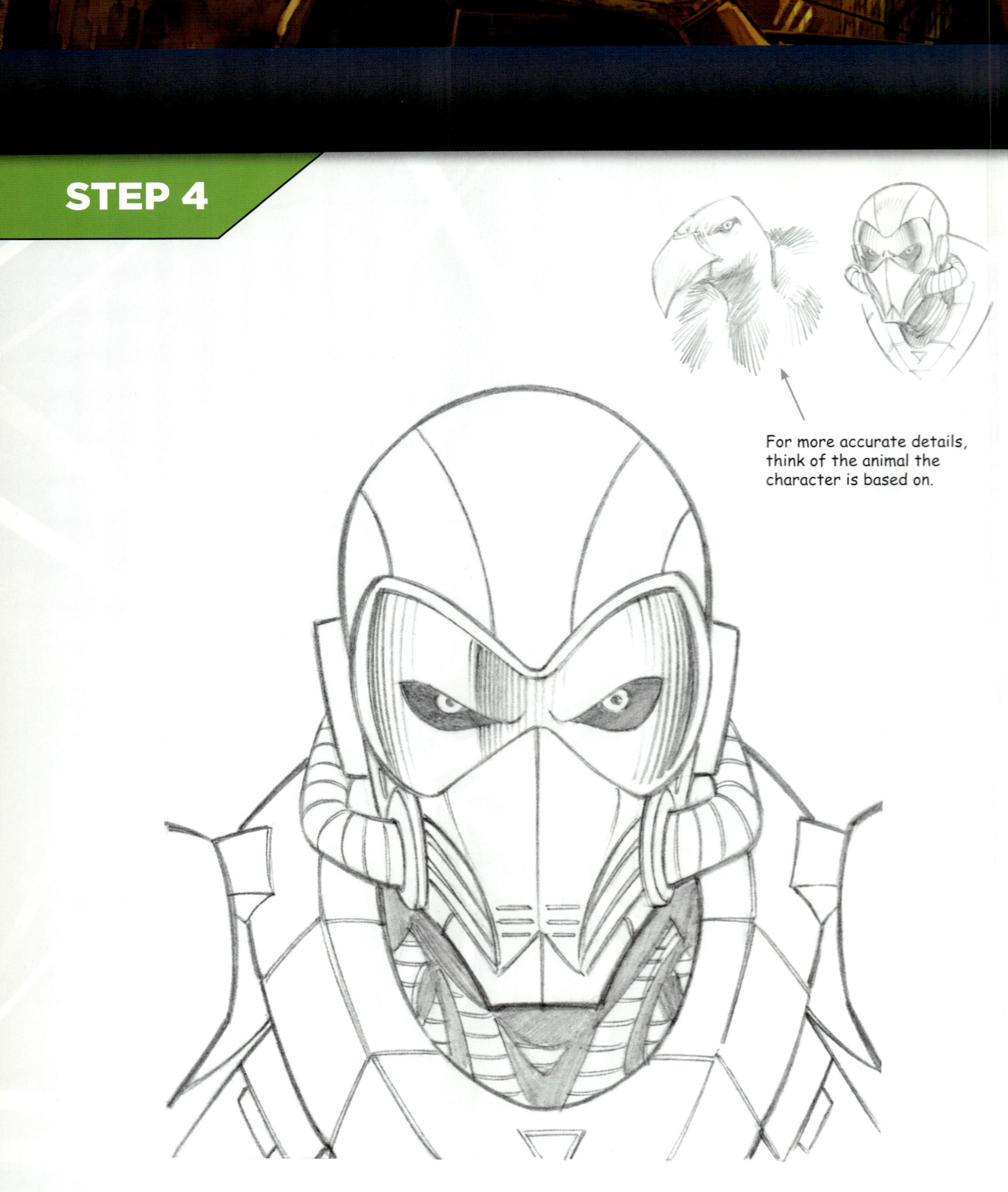

For more accurate details, think of the animal the character is based on.

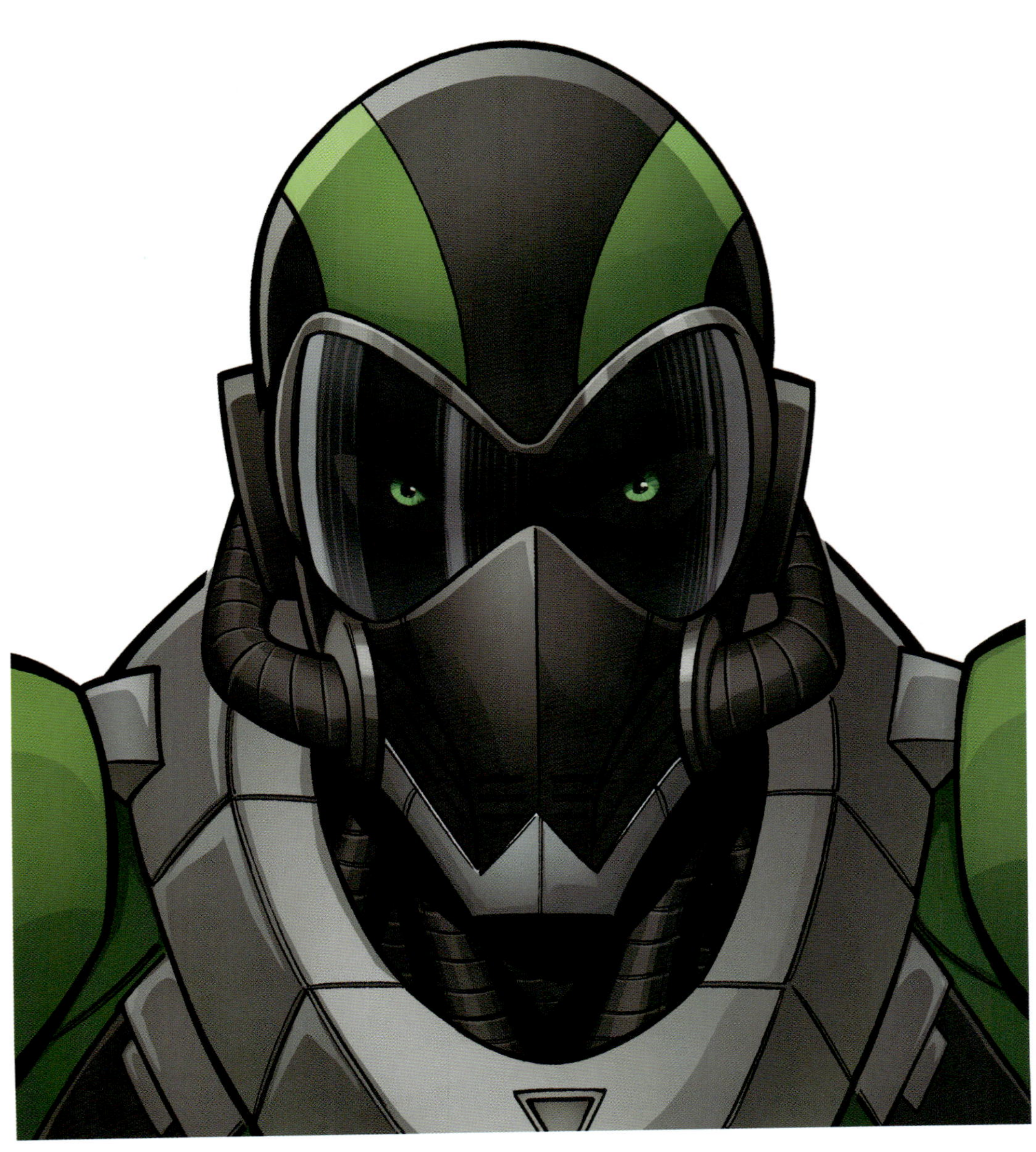

STEP 1

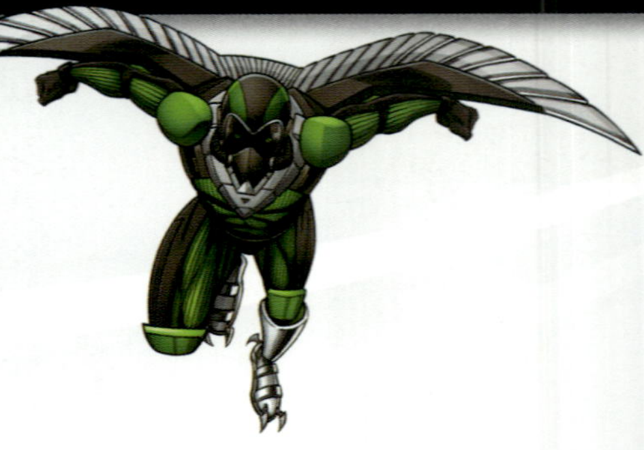

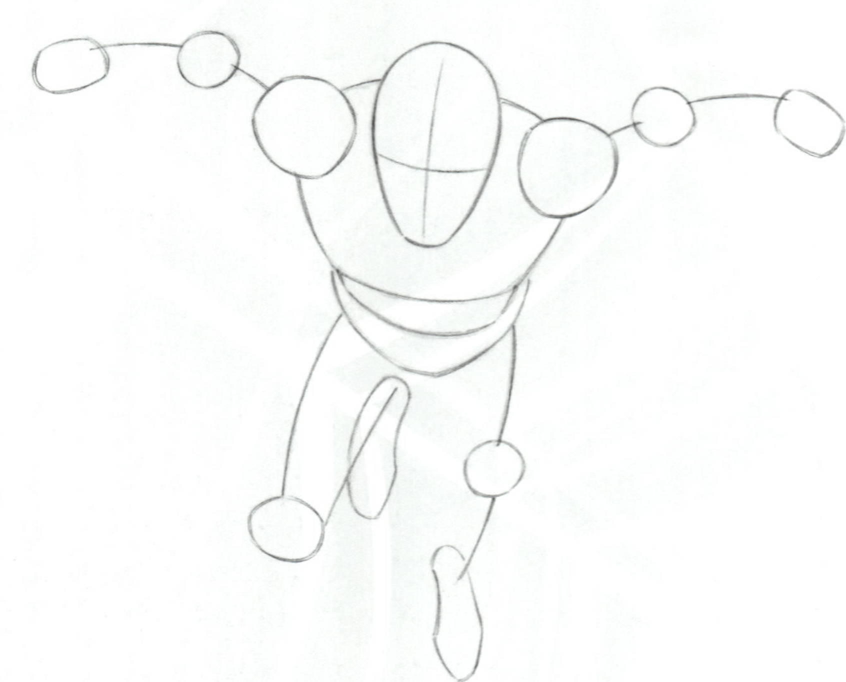

Adrian Toomes is old and in ill health, but the special wings he's made provide him with temporary youth, increased physical strength, and the ability to fly. These enhancements slowly fade once he takes the wings off.

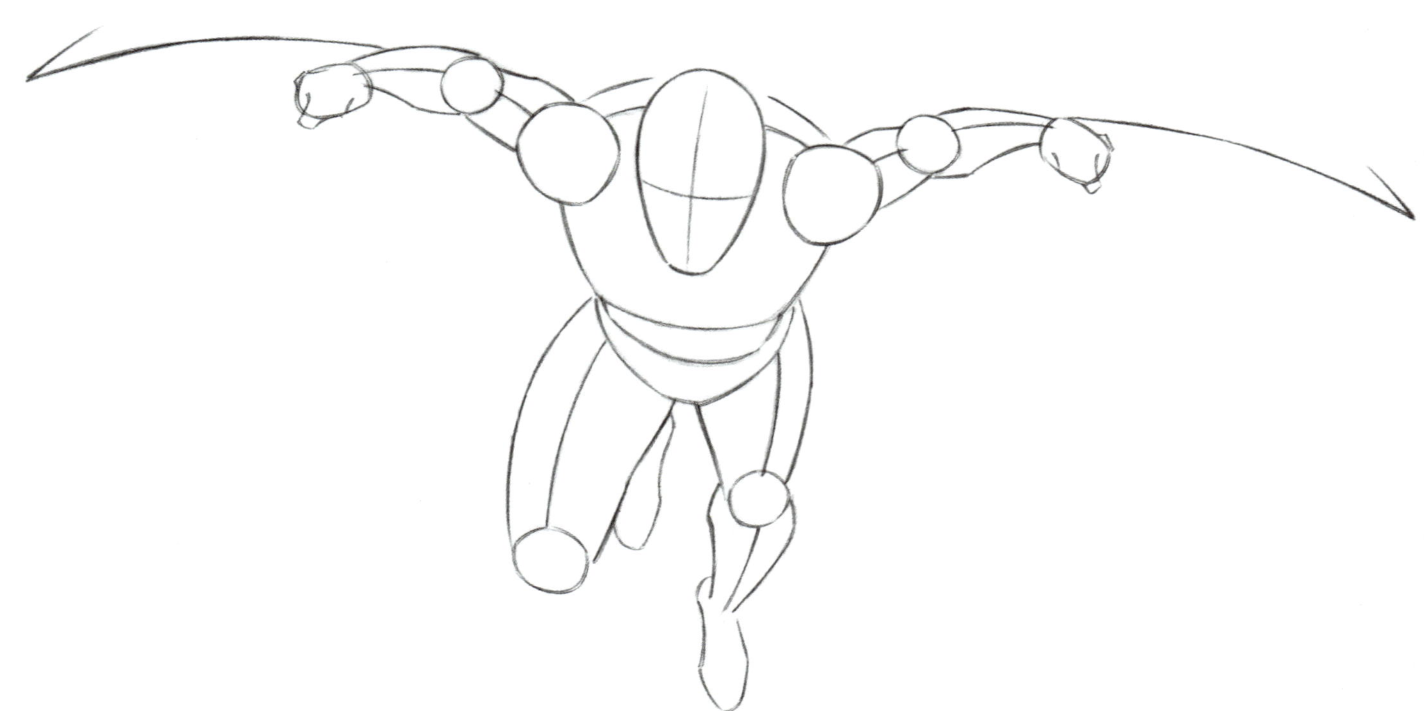

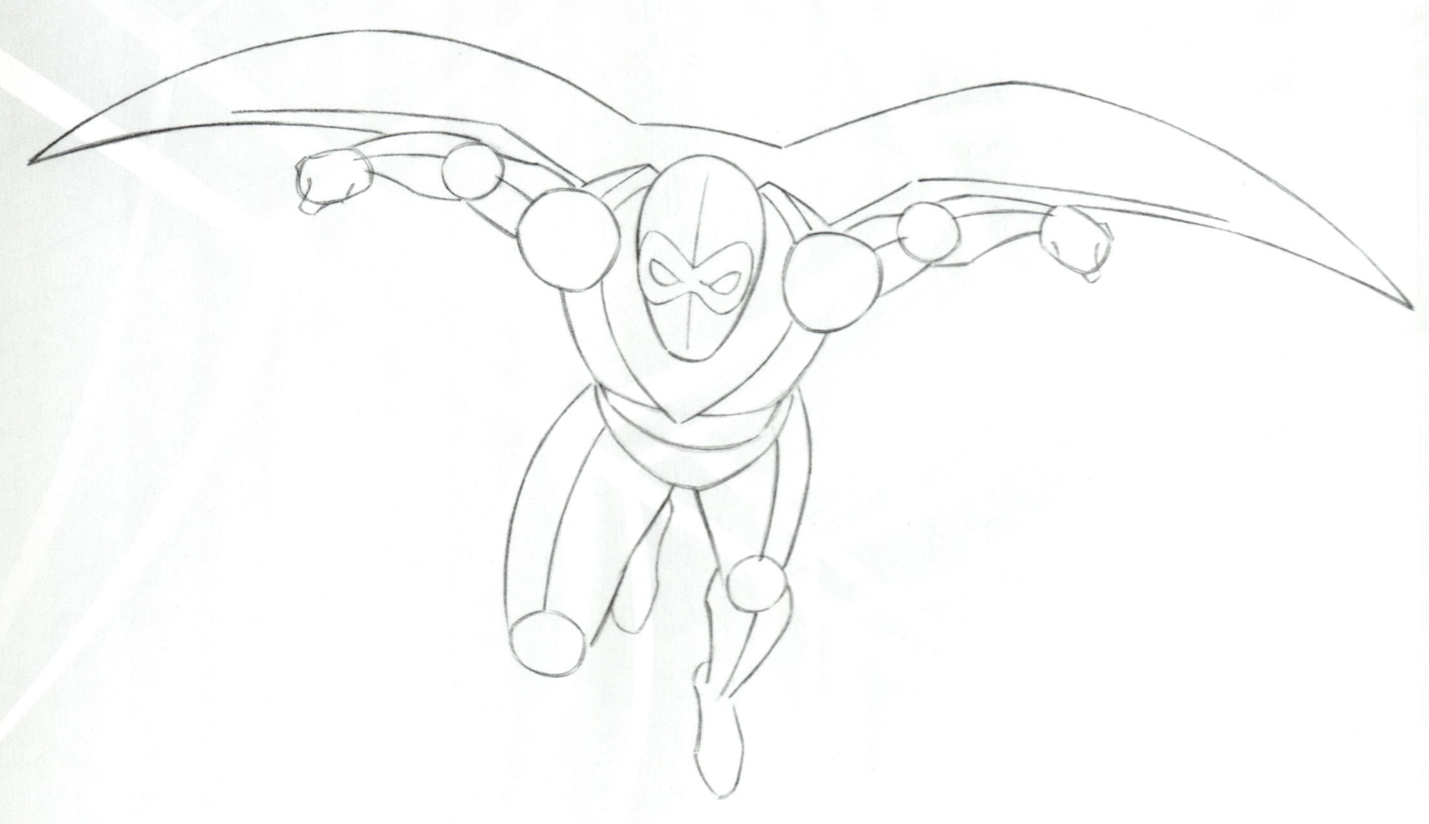

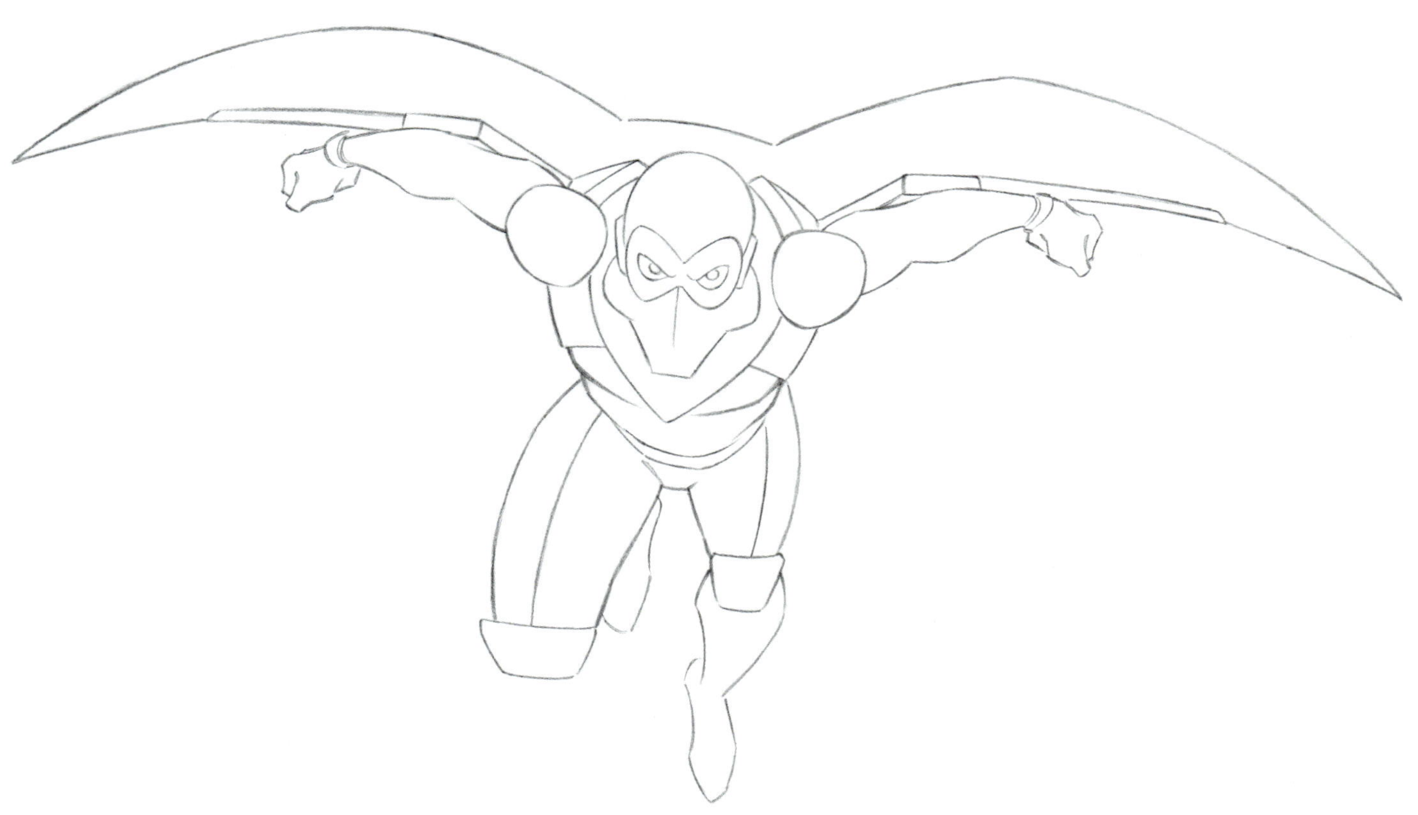

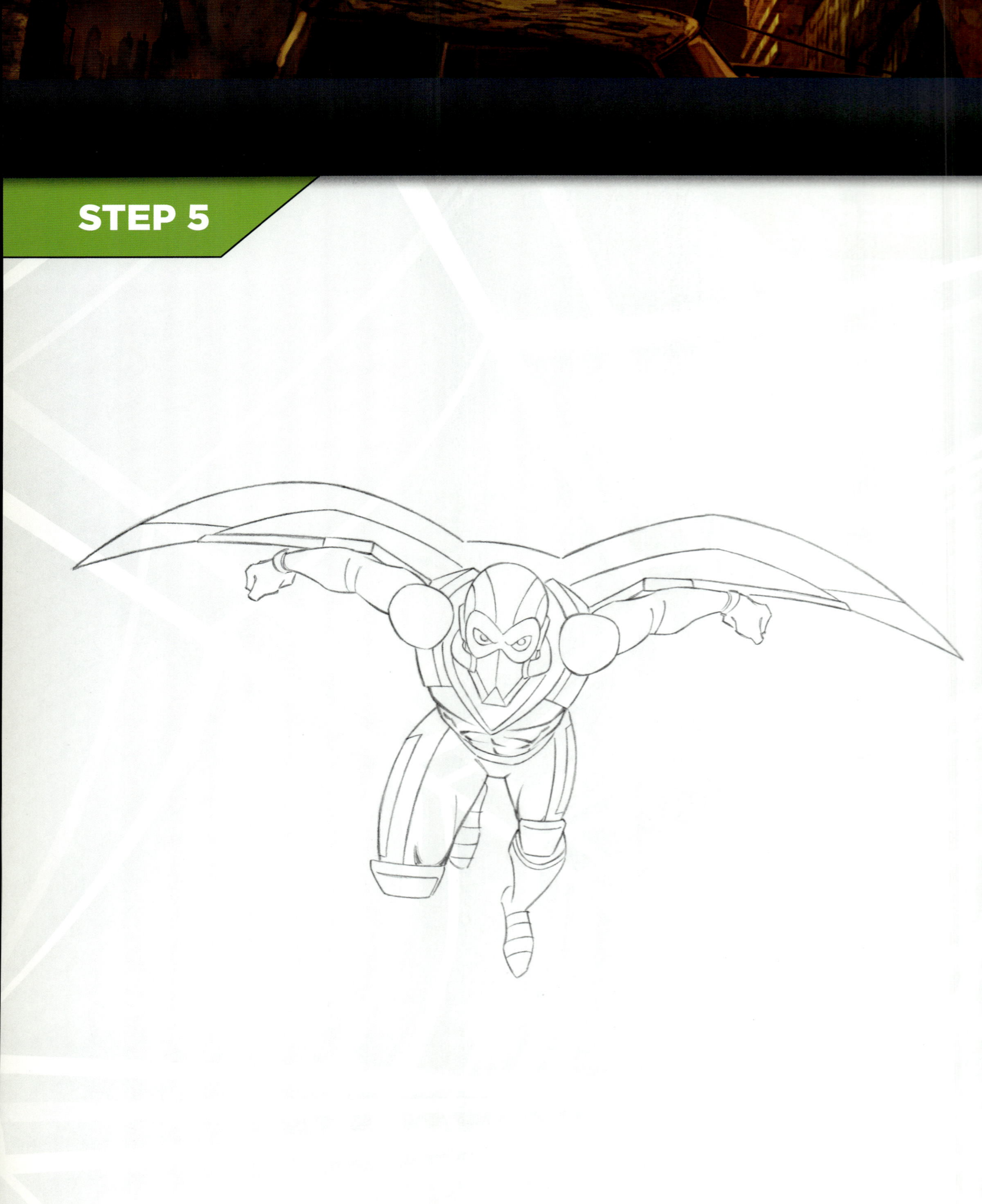

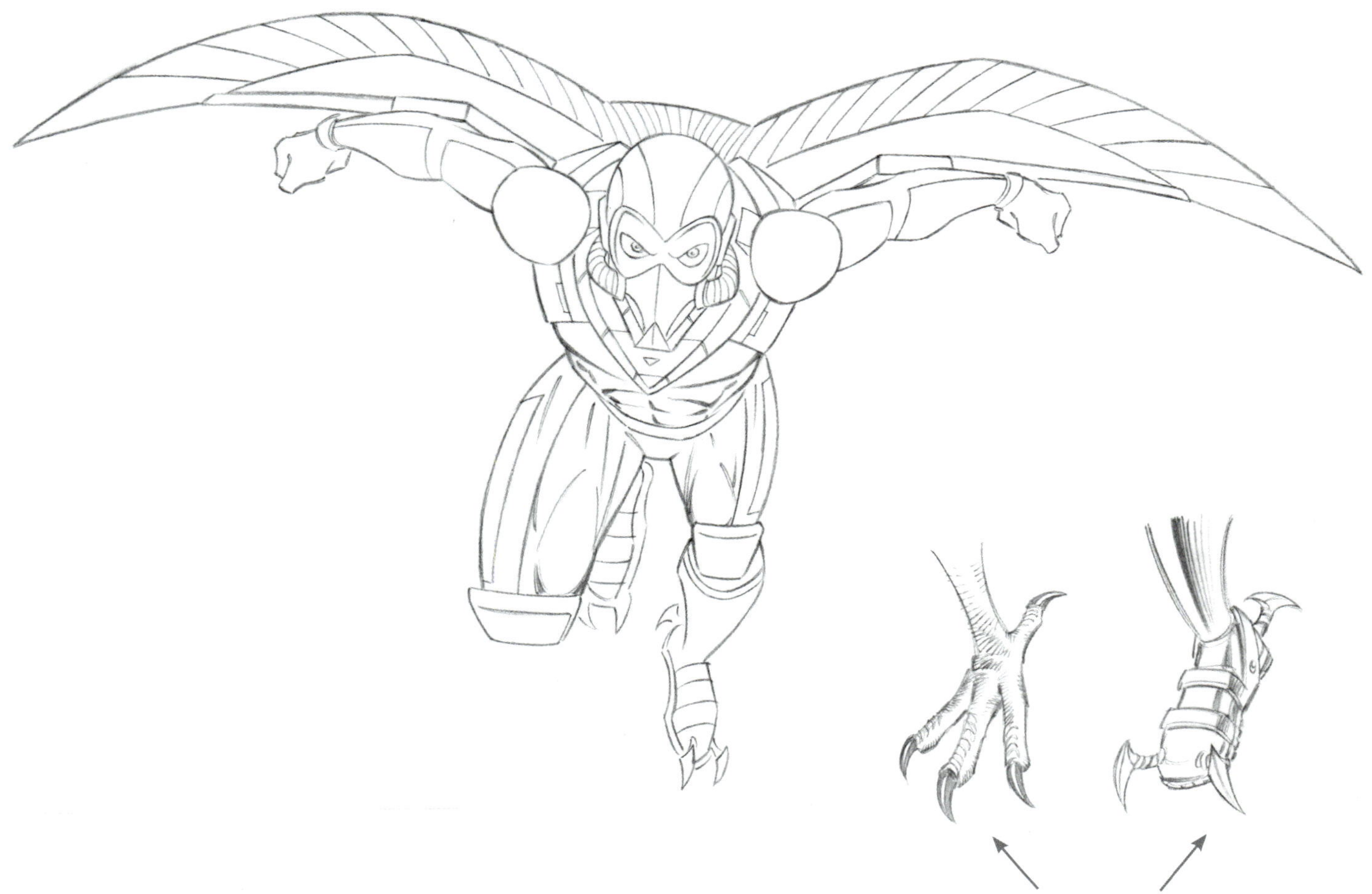

See how the Vulture's man-made talons compare to those of a real vulture.

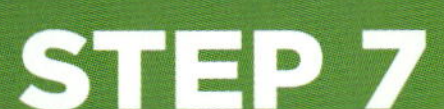

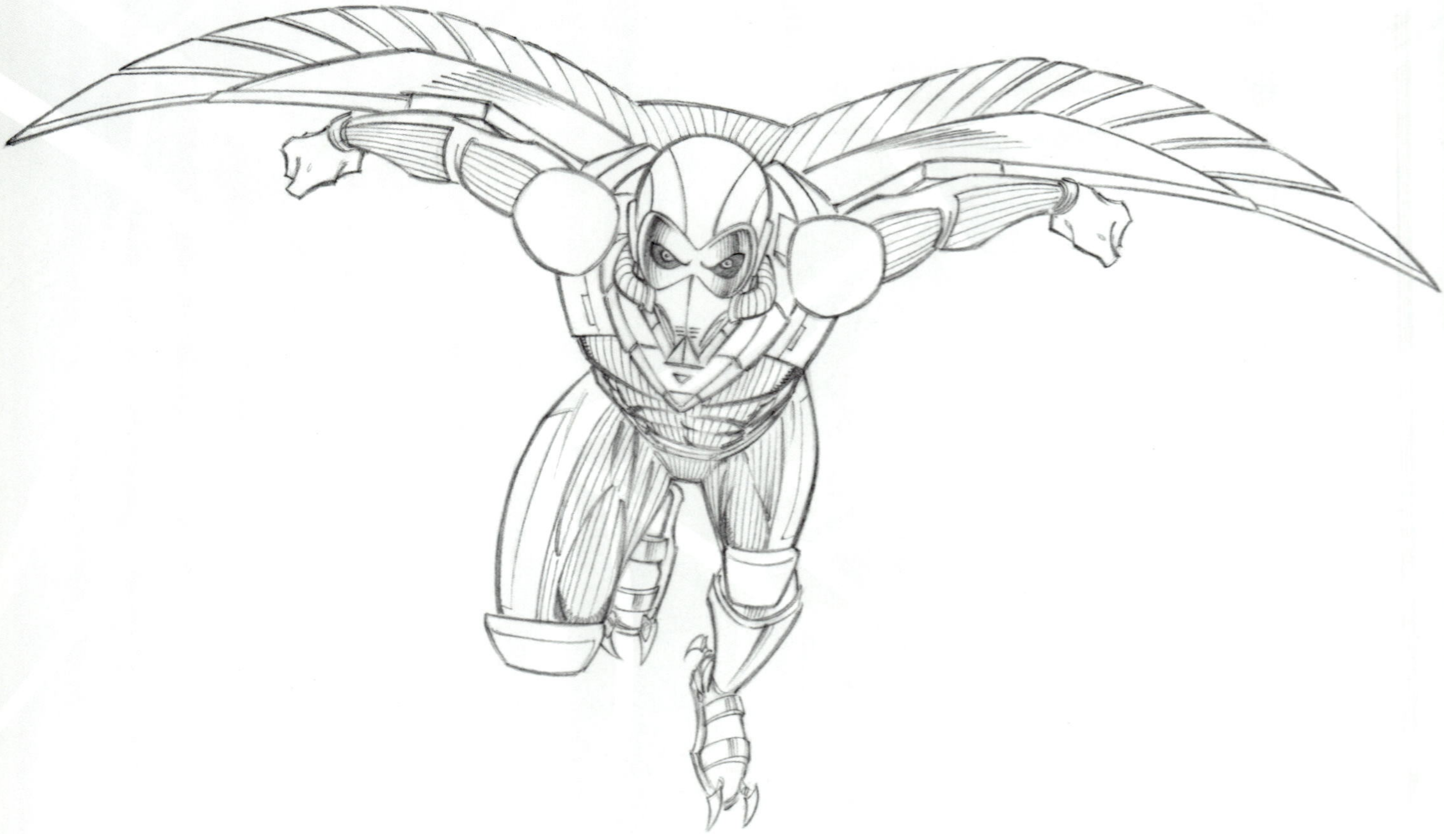

The Vulture's first appearance was in issue #2 of *The Amazing Spider-Man*.

STEP 8

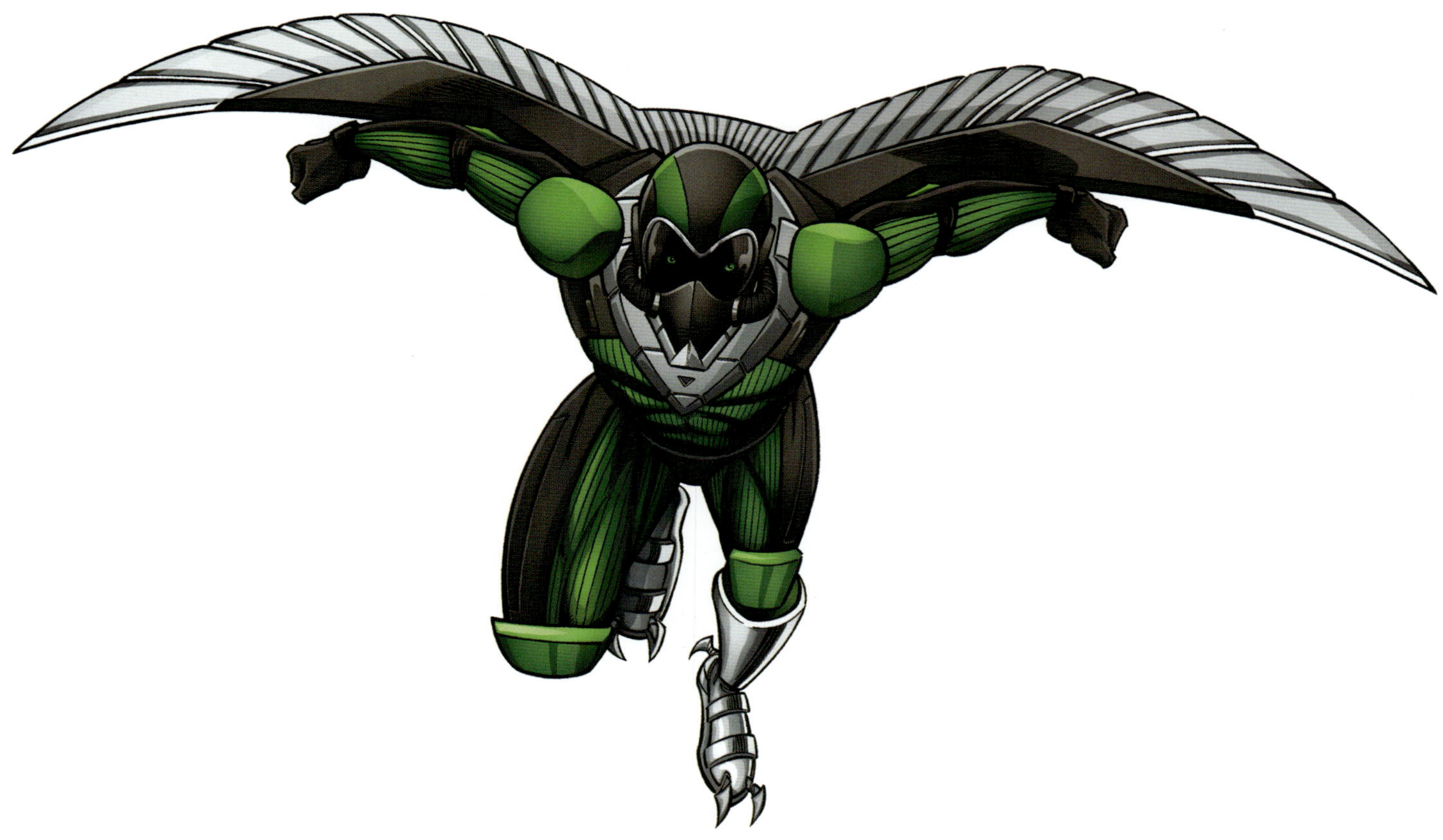

RHINO

Aleksei Sytsevich, a common thug in the Russian mafia, is selected by a collective of professional spies because of his muscular physique and low intelligence, which they believe will ensure his loyalty. They promise Aleksei wealth and power to undergo a life-threatening series of chemical and radiation treatments, which transform him into a superhumanly strong agent. Aleksei's powerful armor, modeled after the hide of a rhinoceros, is permanently bonded to his body.

STEP 1

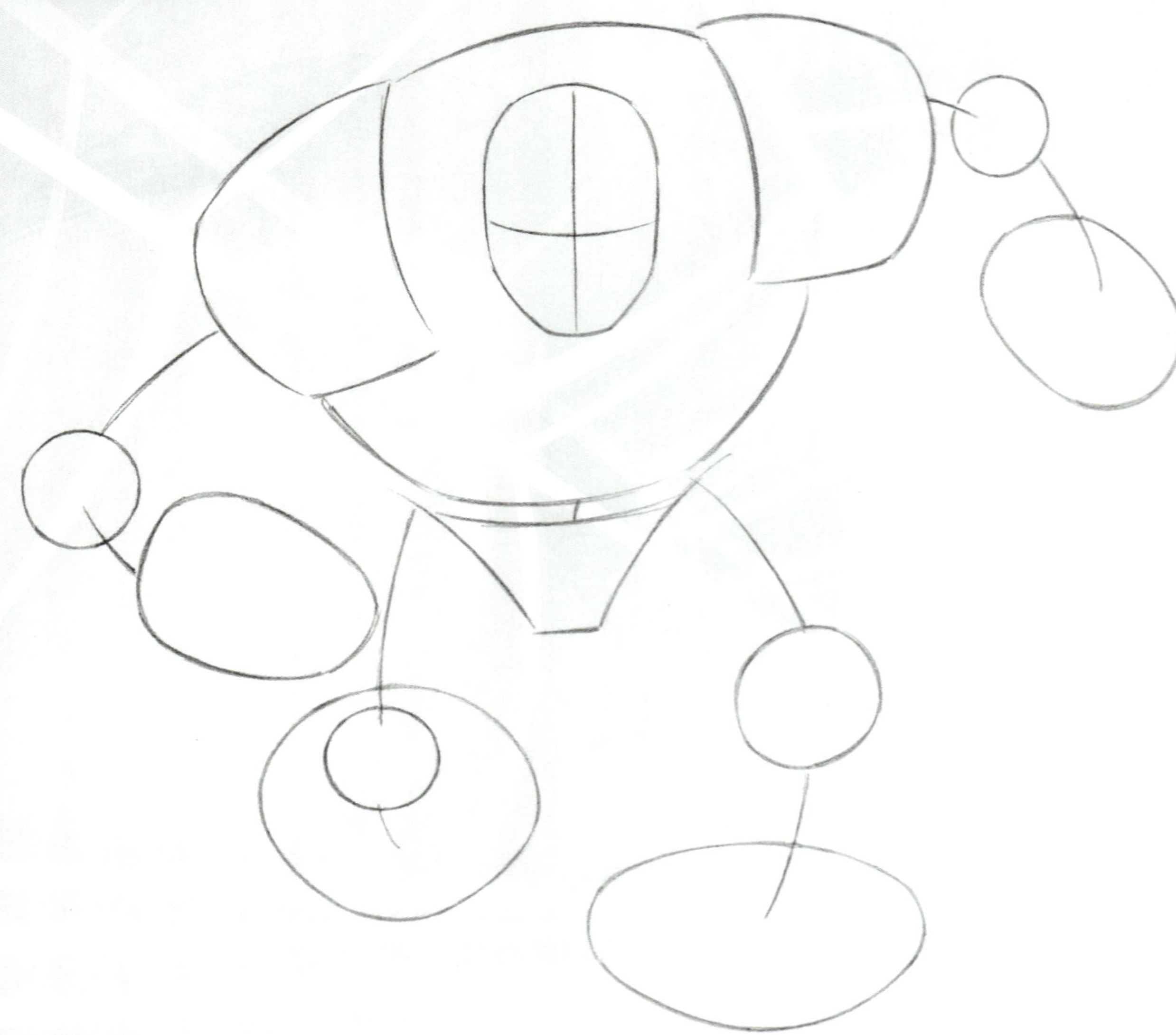

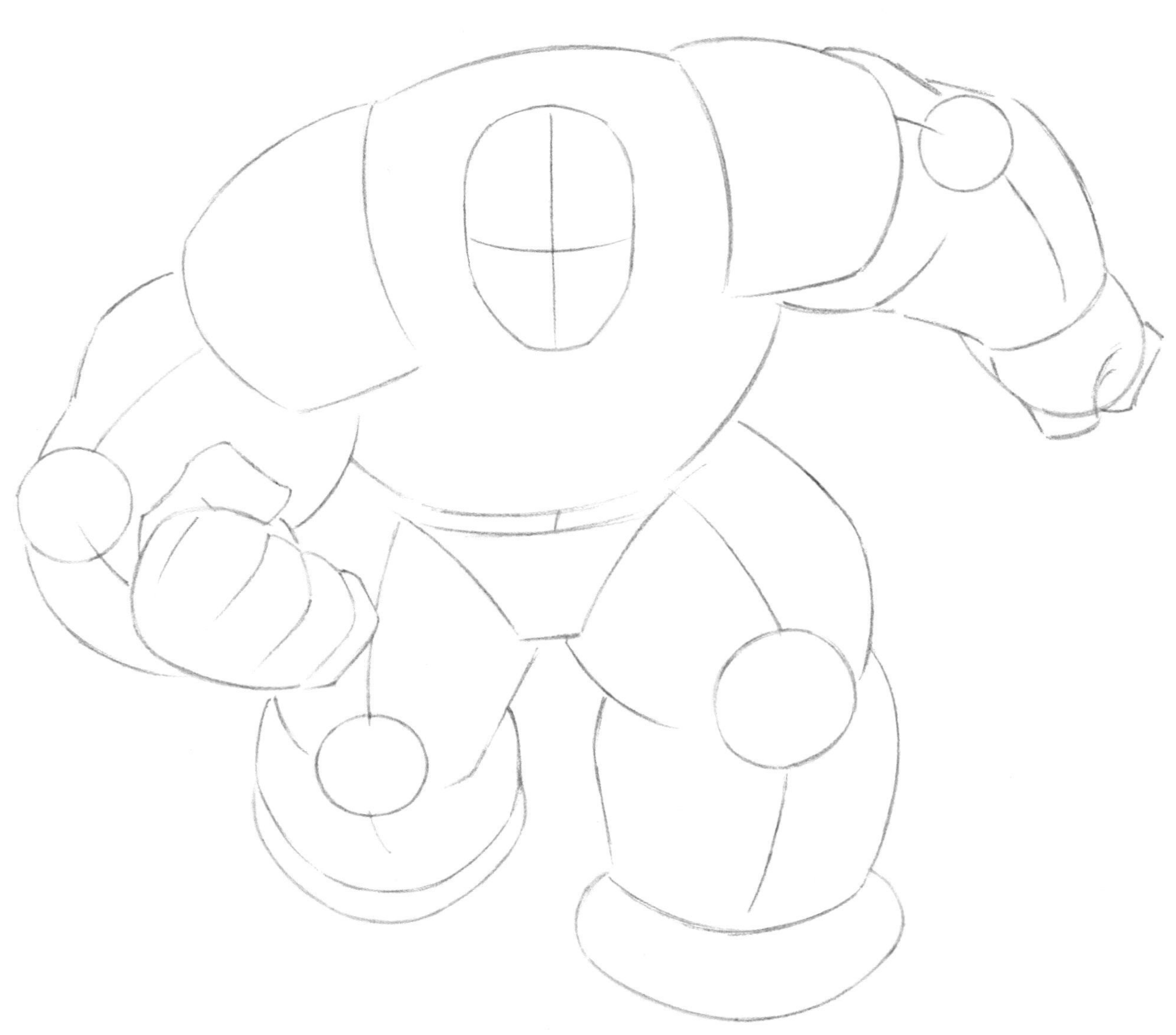

The Rhino suit is virtually indestructible: It is bullet-proof, acid-resistant, and offers protection from explosions and extreme temperatures.

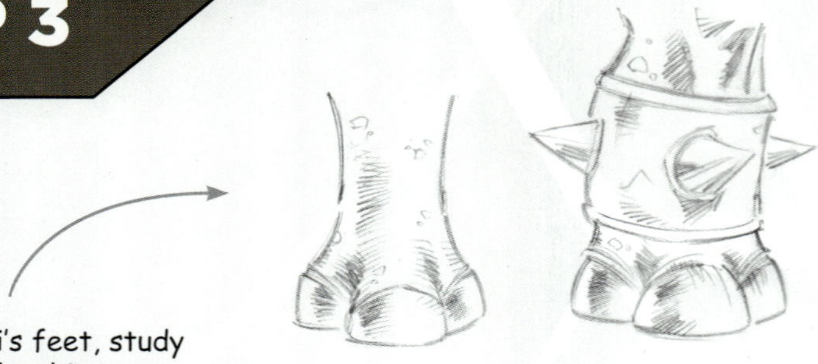

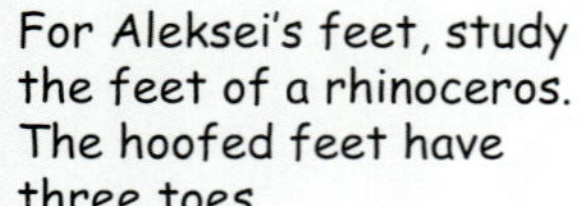

For Aleksei's feet, study the feet of a rhinoceros. The hoofed feet have three toes.

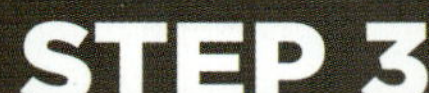

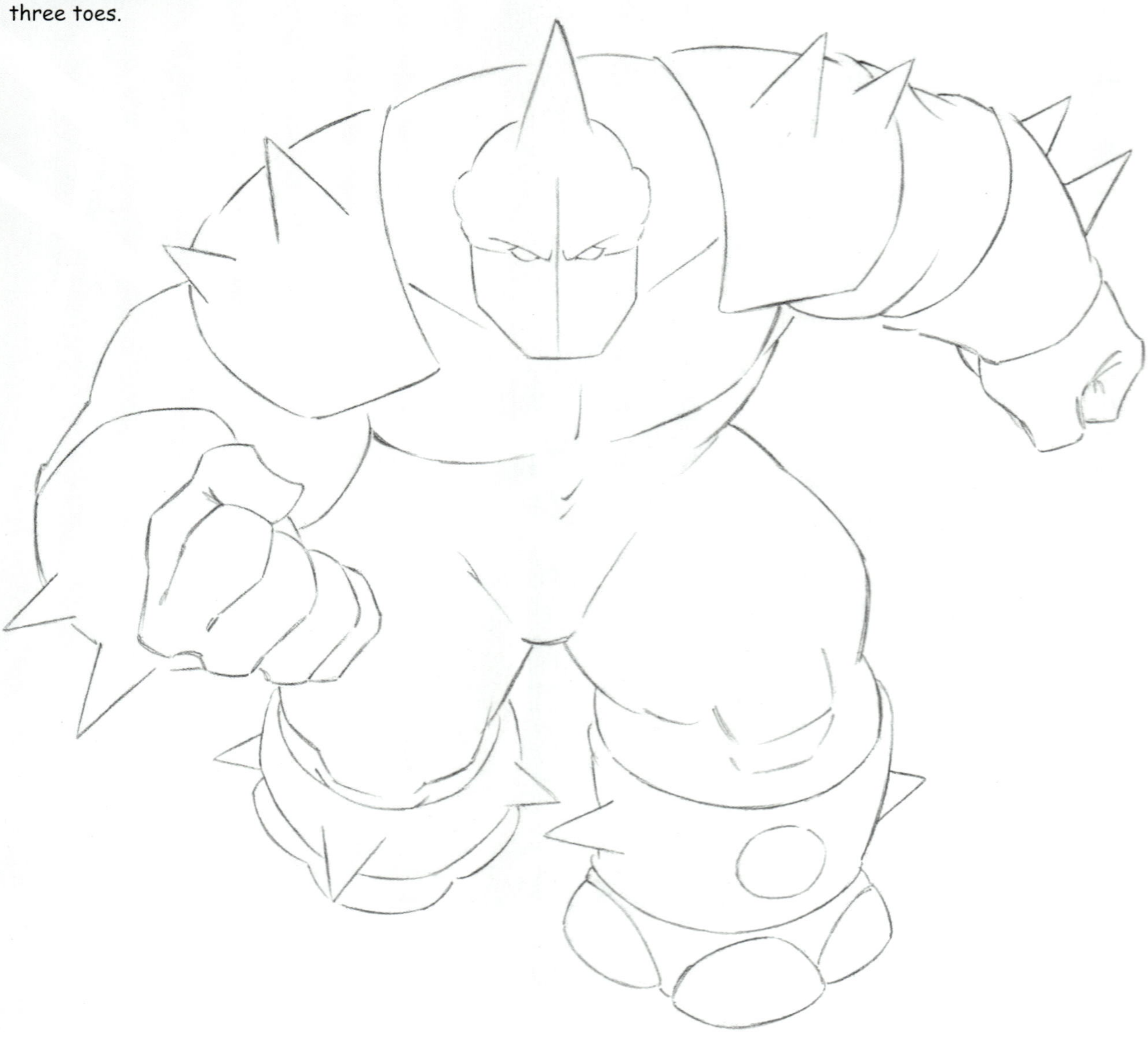

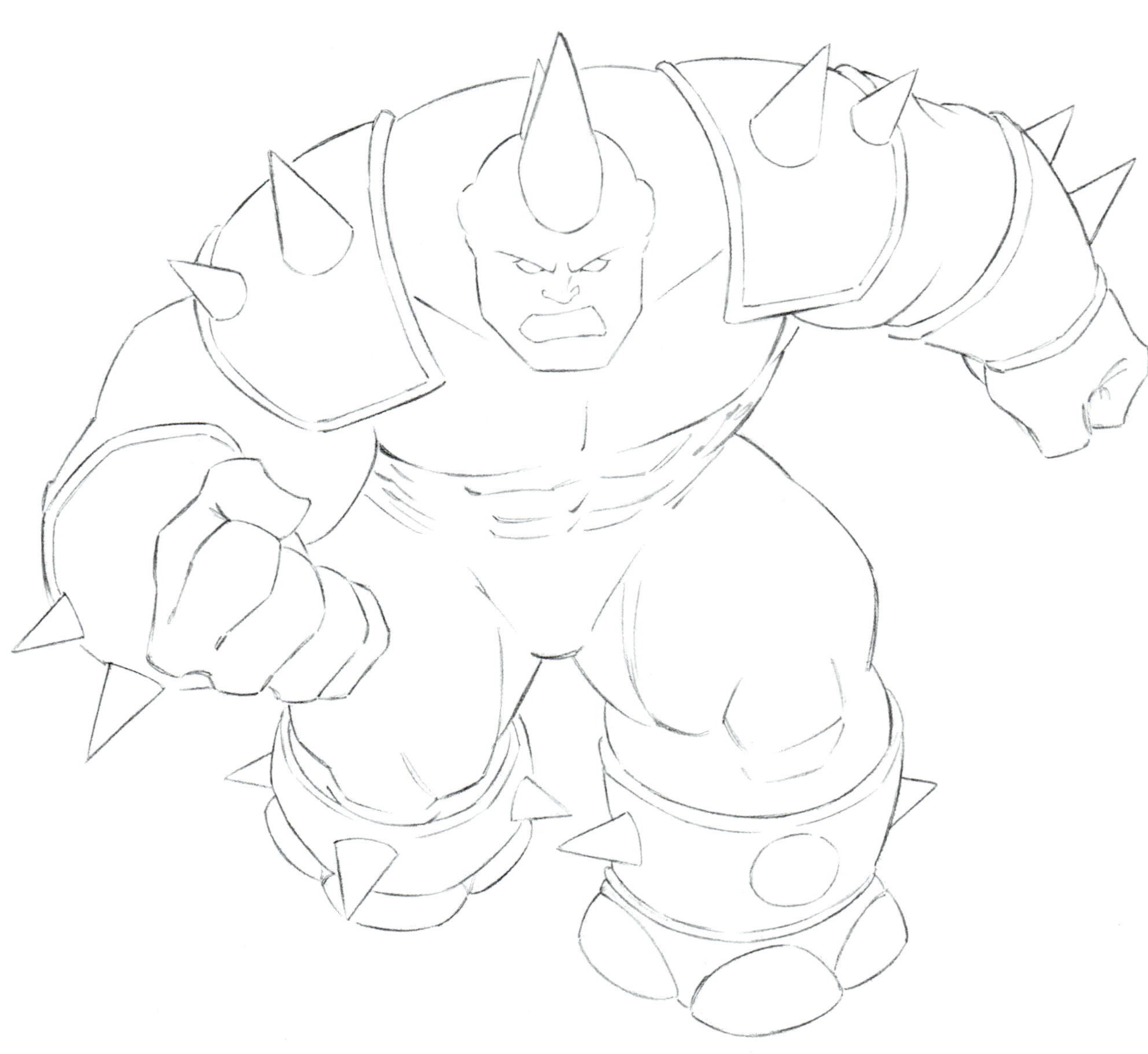

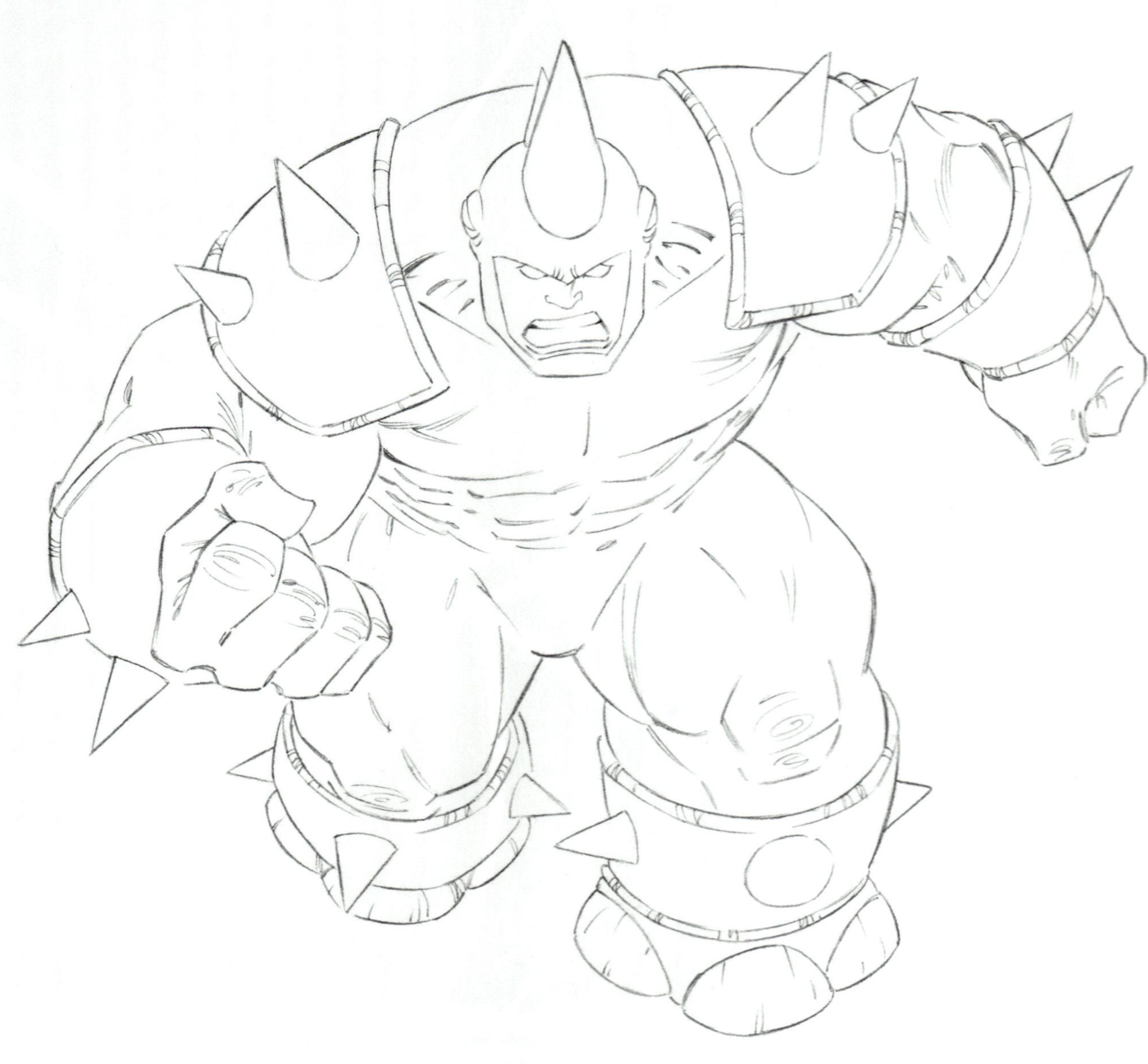

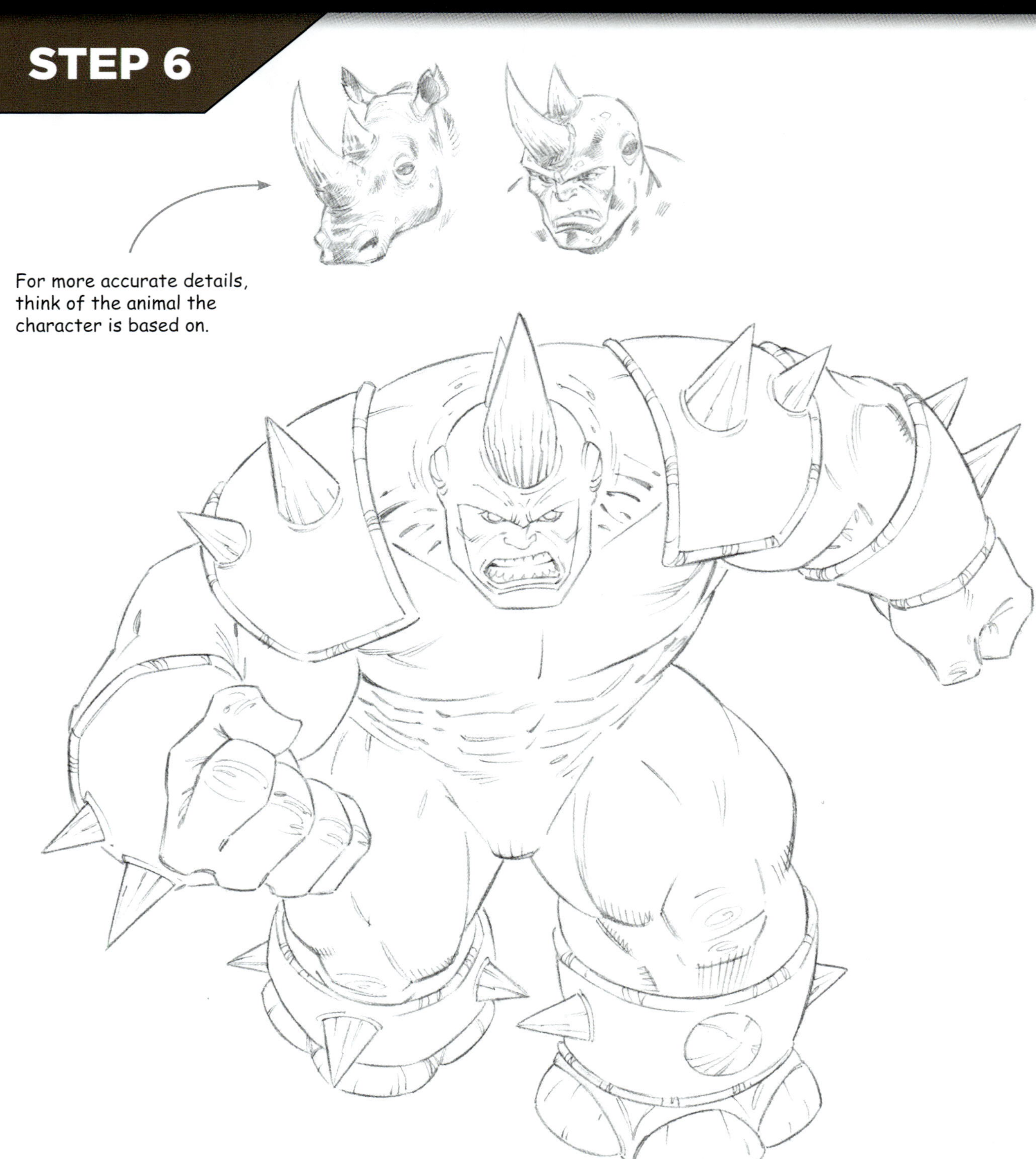

For more accurate details, think of the animal the character is based on.

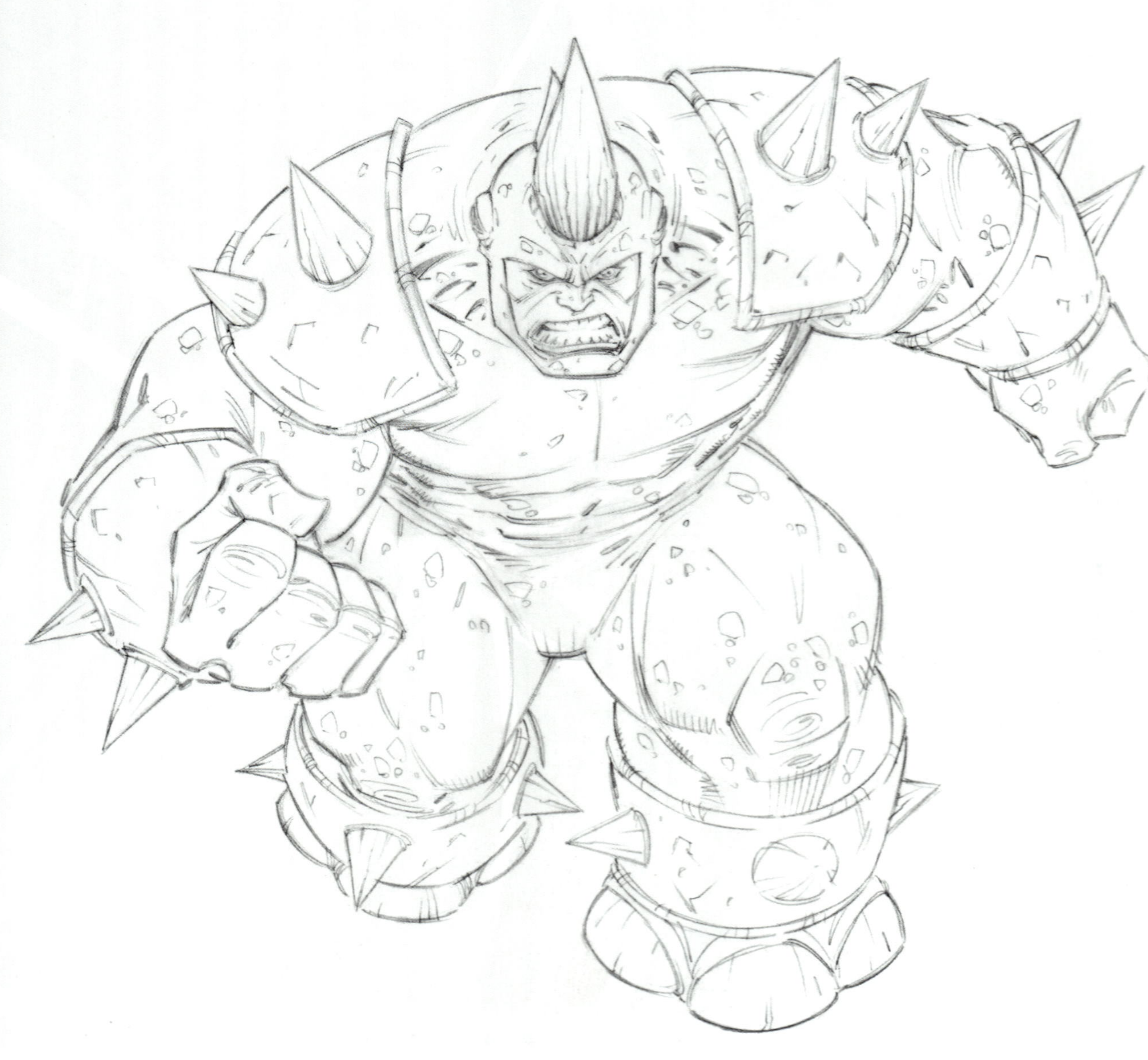

STEP 8

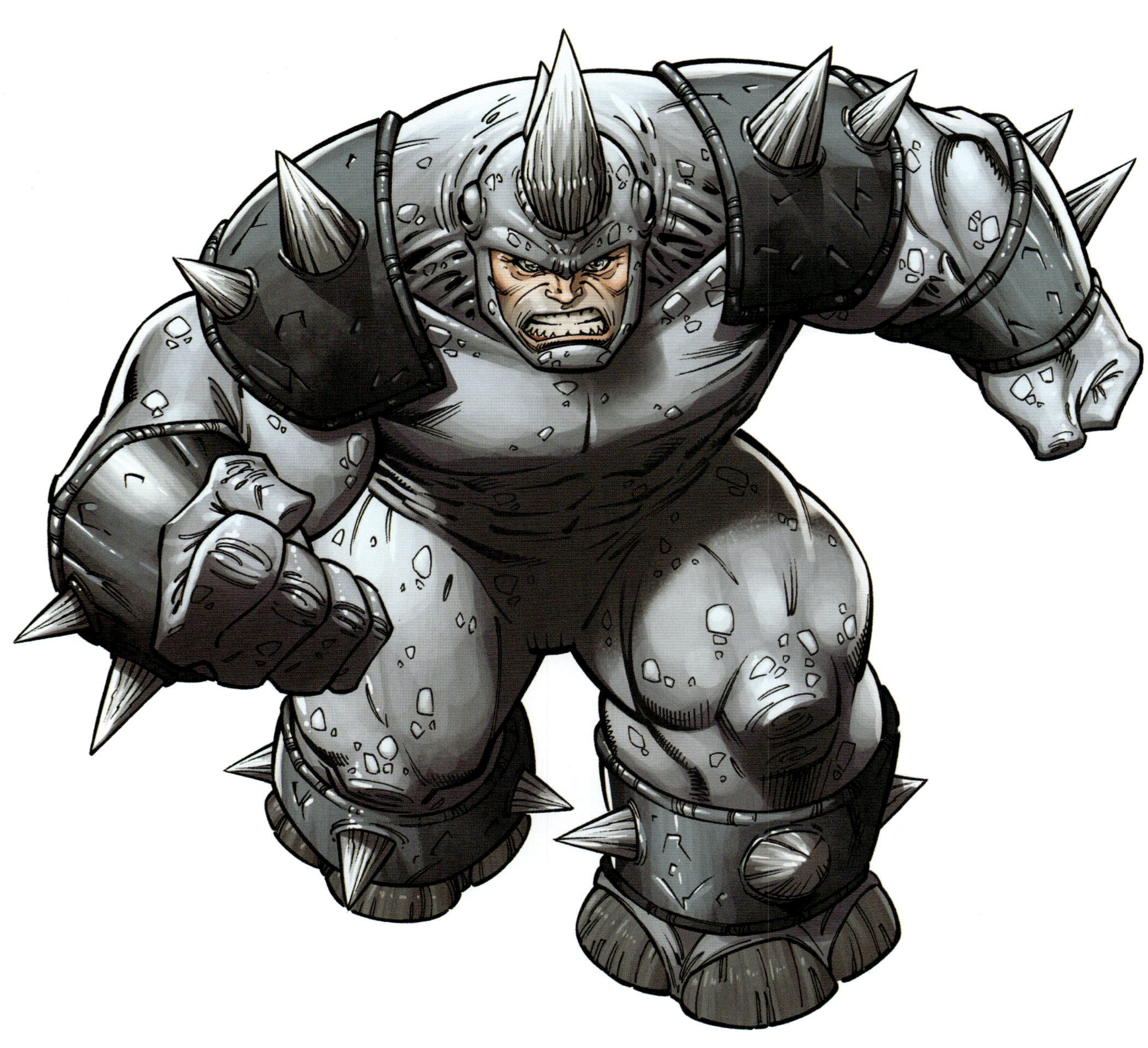

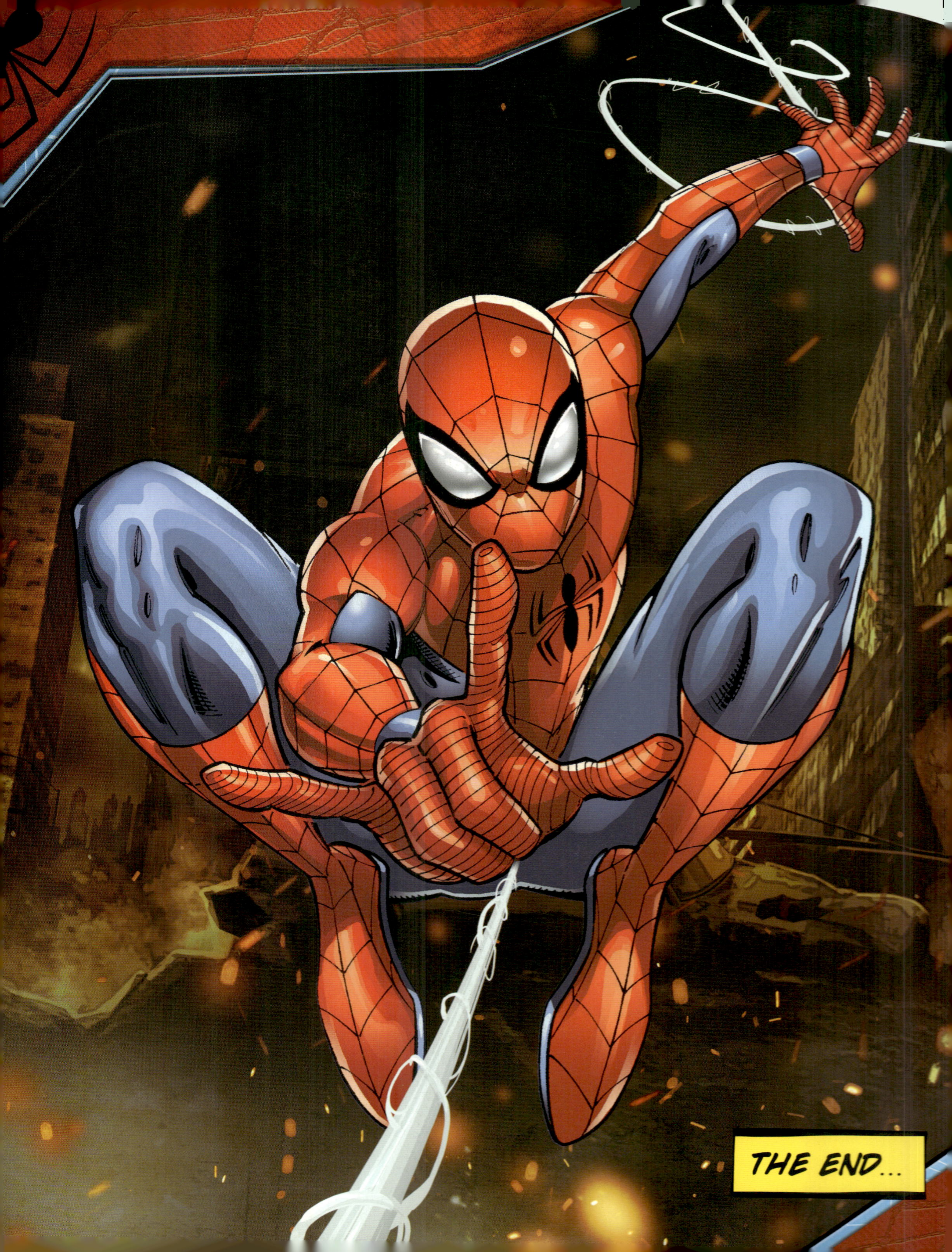
THE END...